The Psychology of Cultural Experience

The essays in this volume focus upon the relationship of individual experience to culture, and chart a new research agenda for psychological anthropology in the twenty-first century. Drawing upon fieldwork in diverse cultural settings, the authors use a range of contemporary perspectives in the field, including person-centered ethnography, activity theory, attachment theory, and cultural schema theory, to describe the ways in which people think, feel, remember, and solve problems. Fascinating insights emerge from these fine-grained accounts of personal experience. The research demonstrates that it is possible to identify cross-cultural universals in psychological development and mental states, and that individual psychology is not determined solely by unique cultural patterns.

CARMELLA C. MOORE is Assistant Research Anthropologist in the Department of Cognitive Sciences at the University of California (Irvine). Her work has been published in the *Encyclopedia of Cultural Anthropology* (1996) and the *Encyclopedia of Psychology* (2000), as well as in a variety of anthropological journals.

HOLLY F. MATHEWS is Professor of Anthropology in the Department of Anthropology at East Carolina University. She has previously edited two books, *Women in the South: An Anthropological Perspective* (1989) and *Herbal and Magical Medicine: Traditional Healing Today* (1992). Her work has also been published in major anthropological journals.

Publications of the Society for Psychological Anthropology

Editor
Naomi Quinn, Department of Cultural Anthropology, Duke University

Editorial board
Daniel Fessler, Department of Anthropology, University of California,
    Los Angeles
Allen W. Johnson, Department of Anthropology, University of
    California, Los Angeles
Takie Sugiyama Lebra, Department of Anthropology, University of
    Hawaii
John Lucy, Committee on Human Development and Department of
    Psychology, University of Chicago
Claudia Strauss, Department of Anthropology, Pitzer College
Harriet Whitehead, Duke University

Publications of the Society for Psychological Anthropology is a joint
initiative of Cambridge University Press and the Society for
Psychological Anthropology, a unit of the American Anthropological
Association. The series has been established to publish books in
psychological anthropology and related fields of cognitive anthropology,
ethnopsychology and cultural psychology. It includes works of original
theory, empirical research, and edited collections that address current
issues. The creation of this series reflects a renewed interest among
culture theorists in ideas about the self, mind–body interaction, social
cognition, mental models, processes of cultural acquisition, motivation
and agency, gender, and emotion.

1. Roy G. D'Andrade and Claudia Strauss (eds.): *Human motives and
    cultural models*
2. Nancy Rosenberger (ed.): *Japanese sense of self*
3. Theodore Schwartz, Geoffrey M. White and Catherine A. Lutz
    (eds.): *New directions in psychological anthropology*
4. Barbara Diane Miller (ed.): *Sex and gender hierarchies*
5. Peter G. Stromberg: *Language and self-transformation*
6. Eleanor Hollenberg Chasdi (ed.): *Culture and human development*
7. Robert L. Winzeler: *Latah in Southeast Asia: the history and
    ethnography of a culture-bound syndrome*
8. John M. Ingham: *Psychological anthropology reconsidered*
9. Claudia Strauss and Naomi Quinn: *A cognitive theory of cultural
    meaning*
10. Alexander Laban Hinton (ed.): *Biocultural approaches to the
    emotions*
11. Antonius Robben and Marcelo Suãrez-Orozco (eds.): *Cultures under
    siege: Collective violence and trauma in interdisciplinary perspectives*

The Psychology of Cultural Experience

Edited by

Carmella C. Moore
University of California, Irvine

Holly F. Mathews
East Carolina University

CAMBRIDGE
UNIVERSITY PRESS

PUBLISHED BY THE PRESS SYNDICATE OF THE UNIVERSITY OF CAMBRIDGE
The Pitt Building, Trumpington Street, Cambridge, United Kingdom

CAMBRIDGE UNIVERSITY PRESS
The Edinburgh Building, Cambridge CB2 2RU, UK
40 West 20th Street, New York, NY 10011–4211, USA
10 Stamford Road, Oakleigh, VIC 3166, Australia
Ruiz de Alarcón 13, 28014 Madrid, Spain
Dock House, The Waterfront, Cape Town 8001, South Africa

http://www.cambridge.org

First published 2001

Printed in the United Kingdom at the University Press, Cambridge

Typeface Monotype Times NR 10/12pt   *System* QuarkXPress™ [SE]

A catalogue record for this book is available from the British Library

Library of Congress cataloguing in publication data

The psychology of cultural experience / edited by Carmella C. Moore,
Holly F. Mathews.
    p.   cm. – (Publications of the Society for Psychological Anthropology)
Includes bibliographical references and index.
ISBN 0 521 80319 5 – ISBN 0 521 00552 3 (pb.)
1. Ethnopsychology.   2. Personality and culture.   I. Moore, Carmella C. II.
Mathews, Holly F.   III. Series.
GN502.P77   2001
155.8 – dc21   00–067444

ISBN 0 521 80319 5 hardback
ISBN 0 521 00552 3 paperback

To Ruth Munroe (1930–1996)
– Scholar, mentor, and friend

Yet all experience is an arch where-thro'
Gleams that untravell'd world, whose margin fades
Forever and forever when I move.

Tennyson,
Ulysses

Contents

List of figures   *page* xi
List of tables   xii
List of contributors   xiii
Preface   xix

Introduction: the psychology of cultural experience   1
HOLLY F. MATHEWS AND CARMELLA C. MOORE

I Theoretical and methodological approaches to the study of experience

1   Beyond the binary opposition in psychological anthropology:
    integrating contemporary psychoanalysis and cognitive science   21
    DREW WESTEN

2   Developments in person-centered ethnography   48
    DOUGLAS HOLLAN

3   Activity theory and cultural psychology   68
    CARL RATNER

II Acquiring, modifying, and transmitting culture

4   The infant's acquisition of culture: early attachment reexamined
    in anthropological perspective   83
    ROBERT A. LEVINE AND KARIN NORMAN

5   The remembered past in a culturally meaningful life:
    remembering as cultural, social, and cognitive process   105
    LINDA C. GARRO

III Continuity and change in cultural experience

6   The psychology of consensus in a Papua New Guinea Christian
    revival movement   151
    STEPHEN C. LEAVITT

x   Contents

7   God and self: the shaping and sharing of experience in a
    cooperative, religious community   173
    SUSAN LOVE BROWN

IV   A reinvigorated comparative perspective

8   Cross-cultural studies in language and thought: is there a
    metalanguage?   199
    EVE DANZIGER

9   Comparative approaches to psychological anthropology   223
    ROBERT L. MUNROE AND RUTH H. MUNROE

Name index   238
Subject index   240

Figures

4.1 How the social development of infants can be culturally   *page* 92
    shaped
8.1 The Route-Completion task   203
8.2 Various arrangements of man "beside" tree for the Man and   207
    Tree Game
9.1 Alternative spellings for *balam* "jaguar"   228

Tables

9.1 Correlations between father presence/absence in the home   *page* 225
and children's attention to males in their immediate social
environments
9.2 Climate and CV scores   230

Contributors

SUSAN LOVE BROWN received her Ph.D. in Anthropology from the University of California, San Diego in 1992 and is Associate Professor in the Department of Anthropology, Florida Atlantic University (Boca Raton, Florida). She has done ethnographic fieldwork on the study of change at Ananda Village, a New Age religious community in Nevada City, California, and on national identity in Cat Island, Bahamas. She is a psychological and political anthropologist with special interests in intentional communities, individualism and communalism, anarchism, gender, ethnicity, and culture change in the Caribbean and the United States. She is the co-author (with Robert Bates Graber *et al.*) of the new text, *Meeting Anthropology Phase to Phase* (Carolina Academic Press, 2000).

EVE DANZIGER received her Ph.D. in Anthropology from the University of Pennsylvania in 1991, and is Assistant Professor in the Department of Anthropology, University of Virginia (Charlottesville, Virginia). Since 1986, her research has been informed by ethnographic and linguistic fieldwork with the Mopan Mayan people of Belize, Central America. Her interests revolve around the three-way interface of language, social identity, and thought, and include publications in the areas of social practice and social organization, the linguistics of Mopan, and the role of language in cognition. Her work has appeared in *Ethos*, the *International Journal of American Linguistics*, and the *Journal of the Royal Anthropological Institute (NS)*, and she is the author of *Relatively Speaking: Language, Thought, and Kinship Among the Mopan Maya* (Oxford University Press, 2001).

LINDA C. GARRO received Ph.Ds. in Cognitive Psychology from Duke University in 1982, and in Social Sciences, Anthropology, from the University of California, Irvine in 1983. She is Professor in the Department of Anthropology, University of California, Los Angeles (Los Angeles, California). She has been a National Institute of Mental Health Research Fellow in Clinically Relevant Medical Anthropology at

Harvard University and is a past recipient of a five-year National Health Research and Development Program Scholar Award in Canada. Her research in medical and cognitive anthropology focuses on intracultural variation in the representation of cultural knowledge. Her field research sites include a Purépecha (Tarascan) community in Mexico and several Anishinaabe (Ojibway) communities in Canada. Among other journals, her work has appeared in the *American Anthropologist*, and *Culture, Medicine, and Psychiatry*, and she is co-editor (with Cheryl Mattingly) of the recent volume, *Narrative and the Cultural Construction of Illness and Healing* (University of California Press, 2000). She is also the 1999 recipient of the Stirling Award from the Society for Psychological Anthropology.

DOUGLAS HOLLAN received Ph.Ds. in Anthropology from the University of California, San Diego in 1984 and in Psychoanalysis from the Southern California Psychoanalytic Institute in 1997. He is Professor and Luckman Distinguished Teacher in the Department of Anthropology, University of California, Los Angeles (California) and senior instructor at the Southern California Psychoanalytic Institute. He has done extended fieldwork among the Toraja of South Sulawesi, Indonesia, and is the author of numerous articles on the relationships between cultural and psychological processes, which have appeared in various journals including the *American Ethnologist*, *Ethnology*, and the *Journal of Anthropological Research*. He is co-author (with Jane Wellenkamp) of two monographs, *Contentment and Suffering: Culture and Experience in Toraja* (Columbia University Press, 1994), and *The Thread of Life: Toraja Reflections on the Life Cycle* (University of Hawai'i Press, 1996).

STEPHEN C. LEAVITT received his Ph.D. in Anthropology from the University of California, San Diego in 1989, and is Associate Professor in the Department of Anthropology, Union College (Schenectady, New York). In ethnographic field research among the Bumbita Arapesh of Papua New Guinea in 1984–86, he focused on individual reactions to a local Christian revival movement. He has also written on Bumbita sexuality, adolescence, and bereavement. He is co-editor (with Gilbert Herdt) of the recent volume, *Adolescence in Pacific Island Societies* (University of Pittsburgh Press, 1998), and guest editor (with Karen Brison) of a special issue of *Ethos*, "On Coping with Bereavement." His most recent field research is with ethnic Fijians in Fiji.

ROBERT A. LEVINE received his Ph.D. in Social Anthropology from the Department of Social Relations, Harvard University in 1958. He is currently Roy E. Larsen Professor of Education and Human Development,

Emeritus, and Professor of Anthropology, Emeritus, at Harvard University (Cambridge, Massachusetts). During the early 1960s, he did ethnographic fieldwork among the Nyansongo, a Gusii community in Kenya, in collaboration with John and Beatrice Whiting's Children of Six Cultures study. He has continued to study Gusii culture, as well as to do fieldwork in other areas of the world including Asia and North and Central America. He has written about topics as diverse as witchcraft accusations, demographic transition, political authority systems, and psychoanalysis that have been published in many journals including the *American Anthropologist*. He is co-author of the monograph, *Child Care and Culture: Lessons from Africa* (Cambridge University Press, 1994), and co-editor of *Parental Behavior in Diverse Societies* (Jossey-Bass, 1988). He was chairman of the Social Science Research Council, 1980–83, and served as president of the Society for Psychological Anthropology, 1980–81. He received the Distinguished Career Contributions award from the society in 1997.

HOLLY F. MATHEWS received her Ph.D. in Anthropology from Duke University in 1982, and is Professor in the Department of Anthropology, East Carolina University (Greenville, North Carolina). She has done ethnographic fieldwork with the Zapotec in Oaxaca, Mexico, among Afro-Caribbean peoples in Costa Rica, and in rural communities in the southeastern United States. Her research interests include cultural models, cognitive processes of reasoning and decision-making, medical anthropology, and gender roles. Her work has appeared in numerous journals including the *American Anthropologist*, the *American Ethnologist*, and the *Journal of the American Medical Association*.

CARMELLA C. MOORE received her Ph.D. in Social Sciences, Anthropology from the University of California, Irvine (California) in 1991 where she is currently Assistant Researcher in the Department of Cognitive Sciences. Her research interests include the study of personality change in neurological dysfunction, the study of intra- and intercultural agreement and variation in cultural knowledge, and the development and use of quantitative methods for anthropology. She has done fieldwork at clinical sites in Orange County, California, and in Ensenada and Guadalajara, Mexico. Her work has appeared in a number of journals including the *American Anthropologist, Current Anthropology*, and the *Proceedings of the National Academy of Sciences.*

ROBERT L. MUNROE received his Ph.D. in Social Anthropology from the Department of Social Relations, Harvard University in 1964. He was a member of the founding faculty at Pitzer College (of the Claremont

Colleges, Claremont, California), where he is currently Research Professor in the Department of Anthropology. He has carried out field-work in East Africa, Central America, North America, Nepal, and American Samoa. His work has appeared in numerous journals including the *American Anthropologist* and *Cross-Cultural Research*, and he is co-author (with R. H. Munroe) of the monograph, *Cross-Cultural Human Development* (Waveland Press, 1994). He served as president of the *Society for Psychological Anthropology* from 1995 to 1997.

RUTH H. MUNROE received her Ed.D. in Human Development from Harvard University in 1964. A member of the founding faculty at Pitzer College (of the Claremont Colleges, Claremont, California), she was Research Professor of Psychology there at the time of her death in 1996. Her work was published in numerous anthropological and psychological journals, and she served on the editorial boards of the journals *Cross-Cultural Research*, *Ethos*, and the *Journal of Cross-Cultural Psychology*. In 1971 she introduced to the literature the spot- observation technique, a systematic observational tool designed for use in naturalistic research. Central use of that technique was made in her last major publication, a monograph on time use among the Newars of the Katmandu Valley, *Newar Time Allocation* (R. H. Munroe *et al.*, HRAF Press, 1997).

KARIN NORMAN received her Ph.D. in Anthropology from Stockholm University (Stockholm, Sweden) in 1991 where she is currently Associate Professor in the Department of Social Anthropology. Her research interests concern issues on children's lives and socialization; displacement and refugee studies; and problems of method. She has conducted fieldwork in Sweden and Germany, and is planning research in Kosovo, former Yugoslavia. She has published on various topics in English and Swedish and has recently published a monograph in Swedish on cultural ideas about children and childhood. She is currently working on a book of essays (in English) on different experiences and interpretations of exile from the vantage point of two Kosovo Albanian families in Sweden.

CARL RATNER received his Ph.D. in Social Psychology from the State University of New York, Buffalo in 1970. Recently retired from the Department of Psychology, Humboldt State University, he continues to write and do research from his home in Trinidad, California. Early in his career, he spent two years as a visiting scholar in China, teaching psychology and editing a social science journal. His research interests include cultural psychology and qualitative methodology. His work has appeared in a number of journals including *Culture and Psychology*, and the *Journal of Personality and Social Psychology*. He is author of the monograph, *Vvgotsky's Sociohistorical Psychology and its Contemporary Applications* (Plenum Press, 1991), and of the forthcoming work, *Cultural Psychology: Theory and Method* (Plenum Press, 2001).

DREW WESTEN received his Ph.D. in Clinical Psychology from the University of Michigan in 1985, and is Research Associate Professor in the Department of Psychology, and Director of the Adolescent and Adult Personality Programs at the Center for Anxiety and Related Disorders at Boston University (Boston, Massachusetts). His primary areas of research are personality disorders, emotion regulation, and integrations of cognitive neuroscience and psychoanalysis. His work has appeared in many journals including the *American Journal of Psychiatry*, *Journal of the American Psychoanalytic Association*, and *Psychological Science*. He is author of the monograph, *Self and Society: Narcissism, Collectivism, and the Development of Morals* (Cambridge University Press, 1985), as well as of the recent introductory text, *Psychology: Mind, Brain, and Culture* (Wiley, 1999).

Preface

The idea for this collection originated at the 4th Biennial Meeting of the Society for Psychological Anthropology held during early October, 1995 in San Juan, Puerto Rico. At the meeting, SPA President and Program Chair, Naomi Quinn, chose the sessions and selected the papers to be presented, with the goal of assessing the state of the field of psychological anthropology. One thematic interest emerging in several sessions was the relationship of individual experience to culture. We identified key contributions by authors Brown, Danziger, Hollan, Leavitt, LeVine and Norman, and the Munroes and asked them to revise and expand their meeting papers to address this theme more explicitly. Author Westen was the featured speaker at the meeting banquet, and he agreed to develop a contribution for this volume based upon his presentation. Finally, we invited papers from Garro and Ratner because their research on individual experience derived from theoretical perspectives different from those of the other contributors to this volume.

Our aim in developing this volume was to represent the theoretically diverse and methodologically sophisticated analyses emerging from the study of culture and experience and to demonstrate that a renewed commitment to careful, empirical analyses and the comparative perspective can yield important data essential to outlining an agenda for research in psychological anthropology in the twenty-first century. We also hope these chapters will demonstrate to graduate students with psychological interests that there are many "researchable" questions to be both asked and answered, and that the research process is both contemporary and cumulative.

These chapters have necessarily undergone numerous transformations since their original inceptions as kernels of ideas presented at a meeting, and we thank our authors for their efforts and tolerance during the revision process, as well as the three anonymous reviewers who made very helpful comments and criticisms on the manuscript. We especially thank SPA Book Series Editor, Naomi Quinn, for her guidance through this process and for her assistance in revising the manuscript. We also thank Professor Roy G. D'Andrade and Professor Robert L. Munroe for their suggestions and encouragement during the preparation of this volume, as well as Ti-lien Hsia, Sarah Miller, and Amy Willoughby for editorial assistance. In addition we thank Jessica Kuper and Cambridge University Press for invaluable help in the publication process. We also appreciate the support for the volume provided by our respective universities as well as assistance from National Science Foundation grant SBR-9730831 to C. C. Moore.

During the course of producing this volume, one of our authors, Ruth H. Munroe, a distinguished psychologist, passed away after suffering from a long illness. Ruth was a dedicated scholar and scientist, as well as a mentor and friend to many contemporary psychological anthropologists. She will be greatly missed. We hope that her message of sensitivity to the cultural context, coupled with an openness to the comparative method, will provide an example and an inspiration to all of us as we move into the twenty-first century and into the next century of psychological anthropology.

Introduction: the psychology of cultural experience

Holly F. Mathews and Carmella C. Moore

The complicated relationship that obtains between psychology and culture is revealed in the lived experience of active, purposive individuals. Paradoxically, however, the past two decades have seen a constructivist view of cultural meaning and practice triumph over other approaches in the field, leading many investigators to overemphasize the magnitude and importance of cultural diversity and conclude, often on the basis of little evidence, that each culture constructs its own unique psychology (Abu-Lughod 1991, Clifford 1986, Crapanzano 1980, Kondo 1990, Lutz 1988, Rosaldo 1989, Shweder 1990, 1991, 1999). As Spiro (1999: 13) has observed, the epistemological fallout from such a thesis of cultural and psychological incommensurability is the conclusion on the part of many that a genuinely comparative psychological anthropology is impossible to achieve (see also LeVine 1999: 18).

Although constructivist theorists stress attention to individual agency, many of them are avowedly antipsychological in their approach. Thus their studies tend to describe local cultural content derived largely from analyses of public symbols and texts (see also Ingham 1996: 4–8) and to depict individuals as either passively absorbing (Bourdieu 1977, Butler 1990, Ortner 1990) or reflexively resisting (Abu-Lughod 1990, Comaroff 1985, Martin 1987, Scott 1985, Willis 1977) such cultural content (see also, Strauss 1992, Strauss and Quinn 1997: 12–44). Absent from these accounts are empirical descriptions of the ways in which active, creative individuals meet the everyday challenges of thinking, feeling, remembering, and solving problems. Yet such descriptions are vital to the development of a vigorous psychological anthropology capable of theorizing in new ways about the complex relationship that obtains between individual psychology, culture, and lived experience (Schwartz 1999: 58–59).

Rather than accept cultural and psychological incommensurability as a given, the authors represented in this volume view it as an empirical question requiring rigorous, case by case, and comparatively oriented investigation (cf. Nuckolls 1998: 42). They reject the postmodern notion of "fundamental otherness" which has led many in the larger discipline of cultural anthropology to eschew the validity of long-term ethnographic

1

fieldwork and comparative analysis (e.g., Clifford 1998). Instead, these defining chapters by established scholars demonstrate that sound scientific methodologies can yield important data about the mutually constituted nature of culture and individual experience, and they reaffirm the possibility of identifying cross-cultural universals in psychological development and mental states. In so doing, these contributors also articulate an agenda for psychological anthropology in the twenty-first century.

Instead of replicating old and oftentimes destructive divisions between variant theoretical perspectives in the wider field of anthropology (i.e., cognitive, psychoanalytic, evolutionary, constructivist, postmodern etc.), these authors emphasize the importance of forging a cooperative, multidisciplinary approach (see also, Edgerton 1999, Munroe 1999). They draw upon exciting new developments in neurobiology and cognitive science about how minds and brains work; upon recent research in developmental psychology and relational psychoanalysis about the interaction between universal windows of neurological development, intrapsychic drives, and cultural practices in shaping mental development; and upon a body of fine-grained, person-centered ethnographic research that shows how real individuals use, modify, and transmit cultural ideas as they confront the everyday challenges of life. Their findings demonstrate that far from being wholly culturally constructed, individual psychology is also partially explicable in terms of universal patterns of human biological development as well as the similar behavioral and psychological adaptations that groups make to common problems (see also Hinton 1999). As a result, these essays provide an antidote to the existential malaise that has characterized psychological anthropology in the wake of the postmodern onslaught, and they reassert the strengths of the field that pioneered the study of individual experience and its relationship to culture.[1]

In the first section of the volume entitled "Theoretical and Methodological Approaches to the Study of Experience," Westen delineates the implications of a new theoretical model of the mind for recent studies of intra-individual mental and psychological attributes and a growing body of data on daily experience as grounded in culturally and socially meaningful worlds. Authors Hollan and Ratner explore different methodological approaches to the study of culture and experience and consider the implications of the subjective, behavioral, and embodied aspects of individual experience for theories of cultural meaning and practice. In part II, authors Garro, and LeVine and Norman present detailed empirical studies of the ways in which individuals act to acquire, modify, and transmit culture in specific contexts. Part III of the volume focuses on continuity and change in cultural experience. Authors Leavitt and Brown examine how intrapsychic conflicts stemming from disjunctions in cultural values and individual experiences act to motivate and shape the content of social movements. In the final part, authors Danziger, and Munroe and Munroe articulate the need for a reinvigorated comparative perspective in contemporary psychological anthropology. Their data demonstrate that it is possible to be sensitive to cultural context in constructing valid categories for comparison while still embracing the search for regularities in human thought and behavior as a central anthropological goal.

Taken together, these chapters outline an important and exciting new research agenda for psychological anthropology and illustrate some methodological approaches and types of data that characterize it. The first component of the new agenda is the exploration of the interconnections that exist between the use of systematic methods for the study of individual experience and the theoretical insights that emerge from the resultant rich corpus of experience-near data gathered in a variety of cultural contexts. In particular, this agenda attempts to model a new theoretical connection between mind, psyche, and culture that helps us reconceptualize the relationships of mental models to experience. This new model of the mind shifts the underlying view of knowledge from one of sequentially stored lists of propositions to one of information, feelings, and motives stored along networks of association built up by their repeated conjunction in individual thought and experience. Because such networks of association may operate either unconsciously or implicitly, it becomes imperative for the second part of the new agenda to include the development of a battery of methodological techniques capable of uncovering and theorizing about the relations that obtain between the subjective, behavioral, and embodied aspects of individual experience. A third component of this new agenda, as these essays demonstrate, involves using such methodologically sophisticated approaches to better understand internal psychological states and the individual bases of group behavior, paving the way for a more comprehensive theory of culture change as both motivating and motivated by everyday experience. Finally, the agenda articulated by these authors outlines a way to reconcile the desire of many psychological anthropologists to combine person-centered studies with a return to the use of explicit comparative frameworks. By carefully attending to the design of relevant measures in different cultural contexts, these authors demonstrate how categories of comparison can emerge from the lived experience of the people studied and thus form the basis upon which more sophisticated cross-cultural studies can be designed. The remainder of this introduction outlines in more detail the four items of the new agenda and discusses some of the key theoretical insights and empirical findings emerging from the application of this agenda to the volume authors' recent research in psychological anthropology.

Implications of a new theoretical model of the mind

In the first part of this volume, Drew Westen synthesizes recent developments in neuroscience, cognitive psychology, and psychoanalysis to demonstrate how a newly emergent theoretical model of the mind is capable of integrating insights about intra-individual mental processes with anthropological data on culturally and socially constructed schemas of meaning (see also Strauss and Quinn 1997: 48–84). Known in cognitive science as connectionism or parallel distributed processing, this model, Westen notes, is based on the assumption that many cognitive processes occur simultaneously and in parallel, rather than sequentially, and that the meaning of an object or concept is not contained in any single unit (Rumelhart, McClelland, and the PDP Research Group 1986, Read, Vanman, and Miller 1997, Smith 1998). Rather, he writes, "it is spread out, or *distributed*, across a network of processing units that, through experience, become activated in tandem" (p. 30). As a heuristic device, this model helps us conceptualize the relationship of mental models to experience in a new way because it shifts the underlying view of knowledge from sequentially stored lists of propositions to one of information stored along networks of association that operate unconsciously or implicitly. In general, Westen notes, the associative links between units of information are strengthened by their repeated conjunction, either in thought or in reality.

Strauss and Quinn (1997) have drawn upon this connectionist model of mind to define learned schemas as dense networks of strong associations built up from experience. Whatever co-occurs in experience, including thoughts, emotions, motivations, and the nonverbalized or preverbal, will become incorporated in a schema. Once a strong network of associations has been created, moreover, it fills in missing or ambiguous information by activating all the units in an interconnected network, even those not directly stimulated by current experience. Schemas or networks thereby come to be mediating devices through which subsequent experiences are rendered meaningful. To the extent that individuals share experiences, such as common patterns of childhood socialization, they will share schemas. Culture, from this perspective, consists of people's shared experiences and the schemas they acquire on the basis of those experiences (Strauss and Quinn 1997: 7). Thus certain aspects of cultural experience may be more widely shared than others.

A key implication of such a connectionist view of mind is that not only do individual experiences form the basis for shared cultural beliefs and behaviors but cultural forms, in turn, act to subtly shape the perceptions and understandings of individual culture members. Stephen Leavitt's chapter on a Christian revival movement in Papua, New Guinea, demonstrates empirically this interconnection between experience and culture. He found that the Bumbita enthusiastically embraced a Christian revival movement out of a desire to attain consensus and social harmony. This desire for consensus derived initially from individual needs and experiences as structured by cultural conceptions of the self. For the Bumbita, Leavitt writes, self schemas set up a tension between a desire for personal autonomy and the sense that one is, in fact, defined by relations to others so that no act can be undertaken without consideration of its potential impact on relatives and associates. This tension leads the Bumbita to be guarded in their dealings with others, keeping desires and motives secret as much as possible. In such a situation, Leavitt argues, the idea of consensus becomes appealing precisely because it neutralizes this contradiction born of experience. Everyone is fostering one goal while also preserving a sense of autonomy. Thus shared desires and their formulations in cultural expectations shaped the content of the revival movement. Yet, once it was under way, individual experiences with bickering and distrust led to disillusionment with the movement's promise of consensus, contributing to its failure.

Linda Garro's chapter in this volume provides a detailed, empirical study of the ways in which cultural understandings shape even the memories of individual experiences. Among the Anishinaabe, there is a culturally accepted belief that illness and misfortune often result from the prior mistreatment of animals. In an attempt to explain why his daughter's rash was not responding to medical treatments, one of Garro's informants drew upon this shared notion of causation to search his memory and to produce an emotionally vivid account of his encounter with a snake some twenty-five years previously, which he subsequently decided was the cause of his daughter's illness. Garro notes that such strong cultural expectations serve to highlight individual experiences with animals in part because these experiences engender the emotions of fear and worry, making them more likely to be remembered in the first place. Because these experiences are more salient than are the memories of other unmarked experiences, they may also be recalled more easily when the triggering conditions of an unresolved illness are present. Cultural beliefs, then, can shape the ways that individuals attend to, remember, and then actively reconstruct memories in the process of solving concrete cultural problems.

New approaches to conceptualizing and studying experience

A connectionist model of the mind, according to Westen, illuminates the need for a broader conceptualization of experience and how it is acquired and transmitted. While actual experiences may shape cultural forms, there are many factors that shape the way that such experiences themselves transpire. Implicit associational learning, for example, may occur through everyday actions and experiences while conscious beliefs may be more heavily shaped through explicit teaching. Thus a variety of methodological approaches may be needed to fully explore the complicated interrelationship between culture and experience.

Doug Hollan's chapter in this volume updates Robert LeVine's (1982) review of person-centered ethnography and outlines three methodological approaches that characterize recent research on culture and experience. These three approaches focus attention either on what people say, on what people do, or on how people embody personal experience. The authors represented in this volume use these different methodological approaches; at the same time, their resultant findings extend Hollan's distinction to a theoretical level, demonstrating that a more complete understanding of personal experience is dependent upon efforts to untangle the interconnections that obtain between its subjective, behavioral, and embodied aspects.

Analyzing the subjective aspects of individual experience

Traditionally, Hollan writes, person-centered researchers like volume authors Garro and Leavitt have attended primarily to what people say about their subjective experiences and have examined these verbal reports for what they reveal about the relationships between such experiences and the larger cultural context. One reason this strategy is so important, Hollan notes, is because verbal report remains the only means we have of directly sampling a phenomenon like personal experience, which is very difficult to study. This approach, moreover, can reveal quite explicitly the mutually constituted nature of cultural representations and individual experience as illustrated in the examples discussed previously from the work of Leavitt and Garro.

Yet, as Hollan points out, the relationship between verbal utterance and subjective experience is an extremely complicated one that may be affected by the difficulty of expressing certain types of experiences and by the narrative conventions and social constraints guiding the purpose and scope of verbal interactions. Garro's example discussed above of the informant who attributed his daughter's illness to his own encounter with a snake demonstrates the need to attend carefully to both the social setting and the task being pursued by the individual as these comprise the social context of verbal report. As she observes, her informant's recollection was elicited during his visit to a traditional Anishinaabe healer raising the question of the extent to which his account is constructed in response to the suggestions of that healer. A further complicating factor is the degree to which this informant wishes to persuade Garro of the validity of his interpretation of his daughter's illness and thereby also validate the actions he took in response to her condition. All too often a careful consideration of social context is lacking in experience-near approaches, which therefore privilege the study of cultural representations as revealed in discourse over the analysis of the social dynamics affecting the production of such discourse.

Analyzing the behavioral aspects of individual experience

As Hollan points out, a number of person-centered ethnographers currently emphasize the importance of grounding discussions of human experience in the compelling concerns of people's everyday lives by returning to fine-grained, participatory ethnographic work. Volume authors LeVine and Norman, Leavitt, and Brown base their interpretive chapters on long-term fieldwork that includes systematic observation and attends to the intersection of lived experience and verbal report. As a result, their data provide the basis for more complex conceptualizations of implicit learning.

Authors LeVine and Norman, for example, analyze the ways in which the concrete practices of German mothers affect the implicit associational learning of their infants, and then go further to explore the motivational sources of these mothers' behaviors. German infants, the authors contend, develop a strong sense of self-reliance from an early age because of their mothers' socialization practices. These mothers, for example, often let their young infants cry in their cribs for an hour or more in the morning before attending to them, and they leave the infants at home alone while they are out shopping and visiting. When they are home, moreover, they frequently ignore the demands of infants, especially when these are considered to be excessive cries for attention. As a result, the authors argue, these infants develop an implicit disposition toward self-reliance from actual experience and this disposition, in turn, shapes the infants' subsequent behavioral responses to caregivers.

Yet this documentation of implicit learning only provides a partial glimpse into the complex relationship that obtains between culture and experience, the authors contend, because the socialization environment itself is constructed largely by parents who are motivated to rear children in a certain way. Specifically, the authors argue that a model stressing the need for parents to promote virtue by bringing up a child to be "fit for life" combined with shared German cultural values emphasizing self-reliance and the love of order, shape maternal ideas and caretaking behaviors. Thus while regularities in the socialization environment of these German infants may determine the precocious dispositions they acquire, these regularities of pattern are themselves generated out of the conscious, intentional acts of mothers who are motivated by both explicitly taught and implicitly acquired German cultural values and patterns of caretaking.

In another chapter, Carl Ratner critiques behavioral studies that focus exclusively on global experience without attending to particular tasks and the environments in which these are performed. He proposes an alternative perspective, activity theory, for gaining a broader understanding of the relation of experience to culture. Activity theorists contend that culture consists fundamentally of socially organized practical activity, and that the specific activities individuals pursue are likely to influence the aspects of the cultural pattern they attend to and absorb. Ratner follows Bourdieu (1984) in noting that the activities individuals find meaningful and choose to pursue are themselves a product of a concrete socioeconomic system grounded in a particular historical epoch. It is the social organization of an activity and the cultural instruments used to carry it out, moreover, that activity theorists assume stimulate and organize psychological phenomena. Thus, Ratner, echoing the ecological theory of an earlier generation of anthropologists like Kardiner (1945) and the Whitings (1975), argues that changes in the social environment may subtly alter the nature of specific activities and the groups of people who perform them, thereby transforming the implicitly acquired psychological dispositions of individual culture members. A key theoretical insight emerging from studies of concrete individual activities, Ratner maintains, is the demonstration that individual psychological change is tied to societal change. Since concepts and psychological phenomena are shaped by practical activities which are grounded in concrete social patterns, significant psychological change requires corresponding changes in the organization of social life.

While the theoretical perspectives articulated by Ratner and by LeVine and Norman differ in some important respects, they complement each other. Clearly, LeVine and Norman's research findings demonstrate the importance of the concrete activities of German mothers in shaping the behavioral responses and implicit psychological dispositions of their infants. However, LeVine and Norman go beyond activity theory to explore the importance of a shared cultural ideology in shaping specific maternal ideas and in determining the common behavioral strategies that structure the infants' environment. In so doing, they challenge Ratner's unicausal direction of change and emphasize, instead, the reciprocal feedback that continually occurs between cultural ideals, individual motivations, and the social environment in which concrete activities take place.

On the other hand, LeVine and Norman's review of the historical evolution of child-rearing attitudes and practices in the United States clearly illustrates the importance of Ratner's insight that individual psychological change is tied ultimately to changes in the larger social environment as mediated through shifts in patterns of activity. LeVine and Norman report, for example, that child-rearing during the early part of this century was "medicalized" as a response to the threat of infectious disease, and that pediatricians advised mothers to maintain a hygienic environment for infants, which included keeping them on inflexible routines for feeding, sleeping and bodily contact. These activities subsequently cultivated a psychological disposition toward self-reliance in American infants similar to that seen in German infants today.

Analyzing the embodied aspects of individual experience

As Hollan notes in his chapter, person-centered ethnographers have begun to pay increasing attention to the ways in which subjective experience is "embodied," that is, to "how the senses and perceptions of the body are culturally elaborated into the experience of self and other" (p. 56). This area has long been neglected by traditional ethnographers who have focused, instead, Hollan reports, on talk and on linear, discursive, and cognized forms of data collection and analysis. As a consequence, anthropology has neglected other potentially important aspects of personal experience that are more tacit, visceral, imaginal, and "preobjective" (p. 57).

While researchers interested in the study of embodiment generally agree that minds cannot be studied independently of the bodies that they occupy, the difficulty of apprehending and representing embodied forms of experience is a considerable methodological obstacle. Hollan reports that person-centered ethnographers have generally pursued three approaches to the study of embodied experience. These include formal phenomenological studies of how perception and consciousness are created and maintained, more qualitative studies of how bodily senses become culturally elaborated in different ways, and studies in which bodies are used as a way of gaining privileged access to aspects of subjective experience that are otherwise unknowable or unspoken.

Westen contends that connectionist models of the mind are particularly well suited to theorizing about the creation and maintenance of perception and consciousness because they have the potential to integrate psychoanalytic insights about affect and motivation with cognitive insights into the acquisition and organization of knowledge. He cites examples of recent experiments demonstrating the existence of implicit or unconscious affective and motivational processes and argues that because feelings, wishes, and fears are associated with representations of people, situations, and abstract concepts, they will be activated unconsciously along with other forms of information when an associative neural network is stimulated by something in the person's environment.

Theorists have often disagreed, however, about the conditions that bring information stored in networks of association into consciousness. While cognitive theorists assume that information becomes conscious when its activation exceeds some threshold, psychoanalytic theorists, Westen writes, contend that important or significant information is more likely to become conscious (except when it is emotionally threatening). For Westen, then, consciousness is a joint function of level of cognitive activation, level of emotional significance, and affective quality that can either excite or inhibit representations from becoming conscious. The implication of his view is that affects are not only associatively *linked* to ideas but also *shape* them. Thus, for Garro's Anishinaabe informant discussed previously, the stress and despair arising from an unresolved illness activated the memory of an associationally linked experience with a snake that was itself marked in memory because of the fear and anxiety the individual experienced twenty-five years previously.

An emerging area of interest in studies of embodiment is how the senses and perceptions of the body affect and are affected by culturally mediated experiences. In a 1992 review article on the relationship of biological to psychological anthropology, Worthman argues that "physical states may mediate effects exerted by experience; social construction of experience may be designed to enhance these effects" (1992: 158). The implication, Worthman suggests, is that the timing of experience relative to physical development will have important effects on cognition, affect, and behavior. Thus, critical or sensitive periods, she writes, "open windows of differential sensitivity or developmental vulnerability to environmental inputs" (1992: 159). While LeVine and Norman do not deal directly with the embodied aspects of infant experiences in Germany, Worthman's contention is suggestive about the importance of timing and the physical aspects of the socialization practices of German mothers. Attempts to instill self-reliance begin in infancy, when German mothers selectively both offer and withhold bodily contact and comfort to babies. Thus the precocious self-reliance in the infant is grounded in embodied experiences which serve to link affective responses to the caretaker with a developing sense of self-awareness. This complex of preverbal experiences, in turn, forms the basis from which these children later interpret and respond to environmental stimuli, including the Strange Situation psychological test reported on by LeVine and Norman.

As Hollan notes, one of the key problems in the study of the embodied aspects of experience is ascertaining how we know that the senses, perceptions, and bodily experiences that we have discovered are really those of our subjects and not of ourselves – that is, how do we ensure that our findings are not really our own perceptual projections or preoccupations? This can be particularly difficult because, as Worthman (1992: 152) documents, the body has long been considered by psychological researchers as a significant source of primary metaphors in thought and hence is often assumed by them to be the primary referential locus for everyday experience among all groups of people.

Eve Danziger's chapter on Mopan Maya expressions of spatial relationships questions the prevailing European assumption that the linguistic domain of spatial perception is universally structured by reference points based on the physiological body (i.e., to the left, to the right, in front of, etc.) and invites a reconsideration of Sapir's arguments, later elaborated by Whorf, about the influence of language on perception and cognition (see also Kay and Kempton 1984). Employing a series of experimental tasks, Danziger found that her Mopan speakers did not utilize bodily reference coordinates like "left/right," "north/south" spatial orientations, or other orientation-bound schemas to organize abstract spatial relations. Rather, they tended to specify the relation between two objects in space in an orientation-free way by stating the proximity of one to some part of the other. This is an uncommon use of linguistic expression to encode spatial relations, and Danziger's research demonstrates further that this linguistic variation in spatial description shaped behavioral experience. The Mopan speakers she tested solved cognitive spatial perception tasks in less patterned ways than did speakers of languages with more common orientation-bound systems of spatial expression.

Her data and those of others working on this issue suggest that orientation-bound systems of spatial relations, which most investigators have assumed to be "natural," embodied, perceptual universals, are, in fact, themselves cultural constructs. Thus, Danziger argues, "the particular facts of linguistic encoding not only *structure* conceptualizations within the domain of spatial relations – a domain once thought to be invulnerable to cultural influences – they may actually *create* the domain . . . " (p. 216).

Danziger's work, then, would seem to confirm the worst fears of many ethnopsychologists (that analytical constructs employed by anthropologists would reflect their own culture-bound categories and hence render an understanding of indigenous beliefs and practices impossible), and of cultural psychologists (that the mutually constitutive nature of psychology and culture would render cross-cultural comparison and the search for universals impossible). Yet as Danziger notes, recognition that a domain of knowledge may be contextualized differently in different cultures does *not* make comparison impossible or necessarily invalid. Rather, careful attention to the design of relevant measures in different cultural contexts coupled with the explicit acknowledgment that the existence of universals is an open, empirical question can lead to fruitful results (see also D'Andrade 1995: 251). Like the patterning of human attachment studied by LeVine and Norman, there appears to be more than one way to conceptualize and to communicate about space. At the same time, it is possible that a limited number of variant patterns characterizes each of these domains cross-culturally, suggesting the existence of a universal set of constraints. Without careful comparative study, however, anthropologists could not delineate these differences and might, paradoxically, be more rather than less likely to assume that their own culturally and linguistically constructed domains were universal.

Continuity and change in cultural experience

The use of a variety of methodologically sophisticated approaches to understand internal psychological states and the individual bases of group behavior will ultimately enable psychological anthropologists to contribute to a more comprehensive theory of culture change as both motivating of and motivated by everyday experience. Generally, Westen contends, people are motivated to seek pleasurable states and to avoid painful ones. When they experience painful events, people may attempt to alter the situation to alleviate the painful feeling or, if this cannot be done behaviorally, they may use conscious coping mechanisms or unconscious defensive processes to manage the pain. To the extent that these latter processes are used repeatedly in similar situations, they will themselves come to be associated with the regulation of the feeling and may become a kind of procedural knowledge learned through experience.

While the tendency in psychoanalytic theory is to see these defensive responses as individualized, Westen points out that widespread cultural conflicts within a society can engender collective feelings of intense emotional distress that group members then seek to resolve. In such situations, Westen suggests, pre-packaged solutions are often available in the form of culturally patterned compromise formations (LeVine 1982). In the absence of such a cultural solution, however, groups may create their own. These new solutions to old dilemmas, moreover, may lead eventually to the formation of alternative cultural models that come to motivate and direct individual behavior in novel ways.

Just as Leavitt's Bumbita informants were attracted to a Christian revival movement that seemed to resolve their intrapsychic struggles between the desire for personal autonomy and a cultural concept of self defined in relationship to others, volume author Susan Love Brown's white, middle-class American informants of the "baby boom" generation coped with conflicts in self-representation by joining a utopian religious community. For the Americans she studied, however, the dilemma was the reverse of the one experienced by the Bumbita. Brown argues that the shift from a sociocentric conceptualization of self to an egocentric one based upon the ideal of self-fulfillment, which occurred in the United States between the 1950s and

1970s, created the need for these young Americans to reconcile the perception of an isolated self with their desire to form meaningful attachments to others. Their search for a solution was shaped, Brown argues, by the rise of a psychological consciousness in 1960s America and by their own prior personal experiences with hallucinogenic drugs. For her informants, experience was seen to be the only valid approach to knowledge and truth. Thus the Ananda Village movement attracted them because it was predicated upon the Self-Realization philosophy of Paramahansa Yoganda which emphasized the experiential practice of kriya yoga and meditation as the route to achieving unity with God. Along the lines that Ratner proposed in his chapter for this volume, this shift in religious activity coupled with the adoption of a communal living pattern became an avenue to significant psychological change for these new converts, who began, Brown argues, to alter their base level conceptions of self as well as their ways of establishing connections to others.

Brown's and Leavitt's research demonstrates that inherent conflicts between cultural notions of the self and the group, which become exacerbated under certain social conditions, may motivate people to create new social movements that could function, Westen suggests, as group compromise formations. Many social movements, moreover, are distinctly therapeutic, Brown contends, because they are the means through which psychological security is restored so that people are protected against the turmoil of change. Yet not all movements succeed in resolving the intrapsychic conflicts of adherents. While Brown's Ananda village informants were able to adapt successfully to a new view of self and to a communal way of life, Leavitt's Bumbita informants became disillusioned with the Christian revival movement they embraced so enthusiastically in the beginning.

Once again, the work of Leavitt and of Brown demonstrates the importance of careful case studies as the basis for fruitful comparison. In contradistinction to a wholly constructivist explanation for social action, these authors demonstrate empirically that the members of both groups were motivated to join social movements by their common experience of intrapsychic conflicts stemming from disjunctions between individual desires and cultural conceptions of self. Clearly, however, variant cultural notions of self and changing social conditions did shape the content of the conflicts experienced by each group and of the solutions each found meaningful. Without such fine-grained comparison, moreover, it is impossible, as De Vos (1999: 33) points out, to assess the relative adequacy or inadequacy of different cultural adaptations in achieving mental and emotional balance for individual culture members. Yet such assessments are crucial to determining why the Ananda Village movement was able to provide therapeutic resolution for its converts while the Bumbita Christian revival movement was not.

The need for a reinvigorated comparative perspective in psychological anthropology

As the preceding discussion indicates, the possibility of valid comparative study is of central concern in psychological anthropology today. While a justified anthropological wariness has grown up about the possibility of any genuinely culturally sensitive comparative research, Danziger argues that it is critical that psychological anthropology, in particular, once again take up the comparative challenge. Because it is often difficult for the single researcher to attend to all the interconnections that obtain between the structure and apprehension of experience, comparative syntheses of multiple field studies are essential if we are to advance our theoretical understandings about the interconnections between culture and experience. As Danziger writes, summarizing the sentiments of many of the authors in this volume:

Although one response to the realization that there is no such thing as decontextualized knowing is to cease to desire to know, another is to seek an identifiable context for one's own intellectual program, and to accept the contextualized nature of one's discoveries without rejecting them because they are contextualized. (p. 200)

In their chapter documenting the history of comparative studies in psychological anthropology, Robert and Ruth Munroe point out that even those anthropologists who eschew the making of cross-cultural comparisons often do so implicitly by using their own culture as the unstated but assumed baseline against which the "other" is assessed (p. 223). While theorists in this latter group fear that comparison will result in the inappropriate reification of Western theoretical concepts, the refusal to make explicit comparison often results, ironically, in implicit biases that stem from the analysts' taken-for-granted assumption that their own culture-bound attitudes and predispositions characterize human behavior everywhere. Alternatively, such anticomparativist sentiments often act selectively to emphasize the alien nature of the "other" and subtly reinforce existing power and prestige differentials between the researcher and the people being studied. The only antidote to such bias is careful, methodologically sophisticated, comparative investigation, whether within single cultures, across specified units, or within a larger cross-cultural framework.

Citing the pioneering work of John Whiting, the Munroes emphasize two major advantages to systematic comparative investigation: it provides an increased range of variation in human behavior and it can answer the question of generality – that is, whether a finding is bound to a single culture or relates to human behavior in general – points both well illustrated in Danziger's comparative study of the linguistic expression of spatial relations, LeVine and Norman's study of patterns of infant attachment in the United States and Germany, and Brown's and Leavitt's essays on social movements in very different cultural contexts.

For the Munroes, another crucial benefit of comparative analysis is the determination of universals in human behavior. Because universals are characterized by the patterns of regularity and similarity they display across cultures, the Munroes argue that they "point us toward robust biopsychological points of reference that are critical and necessary for the framing of generalizations about humankind" (p. 226). Yet the existence of universals also presupposes variation in their magnitude, intensity, or frequency – variation that demonstrates the importance of cultural factors in shaping or "tuning" biopsychological predispositions (see also Johnson and Price-Williams 1996: 99).

One of the most important messages of this volume is that we can combine person-centered studies in experience-near ways (cf. Hollan, this volume) with a return to the use of explicit comparative frameworks. As the Munroes demonstrate in a detailed analysis of research on the topic of emotion, "the comparativist and the ethnographer who works within a single society are divided in their labor, but not necessarily in their aims" (p. 231). Similarly, Hollan (p. 49) argues that person-centered ethnography is not necessarily anticomparative. However, its practitioners stress that the categories of comparison should emerge from the experiential lives of the people studied rather than be imposed by the anthropologist with little reference to that experience. Although the authors included in this volume draw upon various theoretical perspectives, their research demonstrates a renewed commitment to finely contextualized studies of experience as the basis upon which more sophisticated and potentially cross-cultural comparisons can be made. In so doing, their studies demonstrate that far from being wholly culturally constructed, individual psychological predispositions and mental states are also shaped by universal biological attributes and developmental stages; common human activities resulting from shared material adaptations; and culturally specific intrapsychic conflicts stemming from disjunctions between shared cultural values and the realities of everyday experience. The challenge facing psychological anthropology today is to develop a genuinely multidisciplinary perspective capable of analyzing and theorizing in fresh ways the mutually constituted nature of culture and individual experience. The chapters in this volume are an exciting first step in this direction.

Acknowledgments

The authors are grateful to Naomi Quinn, Robert L. Munroe, and three anonymous reviewers for their helpful comments on an earlier version of this chapter.

NOTES

1   The title of this book derives from and pays tribute to the work of two pioneers in the study of culture and personal experience, Edward Sapir and A. Irving Hallowell. Early on, Sapir contended that many of the aspects of individual experience that anthropologists thought of as entirely personal would turn out to have a cultural basis (1994: 177); he also maintained that culture consists of patterns people create such that "culture, like truth, is what we make it" (1994: 245). Some thirty years later, Hallowell formulated the concept of the "behavioral environment of the self" to capture this sense of interaction between cultural representations and the phenomenological world of the individual (1955: 89). Hallowell's essay has been influential among constructivist theorists who derive from his work the notion that individual psychology is culturally constructed and culturally variable. Yet these same scholars often ignore the other key component of Hallowell's theory, its emphasis on the importance of human nature in individual intrapsychic development. Indeed, as Spiro writes, Hallowell advocated a complex conception of individual experience as constructed both from "psychological constants that define the dynamics of a human level of adjustment everywhere, and from cultural dispositions mediated through the behavioral environment of the self" (Spiro 1996: 4–5). The neglected, yet vitally important implication of both Sapir's and Hallowell's work is that it is crucial that we study *the interactions between* the behavioral environments (context and habituation) and cultural expectations that structure experiences *and* the ways in which individuals directly apprehend, explain, and act on those experiences within particular contexts. New theoretical developments in a variety of disciplines coupled with a renewed commitment to case by case, comparatively oriented research provides the basis upon which the authors represented in this volume articulate a new agenda for research on an issue of longstanding interest in psychological anthropology.

REFERENCES

Abu-Lughod, Lila 1990 The Romance of Resistance: Tracing Transformations of Power through Bedouin Women. *American Ethnologist* 17: 41–55.
    1991 Writing Against Culture. In *Recapturing Anthropology: Working in the Present*, R. G. Fox, ed. Santa Fe, NM: School of American Research. Pp. 137–162.
Bourdieu, Pierre 1977 *Outline of a Theory of Practice*, trans. R. Nice. Cambridge: Cambridge University Press.
    1984 *Distinction: A Social Critique of a Judgment of Taste*, trans. R. Nice. Cambridge, MA: Harvard University Press.

Butler, Judith 1990 *Gender Trouble: Feminism and Subversion of Identity*. New York: Routledge.

Clifford, James 1986 Introduction: Partial Truths. In *Writing Culture: The Poetics and Politics of Ethnography*, J. Clifford and G. E. Marcus, eds. Berkeley, CA: University of California Press. Pp. 1–26.

    1998 *Routes: Travel and Translation in the Late Twentieth Century*. Cambridge, MA: Harvard University Press.

Comaroff, Jean 1985 *Body of Power, Spirit of Resistance*. Chicago, IL: University of Chicago Press.

Crapanzano, Vincent 1980 *Tuhami: A Portrait of a Moroccan*. Chicago, IL: University of Chicago Press.

D'Andrade, Roy G. 1995 *The Development of Cognitive Anthropology*. Cambridge: Cambridge University Press.

De Vos, George A. 1999 Toward an Integrated Social Science. *Ethos* 27: 33–48.

Edgerton, Robert B. 1999 Perspectives from a Varied Career. *Ethos* 27: 49–53.

Hallowell, A. Irving 1955 The Self and Its Behavioral Environment. In Hallowell, *Culture and Experience*. Philadelphia, PA: University of Pennsylvania Press. Pp. 75–111.

Hinton, Alexander Labon, ed. 1999 *Biocultural Approaches to the Emotions*. Cambridge: Cambridge University Press.

Ingham, John M. 1996 *Psychological Anthropology Reconsidered*. Cambridge: Cambridge University Press.

Johnson, Allen W. and Douglass Price-Williams 1996 *Oedipus Ubiquitous – The Family Complex in World Folk Literature*. Stanford, CA: Stanford University Press.

Kardiner, Abram with the collaboration of R. Linton, C. DuBois, and J. West 1945 *The Psychological Frontiers of Society*. New York and London: Columbia University Press.

Kay, Paul D. and Willet Kempton 1984 What is the Sapir–Whorf Hypothesis? *American Anthropologist* 86: 65–79.

Kondo, Dorinne K. 1990 *Crafting Selves*. Chicago, IL: University of Chicago Press.

LeVine, Robert L. 1982 *Culture, Behavior, and Personality*. 2nd edn. Chicago, IL: Aldine.

    1999 An Agenda for Psychological Anthropology. *Ethos* 27: 15–24.

Lutz, Catherine 1988 *Unnatural Emotions: Everyday Sentiments on a Micronesian Atoll and Their Challenge to Western Theory*. Chicago, IL: University of Chicago Press.

Martin, Emily 1987 *The Woman in the Body: A Cultural Analysis of Reproduction*. Boston, MA: Beacon Press.

Munroe, Robert L. 1999 A Behavioral Orientation. *Ethos* 27: 104–114.

Nuckolls, Charles W. 1998 *Culture: A Problem That Cannot Be Solved*. Madison, WI: The University of Wisconsin Press.

Ortner, Sherry 1990 Patterns of History: Cultural Schemas in the Foundings of Sherpa Religious Institutions. In *Culture Through Time: Anthropological Approaches*, E. Ohnuki-Tierney, ed. Stanford, CA: Stanford University Press. Pp. 57–93.

Read, Stephen, E. J. Vanman, and Lynn C. Miller 1997 Connectionism, Parallel Constraint Satisfaction Processes, and Gestalt Principles: (Re)introducing

Cognitive Dynamics to Social Psychology. *Personality and Social Psychology Review* 1: 26–53.

Rosaldo, Renato I. 1989 *Culture and Truth: The Remaking of Social Analysis.* Boston, MA: Beacon Press.

Rumelhart, David E., James L. McClelland, and the PDP Research Group 1986 *Parallel Distributed Processing: Explorations in the Microstructure of Cognition.* vol. I: *Foundations.* Cambridge, MA: MIT Press.

Sapir, Edward 1994 *The Psychology of Culture: A Course of Lectures*, reconstructed and ed. Judith T. Irvine. Berlin and New York: Mouton de Gruyter.

Schwartz, Theodore 1999 Residues of a Career: Reflections on Anthropological Knowledge. *Ethos* 27: 54–61.

Scott, James C. 1985 *Weapons of the Weak*: *Everyday Forms of Peasant Resistance.* New Haven, CT: Yale University Press.

Shweder, Richard A. 1990 Cultural Psychology – What Is It? In *Cultural Psychology: Essays on Comparative Human Development*, J. W. Stigler, R. A. Shweder, and G. Herdt, eds. Cambridge: Cambridge University Press. Pp. 1–43.

1991 *Thinking through Cultures: Expeditions in Cultural Psychology.* Cambridge, MA: Harvard University Press.

1999 Why Cultural Psychology? *Ethos* 27: 62–73.

Smith, Elliot R. 1998 Mental Representation and Memory. In *Handbook of Social Psychology*, vol. I, D. T. Gilbert, S. T. Fiske, and G. Lindzey, eds. New York: McGraw-Hill. Pp. 391–445.

Spiro, Melford E. 1996 The Vision of A. I. Hallowell. Paper presented to the 95th Annual Meeting of the American Anthropological Association, San Francisco, CA.

1999 Anthropology and Human Nature. *Ethos* 27: 7–14.

Strauss, Claudia 1992 Models and Motives. In *Human Motives and Cultural Models*, R. G. D'Andrade and C. Strauss, eds. Cambridge: Cambridge University Press. Pp. 1–20.

Strauss, Claudia and Naomi Quinn 1997 *A Cognitive Theory of Cultural Meaning.* Cambridge: Cambridge University Press.

Whiting, Beatrice B. and John W. M. Whiting 1975 *Children of Six Cultures – A Psychocultural Analysis.* Cambridge, MA: Harvard University Press.

Willis, Paul 1977 *Learning to Labor: How Working Class Kids Get Working Class Jobs.* New York: Columbia University Press.

Worthman, Carol M. 1992 Cupid and Psyche: Investigative Syncretism in Biological and Psychological Anthropology. In *New Directions in Psychological Anthropology*, T. Schwartz, G. M. White, and C. A. Lutz, eds. Cambridge: Cambridge University Press. Pp. 150–180.

Part I

Theoretical and methodological approaches to the study of experience

1 Beyond the binary opposition in psychological anthropology: integrating contemporary psychoanalysis and cognitive science

Drew Westen

Mark Twain once quipped that if capital and labor ever do get together, the rest of us are in trouble. The same may be true today of psychoanalysis and cognitive science. For years, these two approaches have proceeded largely independently of each other, in both psychology and anthropology. And yet, I argue, important aspects of the two approaches are capable of being integrated. This chapter begins by reviewing recent developments in psychoanalysis and cognitive science, focusing on the concepts of associational networks and affect regulation. It then suggests how an integration of these seemingly incompatible views of mind may contribute to contemporary thinking about long-standing questions regarding the relation between culture and individual action. In so doing, it addresses three questions: how cultural models are internalized, how they acquire the capacity to influence behavior, and how individual actors think and behave in the face of conflicting and ambiguous cultural models.

Contemporary psychoanalytic theory

Psychoanalytic theory was once a monolithic approach, identified with Freud and his models of the mind. Although Freud's models have not been abandoned, psychoanalytic theorists have developed alternative models that have not yet been reconciled with those Freud laid out but stand instead in a somewhat uneasy coexistence with their Freudian progenitors. Together, however, these various models provide a useful collage, if not yet a portrait, of the mind, that stresses the mind's emotional and motivational aspects.

From Freud's models to contemporary psychoanalytic theory

Freud's first model, his topographic model, distinguished conscious, preconscious, and unconscious processes (Freud 1953). Whereas preconscious processes are not currently conscious but can be brought to consciousness, unconscious processes are inaccessible to consciousness because they are repressed. Freud's second model, his drive-instinct model, proposed that humans are motivated by sexual and aggressive drives. His third, developmental, model focused on the child's evolving quest for pleasure and recognition of the social limitations of pleasure-seeking. Thus, he tied the development of psychic structure to the development of one of his two drives. Freud's final model, the structural model, reframed the topographic understanding of conflict (between conscious and unconscious processes) into conflict among the id (the wishful, instinctive, repressed part of the psyche), superego (internalized morality), and ego (the poor, hapless executive part of the mind that somehow has to reconcile the demands of the id and superego while simultaneously attending to reality).

These were the models that informed early approaches to psychoanalytic anthropology, and that tended to reduce culture to psychosexual conflicts of one sort or another. Over the last thirty years, however, psychoanalytic models have changed substantially. Whereas Freud's theory focused most on the more primitive and wishful parts of human nature, the ego psychology that emerged in the 1940s out of Freud's tripartite structural model focused on the adaptive capacities of the mind, notably cognition, defense, and impulse control (see Blanck and Blanck 1974, Redl and Wineman 1951, Vaillant 1977, 1992).

Although its roots lay in the same era, object relations theory has clearly been the major development in psychoanalysis over the last three decades (see Greenberg and Mitchell 1983, Mitchell 1988). "Object relations" refers to the representations people hold of themselves, others, and relationships, and to the cognitive, affective, and behavioral processes that interact with, and derive from those representations (Westen 1991). Whereas Freud's theory of development focused on psychosexual stages, object relations theorists (e.g., Fairbairn 1952, Kernberg 1975, 1984) have offered models of the development of the capacity to form mature, intimate relationships with others. Fairbairn, for example, proposed that development entails a movement from immature dependence to mature interdependence.

Another major development in recent years is self psychology, initiated by Heinz Kohut (1971, 1977), which argues that humans have fundamental needs for self-esteem and self-coherence. According to Kohut, unempathic caregiving in the early years of life can lead people to have chronic problems with self-esteem, such as low self-esteem or compensatory grandiose views of themselves. Current "relational" models in psychoanalysis (Aron 1996, Mitchell 1988) represent in many respects a rapprochement of object relations theories, self psychology, and the interpersonal model of Harry Stack Sullivan (1953) (who focused not only on internal representations of others – called object representations in psychoanalytic parlance – but also on the way interactions with others in the environment shape people's fundamental needs, desires, and ways of seeing themselves and the world).

The shift to object-relational, self-psychological, and relational theories of development in psychoanalysis is of considerable relevance to psychoanalytic anthropology, since it changes, or certainly augments, the nature of the questions asked from a cross-cultural perspective. The main questions that motivated a prior generation of psychoanalytic anthropologists centered on issues such as the extent to which certain toilet training practices lead to modal character styles or conflicts, the way different cultures socialize children to handle sexual and aggressive impulses, and the way unacknowledged impulses find expression in myths, rituals, and other cultural practices. These newer, more relational theories add questions about the way representations of the self and others are organized, what people expect from each other, the extent to which styles of attachment are universal or culturally specific, the extent to which similar experiences cross-culturally (such as modes of discipline, loss of a parent, or migration) produce similar responses, and so forth.

Three questions that provide a road map of the mind

This collage, or perhaps kaleidoscope, of psychoanalytic perspectives can lead to differing pictures of an individual or of mental processes more generally, depending on the angle one takes. If one steps back, however, a contemporary psychoanalytic understanding of the mind, or assessment of an individual's personality derived from these approaches, addresses three questions (Westen 1995, 1998a) that define a set of variables that could organize cross-cultural investigation of psychological processes. The first is the question of motivation: what do people wish for, fear, and value? This is the question initially addressed by most of Freud's models of the mind, particularly his drive theory, although many contemporary psychoanalytic theorists no longer accept Freud's drive theory, instead arguing for a variety of motives that influence human behavior, such as self-esteem, needs for relatedness, and needs for competence, as well as Freud's motives for sex and aggression (e.g., Bowlby 1969, 1982, Brenner 1982, Kohut 1977, Lichtenberg 1989, White 1960). At the most basic level, people want some things (wishes), avoid others because they are afraid of or repulsed by them (fears), and morally value some others (values). The range of what can be wanted, feared, and valued obviously varies tremendously according to cultural and ecological demands.

One of the most important contemporary psychoanalytic ideas related to motivation, which maintains Freud's emphasis on conflict, is the concept of compromise formation (Brenner 1982). A compromise formation is a compromise among competing motives (many of which are unconscious) that attempts to optimize their satisfaction. The undoing of some leading televangelists in the United States provides a good example, since these television preachers seemed torn between their sexual desires and their rigid moral values, which prohibited culturally normative expression of sexual feelings and wishes. (We will give Brothers Swaggert and Bakker the benefit of the doubt here and presume they were not simply hypocrites and charlatans who did not believe any of what they preached.) Because of their conflict between Bible thumping and genital throbbing, these televangelists spent much of their time preoccupied with sex, preaching its evils, attacking its manifestations in others, and then finding themselves compelled to engage surreptitiously in one colorful variety of it or another. From a psychoanalytic point of view, this confluence of seemingly contradictory behavior was a compromise formation that, within the constraints set by a hypothalamus that would not relent and moral and religious values that were equally inelastic, permitted them the most satisfaction they could obtain. Like a classic Freudian symptom, however, the compromise did not work well and ended up in their undoing. Many compromise formations are more adaptive, such as the sublimation of power and altruistic motives into a political career. As will be described below, cultures provide ready compromises of this sort to help people solve problems that occur with some frequency (LeVine 1982, Westen 1985).

The second question relates to adaptation: what psychological resources does the person have to cope with internal and external challenges? This is the question addressed by psychoanalytic ego psychology. Several variables on which individuals differ fall under this domain. What cognitive abilities does the person have? What are the individual's prominent belief systems? How does s/he consciously cope with, and unconsciously defend against, threatening thoughts and unpleasant feelings? What emotions does the person chronically experience, and to what degree is s/he comfortable with feeling and expressing these emotions? Finally, what behavioral skills does the person have to deal with adaptational demands? These are, once again, domains that are highly influenced by cultural and ecological circumstances.

The third question relates to modes of interpersonal functioning and the internal processes that mediate that functioning: how does the person experience the self, others, and relationships, and to what degree, and in what ways, is the individual capable of forming relationships with others? This is the domain studied by object relations theorists, self-psychologists, and relational theorists. A number of variables are subsumed under this question: the extent to which representations are complex and differentiated; the affective quality of expectations of relationships; the person's style and capacity for investing in other people; the extent to which the individual is guided in interpersonal relations by moral value systems; the individual's habitual ways of understanding of causality in the social realm; self-esteem; the experience of the self as integrated; the ways the individual manages aggressive impulses that threaten relationships; the identifications with others the individual either embraces or fears (McWilliams 1998); the dominant interpersonal themes and concerns that recur in the person's interpersonal thoughts and experiences; and the person's interpersonal behavior. Once again, these domains differ cross-culturally and could establish an agenda for exploring the interface of culture and personality.

For each of these three sets of questions, a hallmark of the psychoanalytic approach is the assumption that understanding them requires placing them in developmental context. What is their developmental course, both normatively and in cases of less than optimal development? And how do specific experiences, some idiosyncratic and some more broadly distributed throughout a culture, influence subsequent development?

Contemporary cognitive science

In psychology, cognitive science has become the dominant perspective (see Robins and Craik 1994), having displaced behaviorism in a scientific revolution that began in the late 1950s. Based on the metaphor that the mind is a computer, researchers developed a multistage serial processing model of information processing, in which information passes sequentially through a series of memory stores. This has become known as the "modal model," since it is the model that has been largely assumed for thirty years, although, as we will see, psychology is in the midst of a second cognitive revolution, in which this model itself is beginning to unravel.

The modal model

The first stage in the modal model is sensory registration, in which information is held for a flicker of an instant (Sperling 1960), long enough, for example, to maintain in memory the last syllable of a speaker's ongoing flow of words. The next stage is short-term memory, which is equated with consciousness and has more recently become integrated into the broader concept of "working memory" because it provides a work space in which the individual can manipulate current information or information from long-term memory for purposes of problem solving (Baddeley 1995). Short-term memory can maintain information for roughly 30 seconds and can hold approximately seven pieces of information at a time (Miller 1956), such as the digits in a phone number.

The third stage is long-term memory, which can store many pieces of information indefinitely, although information can be unrecoverable for a variety of reasons, such as relative disuse, lack of retrieval cues, or interference from similar memories. Information is stored in long-term memory along associative networks – that is, pieces of information are associatively connected with each other, so that activating one spreads activation to related information – and as schemas, hierarchically organized patterns of thought (such as generalized and specific representations of what women are like). When people want to make a decision, according to this model, they retrieve relevant information from long-term into short-term memory and perform various operations, such as calculating the value and probabilities of various courses of action (Anderson 1993, Newell and Simon 1972).

A changing view of thought and memory

In the last decade this model has undergone considerable evolution in four interrelated respects, which may constitute more of a revolution than evolution in thinking. The first is a shift away from a serial processing model. In the modal model, stages of memory storage and retrieval occur sequentially, one at a time, with information passing from the sensory registers to short-term memory to long-term memory. Retrieval in this model means calling up information from long-term memory and restoring it to short-term memory. In contrast, contemporary memory researchers recognize that things are not so neatly ordered. For example, much of the information that is stored for long-term use has never passed through a stage of active, conscious processing (short-term memory), and the attentional mechanisms that bring some sensory information into consciousness (short-term memory) require activation of information in long-term memory that helps determine the likely importance of various sensory experiences.

Second and related, researchers have come to recognize the extent to which thought processes (such as categorization) and discrete memory systems (components of working memory, various long-term memory subsystems) operate simultaneously, in parallel. For example, when people simultaneously hear words and see lips moving, they process the sound and speech using auditory modules in the left temporal and frontal cortex, identify rapidly changing visual images using visual modules in the occipital and lower (inferior) temporal lobes, and pinpoint the location of the person's face and moving lips in space using a visual-spatial processing module, which runs from the occipital lobes through the upper (superior) temporal and parietal lobes. Neural pathways in the cortex that integrate input from different sensory modes then combine the information and signal any disjunction between the sound and image, for example, that someone else interjected a word.

Third, whereas researchers once focused exclusively on conscious thought and memory processes, such as recollection of word lists and conscious problem-solving efforts, as we will see, researchers now recognize that much of information processing occurs outside of awareness. Not only can memory be expressed in behavior without passing through consciousness, but people often act on the basis of learning that occurs unconsciously, as they register regularities in their environment or learn social rules (such as how much eye contact to make with people of different status or gender) with little or no instruction (Reber 1993).

Finally, as important as these substantive changes is a change in metaphor (which Kuhn [1970] has argued is one of the basic features of a scientific revolution). Impressed by the extraordinary developments in computer science that were just beginning to revolutionize technology in the 1960s, researchers saw in the computer a powerful metaphor for the most impressive computing machine ever designed: the human mind. Today, after a decade of similar progress in neuroscience, cognitive scientists have begun to turn to a different metaphor: mind as brain. Thus, cognitive scientists are less likely to think of representations as located in a particular memory store than as distributed throughout a network of neurons whose simultaneous activation constitutes the memory.

Of particular importance for anthropology are two developments in cognitive science that are part and parcel of this shifting terrain: the distinction between implicit and explicit process (particularly in memory), and the emergence of connectionist models of thought, memory, and representation.

Implicit and explicit memory

Cognitive scientists now distinguish two kinds of thought and memory that have very different properties and different neural substrates. (We focus here on the distinction as it applies to memory.) The first, called explicit memory, is the kind of memory studied throughout most of the history of experimental psychology, in which people can consciously recall or recognize information they have previously learned, such as the name of a ritual studied by Bateson or a series of words presented on a list during an experiment. Sometimes called "declarative" knowledge, because this knowledge can be consciously known and "declared," explicit knowledge can be either generic (originally called "semantic"), such as ideas, facts, and definitions; or episodic, that is, memories of specific events (Tulving 1972).

Implicit memory, in contrast, is memory that is observable in behavior but is not consciously brought to mind (Roediger 1990, Schacter 1992, Schacter and Buckner 1998). One kind of implicit memory is procedural memory, "how to" knowledge of procedures or skills useful in various situations, such as the motor memory involved in throwing a ball or playing a complex piece on the piano, which had once required considerable conscious attention, or behaviorally expressed knowledge of subtle social procedures, such as how close to stand to another person in conversation. People typically cannot report how they carry out these procedures, and when they do, they often make up plausible but incorrect explanations of how they did what they did (see Nisbett and Wilson 1977).

Another kind of implicit memory involves associative memory and is studied in priming experiments. In these experiments, researchers present subjects with a word or picture (the prime) that is associatively connected in some way to a target object (usually a word). Thus, exposing subjects to an infrequently used word like "assassin" among a long list of words renders them more likely a week later to respond with assassin when asked to fill in the missing letters of the word fragment, A–A–IN, despite the fact that, after that time interval, they are unlikely to be able to report whether assassin was on the list they learned a week earlier (Tulving, Schacter, and Stark 1982). Thus, they remember implicitly – because the network of associations still has some residual activation – but not explicitly. Priming effects can also occur subliminally. Subjects exposed subliminally to "dog" who are then asked to press a button as soon as they know whether a set of letters flashed on a screen is a word will show shorter response latencies (that is, a faster response) when presented with the word "terrier." The reason is that terrier is semantically related to dog, so that priming with the word dog activates a network of associations, spreading activation to anything on that network (see Collins and Loftus 1975). Because words like terrier and poodle are already primed, they require less stimulation to be consciously recognized. Implicit learning of this sort occurs as people unconsciously observe regularities in their behavioral environment (to use Hallowell's [1955] term), in experiences ranging from daily occurrences to highly organized rituals that carry implicit messages about emotion, motivation, obligation, identity, and so forth.

Research in cognitive neuroscience, particularly with patients with specific brain lesions leading to problems such as amnesia, has recently discovered the neural underpinnings of the distinction between implicit and explicit memory. Like normal subjects, amnesics show signs of implicit memory even when they lack explicit memories. In a series of studies (see Squire 1986), amnesic and normal subjects studied word lists (e.g., absent, income, hotel). As would be expected, the amnesic subjects had difficulty on tests of explicit memory, such as free recall (asking them to name all the words from the list they could remember) and cued recall (giving them cues, such as the first three letters of the words). However, when subjects were shown word fragments (such as "abs–") and simply asked to complete them with the first word that came to mind, amnesic subjects were just as likely as neurologically intact subjects to use words from the list they had seen. Thus, despite their lack of explicit memory, they manifested few if any deficits in implicit memory. Research with animals involving selective lesioning of different areas of the temporal lobes of the cerebrum has documented the key role of a limbic structure, the hippocampus (and adjacent neural tissue), on explicit, but not implicit memory (Squire 1986, Squire and Zola-Morgan 1991).

As we will see, the distinction between implicit and explicit cognitive processes is important for psychological anthropology for two reasons. The first is that the acknowledgment of the pervasiveness of unconscious (implicit) processes allows for some integration of the understanding of thought processes in cognitive science and the understanding of affective and motivational processes in psychoanalysis, which has always assumed that much of mental life is unconscious. The "cognitive unconscious" and the "dynamic unconscious" are, of course, different in some very important respects. Most importantly, the latter includes disavowed mental contents, and not simply representations at low thresholds of activation. However, some mechanisms described below can help bridge what was once an unbridgeable chasm between experimental and clinical views of the mind. Second, most cultural learning is implicit, and distinguishing aspects of culture that are internalized implicitly and explicitly – and of socialization processes that are implicitly intended, explicitly intended, or accidental by-products of other implicitly or explicitly intended acts – is important for understanding how cultural models become integrated into individuals' belief systems and motives.

Connectionism

A second major development of relevance to anthropology is the development of connectionist models, the best exemplars of which are called parallel distributed processing (PDP) models (Read, Vanman, and Miller 1997, Rumelhart, McClelland, and the PDP Research Group 1986, Smith 1998).[1] PDP models rest upon two fundamental propositions. The first is that many cognitive processes occur simultaneously, *in parallel*. In these models, a serial, conscious cognitive "architecture" is superimposed on a parallel unconscious architecture, which assembles conscious cognitions (and as we will see, affects and motives) outside of awareness. The second premise of connectionist models is that the meaning of an object or concept is not contained in any single unit (either a single node in a computer program, or a single neuron or "engram" in the brain). Rather, it is spread out, or *distributed*, across a network of processing units that, through experience, become activated in tandem. Each of these units attends to some small aspect of the representation, and none alone "stands for" the entire concept.

Although connectionist models emerged in artificial intelligence research as cognitive scientists attempted to model cognitive and perceptual processes, paradoxically they have provided the impetus for the shift in metaphor from mind as computer to mind as brain. Connectionist models assume that when the brain represents knowledge, it does so through the interaction of hundreds, thousands, or millions of neurons, which can either excite or inhibit each other – that is, spread activation to or away from a particular interpretation, categorization, or behavior. Consider, for example, how a person differentiates between the words "got" and "pot" when she sees a handwritten scrawl that says, "Sally . . . -ot paid today," where the initial letter is not entirely clear. Primitive feature-detecting neurons in the thalamus (a neural structure involved primarily in relaying sensory information to the appropriate sections of the cerebral cortex for further processing) detect the contours of the ambiguous letter, determining, for example, that it is one letter rather than two (and hence ruling out the possibility of "shot") and that it includes at least one circular component letter. This spreads activation to both "got" and "pot," although the two may differ in frequency of use and hence receive different levels of activation because one is more chronically activated and hence more rapidly primed.

At the same time, however, two additional processes are operating in parallel. The first is a general context effect that inhibits the categorization of the ambiguous word as "pot," because nothing in the letter has anything to do with either the kitchen, plants, or marijuana. The second is a cognitive matching process that "decides" what possible words could fit into this particular sentence. This process inhibits the "p" and spreads activation to the "g" because only the "g" could work in this sentence. Thus, three processes occur in parallel, none of which is available to consciousness and each of which occurs in a flicker of an instant, leading to immediate interpretation of the ambiguous letter and recognition of the word.

This process is thus one of constraint satisfaction, that is, satisfying as many constraints as possible at the different processing levels, in order to achieve the best fit to the data. The constraints at each level are established by ever-changing "weights" attached to connections between units (or neurons, if one moves to this level of analysis). These weights reflect the extent to which the two units have been typically coactivated, and they increase the more times two units are activated in tandem. Unrelated information will have weights of zero connecting two units, whereas related information (such as "g" presented before "ot") will have strong positive weights, so that activating one will spread activation to the other. If, however, a person's experience changes, so that two objects or representations are no longer activated in tandem with much frequency or are eclipsed by other associations, the weight will gradually move toward zero, become negative, or simply be overshadowed by more powerful weights to other associations. Thus, an anthropologist from the United States who hears the word "hunting" will likely have more ready associations to "gathering" than to "license," even though, prior to entering anthropology, he may have shared culturally distributed networks of association about hunters common in the United States.

Connectionist models thus de-emphasize serial processing, arguing that any information that becomes conscious has already had numerous elements of it processed simultaneously and unconsciously without ever passing through the stages depicted in the modal information-processing model. Advocates of parallel processing models argue that human information processing is simply too fast, and the requirements of the environment too instantaneous, to make serial processing viable as a general way of processing most information. Instead, consciousness serves as a mechanism for focusing special attention on issues of adaptive significance, monitoring relevant parts of the environment, and allowing more carefully considered choices, particularly when standard operating procedures fail or lead to ambiguous results.

Integrating psychodynamic and cognitive theory and research

At first blush, these two approaches – psychoanalysis and cognitive science – look like they have very little to say to each other, and indeed, the number of psychologists conversant in both probably could not make up a barbershop quartet. (For potential members of the quartet, see Bucci 1997, Epstein 1994, Erdelyi 1985, Horowitz 1987, Singer and Salovey 1991, and Westen 1985, 1991, 1998b.) Psychoanalysis is derived from clinical experience and focuses primarily on complex affective and motivational processes, whereas cognitive science is derived from experimental studies and focuses on cognition, much of it relatively simple and hence accessible to experimental investigation. If the mind were divided like Caesar's Gaul into three parts – affect, motivation, and cognition – with no connections among them, these two approaches could probably live happily in their isolation. Unfortunately, that is not how things work, which means that either someone is right and someone is wrong or that adherents of both models might have something to learn from each other. I would argue that the latter is the case (for fuller presentations, see Westen 1998b, 1999).

Why the right hand needs to know what the left hand is doing

One of the greatest strengths of the psychoanalytic approach is its under-standing of motivation. From the start, Freud emphasized three things about human motivation: first, motivation has its origin in our bodies, so that below an elegant cortex that allows us to solve differential equations is a relentless hypothalamus that differs little from that of other primates; second, motives need not develop in harmony with one another and in fact often come into conflict; third, motives need not be conscious. All three assumptions have turned out to be correct (see Westen 1998b, Westen and Gabbard 1999). Cognitive theories, in contrast, have only recently begun to recognize that people think for a reason, and to the extent that they rely on a computer metaphor, they have difficulty doing anything but appending motives onto a model that simply cannot accommodate them.

Our strengths and our weaknesses, however, tend to spring from the same wells, and this is no less true of theories than personalities. Psychoanalysis lacks a coherent theory of thinking, and its preference for motivational explanations has often obscured relevant cognitive explanations. For example, for years psychoanalysts have tried to understand patients with borderline personality disorders, who tend to be impulsive and emotionally labile, and to have difficulty maintaining relationships or jobs because of their inability to maintain constant feelings toward people, relationships, and goals. No theory other than psychoanalysis has explicated the dynam-ics of these patients so well (for the best theoretical work in this area, see Kernberg 1975, 1984). One of the prominent characteristics of these patients is their tendency to expect malevolence in relationships and their capacity to transform a person mentally from someone they love and admire to someone they despise and distrust with remarkable rapidity. With their penchant for motivational explanations, psychoanalysts explained these malevolent shifts in terms of projection of the borderline patient's own aggression, an explanation that certainly fits in some cases. Rarely, however, did they consider a simpler cognitive social-learning explanation, that borderline patients may have a tendency to attribute malevolent intent in part because they have *experienced* it. In fact, in the late 1980s, a series of empirical studies demonstrated that these patients tend to have histories of sexual abuse (Herman, Perry, and van der Kolk 1989, Westen *et al.* 1990).

Matters are not, of course, so simple. Some borderline patients may have a genetic vulnerability to poorly modulated affects, and many have histories of disrupted attachments and poorly attuned caregivers in the first few years of life (and beyond). Children who have difficulty regulating their affects and finding competent, empathic others to help them do so are likely to form representations of relationships as unsafe and unhelpful, to become enraged, and hence to respond in ways that draw precisely the kind of malignant or unempathic responses they most fear. And the kinds of caregivers who are emotionally ill-attuned in the first few years of a child's life are less likely to protect the child later from sexually predatory adults, leading to further confirmation of the child's experience of the world as an unsafe place. The moral of the story is not that psychoanalytic explanations are bad and cognitive explanations are good, or vice versa. Rather, we need to recognize that people feel, wish, fear, and think, and any model of mind that fails to integrate all of these processes and their interactions is going to be highly flawed.

With method as with content, psychoanalysis and cognitive science have complementary strengths and weaknesses. Psychoanalytic theory has always rested primarily on the data base of clinical observation, which resembles anthropological fieldwork in many respects: the analyst or analytic therapist steps into the life world of another individual in order to understand the individual's experience of the self, others, and the world (an "emic" view) and to understand how that person's experience is itself a product of psychological principles that are not entirely "local" (an "etic" view). This approach allows an unparalleled depth of observation, but it shares with ethnography a number of weaknesses, such as lack of replicability, subjectivity and bias in interpretation, and the necessity of inferring rather than observing causal relations. In contrast, the data of cognitive science are experimental, which solves these problems (for example, by varying conditions and hence directly assessing causal hypotheses by examining the impact of experimental manipulations) but runs into difficulties with generalizability, application to phenomena outside the laboratory, and a tendency to study what *can* be studied rather than what *needs* to be studied. Clearly a perspective that draws upon both in-depth examination of case materials and controlled experimentation is preferable to one that chooses between the two.

Associational networks: a common ancestor

One area of potential integration between the two approaches lies in the concept of associational networks. Indeed, associationism is a common ancestor not only of psychoanalysis and cognitive science but of behaviorism as well, and this has substantial import for an integrated theory of mind. Both psychoanalysis and cognitive science propose that much of

knowledge is stored along networks of association, which operate unconsciously (in psychoanalytic language) or implicitly (in cognitive language).
Information becomes organized along associational networks through
experience, although some associations are learned more readily than
others. Behaviorist research has shown, for example, that animals can more
easily learn to associate nausea with gustatory than auditory stimuli
(Garcia and Koelling 1966). This makes evolutionary sense, since nausea is
a feeling that evolved as a mechanism for discouraging animals from eating
foods that are toxic. In general, associative links between units of information are strengthened by their repeated conjunction, either in thought or in
reality.

Although cognitive researchers have paid minimal attention to the *affective* associations that are the focus of psychoanalytic theorizing, many of
the same connectionist principles no doubt apply to affective and motivational processes as to strictly cognitive ones. That is, feelings, wishes, and
fears are associated with representations of people, situations, abstract concepts (e.g., "liberty"), and so forth, and they are activated unconsciously
along with other forms of information when part of the network is primed
by something in the environment or by thought processes that touch on the
network.

Indeed, a considerable body of recent experimental literature documents
the existence of implicit or unconscious affective and motivational processes, much like the implicit cognitive processes studied by cognitive scientists (Westen 1998b). For example, if an experimenter repeatedly pairs a
word (e.g., "dog") with mild electric shock and then presents the word subliminally, subjects will show an electrophysiological response (such as
increased skin conductance, a measure of arousal) even though they have
no conscious awareness of having seen or heard the word that elicited the
affective reaction (e.g., Wong, Shevrin, and Williams 1994). Other research
shows that surreptitiously priming subjects with words related to achievement or affiliation (such as "success" or "friendship") can increase their
striving for success or their affiliative behavior in a subsequent experimental
task (Bargh and Barndollar 1996). Neurophysiological evidence supports
these findings as well. Amnesic subjects with Korsakoff's disorder, who
cannot remember any of the information taught them about two fictional
characters, nevertheless subsequently prefer the character who had been
described more positively (Johnson, Kim, and Risse 1985). Although they
cannot consciously remember anything about the person, they have formed
unconscious affective associations.

Aside from its implications for what we mean when we say that cultural
beliefs and values are "internalized" – that is, they are literally built into
associative networks – another important implication is that implicit asso-

ciative learning occurs through everyday action and experience (cf. Bourdieu's [1977] "habitus"; see also Strauss and Quinn 1997), whereas conscious beliefs are more heavily shaped by explicit teaching. As McClelland, Koestner, and Weinberger (1989) have shown, conscious (self-report) versus unconscious (projective) assessments of motives do not correlate with each other; people who are high on self-reported need for power, for example, are as likely to be low as high on power motivation assessed from their Thematic Apperception Test (TAT) responses. However, both conscious and unconscious motives have predictable (and predictably different) correlates, and their presence in adulthood in Western samples can be predicted from patterns of child-rearing as many as thirty-five years earlier. Over the long run, assessment of motives from TAT stories is much more predictive of variables such as entrepreneurial or managerial success than self-reported need for achievement or power; however, in the short run, conscious achievement motivation is a much better predictor of behavior than achievement motivation assessed projectively when subjects are explicitly told that they are about to take on what it is important that they achieve. By and large, longitudinal research shows that unconscious motives in adulthood are predictable from early childhood experiences, particularly nonverbal ones, whereas conscious motives are predictable from later, more verbally mediated experiences (McClelland *et al.* 1989).

Affect regulation and motivation

One way psychoanalytic and cognitive theories differ substantially is in their theories about the conditions for conscious activation of information stored on networks of association. Cognitive theories tend to presume that information becomes conscious to the extent that its activation exceeds some threshold. Psychoanalytic theory is less explicit, but it emphasizes the emotional significance of information, arguing that information that is particularly important is more likely to become the focus of consciousness *except* to the extent that it would be so emotionally threatening that it is defended against. A more integrative formulation is that consciousness is a joint function of level of cognitive activation, level of emotional significance, and affective quality (which can either excite or inhibit representations from becoming conscious).

From this perspective, and in line with a history of philosophers and psychologists since at least Hobbes, people are motivated to seek pleasurable states and avoid painful ones. (For a modern anthropological rendering of this basic but psychologically central principle, see Boehm 1982.) When they experience painful events, they attempt to alter the situation to alleviate the feeling. If this cannot be done behaviorally, they may use conscious coping mechanisms, such as "reframing" the situation in a more benign way, telling themselves things will be better soon, or praying; or unconscious defensive processes, such as denial or rationalization. To the extent that these procedures work, they will be associated with regulation of the aversive feeling and hence reinforced, that is, made more likely to be used again in analogous situations. And to the extent that they are repeatedly used under certain conditions, the weights connecting the units representing these procedures and those representing the circumstances in which they are elicited will increase. In other words, these affect-regulatory processes will be encoded as automatic procedures elicited when conditions match the prototype of the kind of circumstance in which they have proven useful. Thus, coping and defense mechanisms can be conceived as a form of procedural knowledge, which, like other procedures, are learned through experience (Westen 1985, 1994, 1997). In this view, motivation in large measure reflects efforts at affect regulation.

This view of affect regulation has important implications for cognitive science because it suggests that representations are not independent of the wishes, fears, and values posited by psychoanalysis. Affects are not only associatively *linked* to ideas but also *shape* them. To return to connectionist models, what psychoanalysis adds is a second set of constraints, above and beyond the cognitive constraints posited by connectionist models (Westen 1998b, 1999). Thus, when the mind settles on the "best fit" to the data, this judgment of goodness-of-fit not only reflects processes of *cognitive* constraint satisfaction but also of *affective* constraint satisfaction. Unpleasant feelings, for example, can inhibit conscious activation of part of a neural network to which they are associatively linked, leading to conscious judgments that are biased in a way that diminishes distress. To what extent affective processes inhibit *unconscious* activation or simply block *conscious* representation of inhibited ideas, feelings, or motives is unclear, although research on thought suppression suggests that inhibitory processes actually keep inhibited mental contents *more* rather than less active outside of awareness (Wegner 1992).

Implications for models of culture and cultural models

In recent years, psychological anthropologists have turned considerable attention to the "cultural models" that provide both interpretive frames and directives for action (D'Andrade 1992, D'Andrade and Strauss 1992, Holland and Quinn 1987, Shore 1996, Strauss 1992, Strauss and Quinn 1997), attempting to discern how an emergent property of social interaction can simultaneously be an aspect of individual psychology. From a psychological point of view, this raises three central questions. First, how are cultural models inculcated and internalized? Second, how do cultural models become translated into motives that actually influence an individual's behavior? And third, what happens when cultural models that influence motivated behavior conflict with each other? That is, how does the person choose, interpret, or compromise among multiple competing and often ambiguous cultural directives (Strauss 1992, Strauss and Quinn 1997)? Each of these three questions can be better addressed by integrating cognitive and psychodynamic considerations.

How are cultural models inculcated and internalized?

Some cultural models are directly and intentionally inculcated by socialization agents, such as the La Llorona myth of a Mestizo group in Mexico, described by Mathews (1992), that teaches the evils of straying from the marital bed. Many cultural beliefs and values are transmitted this way, through myths, fairy tales, and direct tutelage. This leads not only to unconscious associations but also to conscious knowledge and moral values. For the Mestizos, the association between a representation of a possible action (infidelity) and a negative affect (fear) through the medium of a morality tale translates a cultural value into a moral motive. Similar processes can account for the influence of cultural models on motives other than values – notably fears and wishes (which involve associations between representations and affects) – that are often overlooked in discussions of the influence of cultural models on motives. Although tutelage of this sort (see Bandura 1986) is the most direct way to impart conscious knowledge, it can also lead to unconscious associations and procedural knowledge, as when a child learns a cultural belief about the dangers inherent in in-group tensions and learns culturally prescribed ways of avoiding them.

Another way cultural models can be learned, which typically produces implicit rather than explicit knowledge, is through direct experience (cf. Bourdieu's concept of habitus [1977: 72]). One way this may occur is via socialization experiences common in a culture, such as early toilet training, early weaning, or sleeping alone – experiences that teach implicit lessons about independence, autonomy, self-control, and personal boundaries. Implicit cultural learning occurs through a variety of culturally patterned experiences, such as role interactions (which teach implicit norms about how each member of a role relationship should behave). Implicit cultural learning also occurs in rituals that instill feelings, for example, about group solidarity or about the dangers of greed (as in many rituals involving redistribution of wealth in agricultural societies). The distinction between implicit and explicit processes is particularly important for anthropology because it suggests that implicit and explicit cultural models can be in conflict, based on different modes of internalization. A psychoanalytic perspective adds that such circumstances are likely to evoke or reflect culturally constituted defenses (to use Spiro's [1965] term). For example, an emerging body of research in social psychology on implicit racial stereotypes demonstrates that people's implicit and explicit attitudes toward various minority groups (as well as toward the sexes) can be quite discrepant, and that, in fact, people with positive conscious attitudes toward minority groups are no less likely than those with negative conscious attitudes to harbor negative unconscious associations (Devine 1989, Fazio *et al.* 1995, Fiske 1998, Greenwald and Banaji 1995).

Members of a culture may develop shared implicit associative structures in another way, involving iterative experiences that are common in a culture, that is, experiences that people in similar circumstances share but that reflect features of the environment rather than cultural values or schemas. For example, children in nomadic cultures may become more adept at forming spatial representations than children in technologically developed societies and thus can be said to share certain cognitive properties. Although these shared cognitive procedures are likely to be structured or elaborated by collective representations or collectively patterned cognitive heuristics, they may also in part reflect responses to similar ecological circumstances that would arise to some degree without any cultural intervention, and in fact are shared by people in similar ecological circumstances thousands of miles apart who cannot be said, strictly speaking, to share cultural models (see also Danziger, this volume).[2]

How do cultural models acquire the capacity to influence behavior?

The presence of a cultural model does not necessarily translate into action (D'Andrade 1992) for two reasons. First, many cultural models are strictly cognitive and hence have no motivational force except in so far as they are used to meet affectively meaningful ends (for example, knowledge of foraging strategies that becomes useful when foraging motives are activated). A mental model, cognitive map, or schema is a representation of things as they are perceived to be. As Tolman (1948) showed years ago, even rats form cognitive maps of the mazes in which psychologists place them, whether or not they have ever been reinforced to do so. A mental map of this sort is never motivating. Knowing kinship terms does nothing to influence behavior *unless* these terms are associated with affectively charged norms of behavior.

Second, cultural models that *do* have affective significance and hence carry motivational implications will only influence behavior to the extent that they are associated with affect *at the level of the individual*. That is, to influence an individual's actions, cultural models need to be represented in the person's associational networks and associated with the appropriate affect. In US culture, for example, athletic prowess is held in high esteem, but people vary in the extent to which this motivates them to engage in athletics. What motivates me to play tennis is a wished-for state endowed with affective significance – that is, an association of tennis with pleasure. This association emerged through a combination of internalization of cultural values (e.g., that men should have athletic prowess, and since I was worthless at most non-racquet sports, I had little choice but to find some gentleman's sport at which to rise at least to mediocrity) and a history of experiences on the court. Had those experiences been repeatedly negative, whether because of constitutional or experiential inadequacies leading to failure or shaming experiences, the affect associated with tennis would be different, and the wish would be extinguished or diverted (e.g., to *watching* sports, preferably some aggressive sport that would allow me to feel manly by my sheer knowledge of and interest in it).

Although cognition and affect are in this sense separable, they are certainly not independent. Someone who loves tennis will generally develop more elaborate declarative representations of tennis-related events, such as knowledge of prominent players, as well as more finely tuned procedural knowledge. Indeed, neurophysiological evidence suggests that the neural connections are denser, and the size of the areas is larger, for parts of the brain that individuals tend to use – such as language areas in professors, and sensory areas devoted to the fingers in Braille readers (e.g., Pascual-Leone *et al.* 1993). People attend to, and hence develop more elaborate schemas for, things that are meaningful to them.

We should be careful, however, when we use the word "meaning," which has two "meanings" that must be carefully distinguished, and that parallel the distinction between the cognitive and motivational aspects of cultural models. Something has meaning in the first sense to the extent that we understand it. The reader either does or does not understand the meaning of my words, whether she or he likes what I have to say. When we speak of something being meaningful to a person, however, we are speaking of its emotional significance. The weaker the affective "charge," the less a mental model or cognitive schema will influence behavior.[3]

Cultural models, then, are functionally inert unless they are imbued with affect at the level of the individual. Antisocial personalities can often respond flawlessly to questions about culturally defined appropriate social behavior, such as what a person "should" do if he finds a stamped, sealed envelope on the ground (the answer is to mail it, for anyone who needs the cueing), but they are unlikely to do so in practice because they lack the *emotional investment* in the rule (Westen 1991). Damasio (1994) has shown that patients with damage to the ventromedial prefrontal cortex, which is involved in integrating knowledge (particularly social knowledge) with affect, are similarly unable to govern their behavior in accord with social rules, or even to behave in ways that maximize their self-interest, because they cannot connect their cognitive knowledge with any experience of affective consequences.

How do people behave when cultural models conflict?

Some cultural models are so widely shared in a social group that we almost conceive of them as incorporeal, as having a life outside the actors who must mentally represent them. Others, such as models of shamanistic knowledge, or gendered knowledge, are shared by only subsets of a society. In large, heterogeneous societies, such as in the technologically developed West, some knowledge is virtually ubiquitous (such as the knowledge that breakfast is the first meal of the day), whereas other information may be shared or inculcated in only certain subcultures, classes, families, or even dyads (who may share private words and rituals that make their relationship feel meaningful and predictable). These differences in the distribution of cultural models may produce minimal conflict, except in so far as models internalized by actors who share membership in multiple subgroups may present conflicting norms or beliefs.

People in all cultures confront contradictions in the cultural models to which they are exposed. In part this reflects the fact that cultural elements are always in flux in response to environmental and intrasocietal changes and thus are not all neatly and coherently arranged. It also reflects the fact that any stimulus for thought or action is likely to have multiple, culturally influenced associations that have different implications. Thus, in deciding whether to make a decision that requires an immediate response, a person in the United States or Britain may have two contradictory aphorisms come to mind: "Haste makes waste" and "He who hesitates is lost." This is the stuff of regret, since we often do not know until afterwards which set of experiences embodied in cultural maxims and personal experiences associated with them was the better guide to judgment.

Another source of conflict in the cultural models guiding individual action is that people in all cultures (though of course to varying degrees) are members of cross-cutting subgroups with different perspectives and interests, which are embodied in sometimes contradictory models. With respect to differing interests, cultural models, especially models about how people *should* behave, are often not only *motivating* but *motivated*. Over time, a group of people will generate, recreate, or gradually adapt an ideology, ritual, or aspect of social structure that meets certain needs or provides solutions to problems of adaptation, whether those needs or solutions are in the interest of most members of society or just a subset. The notion that cultural elements such as rituals are motivated in this sense is obviously a key assumption of functionalist accounts, but it is equally inherent in Marxist accounts, which argue for the origins of ideology in class interest, or other materialist and ecological views that argue for the origins of rituals and ideology in material needs and ecological adaptation (Westen 1985).

For cultural models that serve purposes for segments of a society to be accepted and sustained, conditions must be created that, advertently or inadvertently, make them feel compelling to those who come to internalize and perpetuate them. One cannot adequately account for attitudes of the working class that conflict with their material interests by turning to concepts such as false consciousness without explaining, from an emotional perspective, what the *individual* on the assembly line gets from committing to that ideology and transmitting it to his or her children. The problem is essentially the same as in cognitive explanations of why people stay in abusive relationships or continually berate themselves. Being attacked, or attacking oneself, is painful enough that over time any cognitions supporting it (e.g., "negative schemas" about the self) would be extinguished through simple operant conditioning mechanisms if these cognitions themselves were not associated with countervailing motives.

When a conflict is widespread in a society, "pre-packaged" solutions are often available in the form of culturally patterned compromise formations (LeVine 1982, Westen 1985), as when a woman in the West who has internalized conflicting views of female sexuality (which extol both purity and sexiness) is beginning to enter into a sexual relationship with a man and protests that "I don't often do this kind of thing." This compromise works for both her and her partner, who similarly wants his lover to be both chaste and sexy, so that the strategy provides a successful solution for both partners, who thus accept a culturally prescribed mutual deception. Many times, however, culture does not offer satisfying compromise solutions, and people have to create their own, which can range from highly adaptive to highly maladaptive (as in the classical psychoanalytic explanation of symptoms as maladaptive compromise formations).

Distinguishing culturally patterned compromise formations from idiosyncratic compromise formations that draw on cultural idioms but are iteratively developed autonomously by multiple members of a society can be difficult empirically but is conceptually important. For example, cultural models of female beauty over the last thirty years in the West have emphasized thinness. All women are exposed to these models, and no evidence has ever been produced to show that women who develop anorexia have had greater exposure to them than other women. Thus, popular explanations to the effect that "anorexia is caused by cur culture's extreme emphasis on thinness" are, at the very least, very incomplete. In a culture that stresses female thinness, self-starvation can readily become a symptomatic idiom with which to express fears of sexuality (by desexualizing the body so that it resembles a non-gendered prepubescent child, and perhaps even caricaturing norms of attractiveness), conflicts around control and animality (expressed by taking control over the most inexorable biological process there is), competitiveness with other females (taking the norm of controlling weight to an extreme to which other females cannot or will not go), and other personal conflicts and concerns. Many anorexic girls, and certainly those who developed anorexia before there was widespread attention to the disorder, develop this compromise formation independently, making dysfunctional use of what are arguably dysfunctional cultural models. That the disorder is especially widespread in the West does not, however, suggest that anorexia is primarily a result of norms of beauty, any more than the fact that a patient with schizophrenia evaluated in the mid 1980s claimed to be a Cabbage Patch Kid proves that schizophrenia can be blamed on toy manufacturers.

Conclusion

An integration of psychoanalytic and cognitive theory and research cannot provide all the answers, but it can clearly contribute to a better articulated view of what culture is (in terms of patterned associative networks that both reflect and produce patterned behavioral events; see Strauss and Quinn 1997), how it is internalized, and how it gains force in directing human action. People form associative networks that influence the way they process information, and these networks are shaped by explicit and implicit learning, much of it cultural. The feelings associated with representations motivate individual actors toward and away from various ways of thinking and behaving. At the individual level, the cognitive-affective schemas and affect-regulatory procedures that guide behavior are highly influenced by shared associations, as are the compromise solutions people consciously or unconsciously select as a way of managing their own personality conflicts, many of which reflect in part conflicting models provided by their culture.

Nothing guarantees that cultural models are coherent and lacking in contradiction. Cultures change, come into contact with others, and accommodate the interests of subgroups that (consciously or unconsciously) find their way into culturally patterned ways of thinking, feeling, and behaving. To the extent that cultural models tend toward coherence, they do so because enough individual actors, with enough power, find the contradictions distressing and begin to alter their beliefs, values, fears, and wishes, and transmit these altered attitudes to other members of their culture. If we are to understand how these altered cultural models and compromise formations, like the models and compromises that precede them, direct concrete behavior, we need to know the extent to which these collective phenomena are distributed across the culture and the extent to which they are associated with affect or its regulation for the individual actor.

Acknowledgments

The author thanks Holly F. Mathews, Carmella C. Moore, Claudia Strauss, and two anonymous reviewers for their useful comments on a draft of this chapter.

NOTES

1 In an extraordinary book, Strauss and Quinn (1997) have applied connectionist theory to cultural phenomena in a way that sheds new light on the nature of culture and its links to individual action.
2 The existence of shared "cultural" elements that may arise independently of social interaction raises some interesting questions about the boundaries of the culture concept. For example, to what extent should we apply the concept of "deaf culture" to the results of shared iterative experiences that would exist whether or not members of the deaf community shared a common identity and chose to interact with one another? Is a deaf woman who does not identify with being deaf and eschews any connection to the deaf community nevertheless a member of that subculture? Making matters more complicated still, the deaf community may be a negative reference group for her and hence influence her action by her attempts to distance herself from it. Thus, even if she did not actually associate with other deaf people, the deaf subculture would still influence her action through her warded-off identification with it. In that case, however, her motivation would probably be better understood in terms of internalization of the stigma attached to deafness by the dominant culture and her own efforts to forge a positive identity in the face of being a member of a devalued group.
3 See also Spiro's (1987) discussion of levels of internalization, from simple knowledge of a cultural model, through lip service to it, to its influence as a salient, emotionally meaningful value.

REFERENCES

Anderson, John 1993 Problem Solving and Learning. *American Psychologist* 48: 35–44.
Aron, Lewis 1996 *A Meeting of Minds: Mutuality in Psychoanalysis*. Hillside, NJ: Analytic Press.
Baddeley, Alan D. 1995 Working Memory. In *The Cognitive Neurosciences*, M. Gazzaniga, ed. Cambridge, MA: MIT/Bradford Press. Pp. 754–764.

Bandura, Albert 1986 *Social Foundations of Thought and Action*. Englewood Cliffs, NJ: Prentice-Hall.

Bargh, John and Kim Barndollar 1996 Automaticity in Action: The Unconscious as Repository of Chronic Goals and Motives. In *The Psychology of Action*, P. M. Gollwitzer and J. Bargh, eds. New York: Guilford. Pp. 457–481.

Blanck, Gertrude and Rubin Blanck 1974 *Ego Psychology: Theory and Practice*. New York: Columbia University Press.

Boehm, Christopher 1982 A Fresh Outlook on Cultural Selection. *American Anthropologist* 84: 105–125.

Bourdieu, Pierre 1977 *Outline of a Theory of Practice*. trans. R. Nice. Cambridge: Cambridge University Press.

Bowlby, John 1969 *Attachment and Loss*, vol. I: *Attachment*. New York: Basic Books.

   1982 Attachment and Loss: Retrospect and Prospect. *American Journal of Orthopsychiatry* 52: 664–678.

Brenner, Charles 1982 *The Mind in Conflict*. New York: International Universities Press.

Bucci, Wilma 1997 *Psychoanalysis and Cognitive Science: A Multiple Code Theory*. New York: Guilford.

Collins, Allan M. and Elizabeth F. Loftus 1975 A Spreading-Activation Theory of Semantic Processing. *Psychological Review* 82: 407– 428.

D'Andrade, Roy G. 1992 Schemas and Motivation. In *Human Motives and Cultural Models*, R. G. D'Andrade and C. Strauss, eds. New York: Cambridge University Press. Pp. 23–44.

D'Andrade, Roy and Claudia Strauss, eds. 1992 *Human Motives and Cultural Models*. New York: Cambridge University Press.

Damasio, Antonio 1994 *Descartes' Error: Emotion, Reason, and the Human Brain*. New York: Grosset/Putnam.

Devine, Patricia 1989 Stereotypes and Prejudice: Their Automatic and Controlled Components. *Journal of Personality and Social Psychology* 56: 5–18.

Epstein, Seymour 1994 Integration of the Cognitive and the Psychodynamic Unconscious. *American Psychologist* 49: 709–724.

Erdelyi, Matthew 1985 *Psychoanalysis: Freud's Cognitive Psychology*. New York: Freeman.

Fairbairn, W. Ronald D. 1952 *Psychoanalytic Studies of the Personality*. London: Routledge and Kegan Paul.

Fazio, Russell, Joni R. Jackson, Bridget C. Dunton, and Carol J. Williams 1996 Variability in Automatic Activation as an Unobtrusive Measure of Racial Attitudes: A Bona Fide Pipeline? *Journal Of Personality and Social Psychology* 69: 1013–1027.

Fiske, Susan 1998 Stereotyping, Prejudice, and Discrimination. In *Handbook of Social Psychology*, vol. 2, D. T. Gilbert, S. T. Fiske, and G. Lindzey, eds. New York: McGraw-Hill. Pp. 357–413.

Freud, Sigmund 1953 *The Interpretation of Dreams*. In *The Standard Edition of the Complete Psychological Works of Sigmund Freud*, vol. 4, J. Strachey ed. and trans. London: Hogarth Press (originally published 1900).

Garcia, John and Robert A. Koelling 1966 Relation of Cue to Consequence in Avoidance Learning. *Psychonomic Science* 4: 123– 124.

Greenberg, Jay R. and Stephen Mitchell 1983 *Object Relations in Psychoanalytic Theory*. Cambridge, MA: Harvard University Press.

Greenwald, Anthony and Mahzarin Banaji 1995 Implicit Social Cognition: Attitudes, Self-Esteem, and Stereotypes. *Psychological Review* 102: 4–27.

Hallowell, A. Irving 1955 *Culture and Experience*. Philadelphia, PA: University of Pennsylvania Press.

Herman, Judith, J. Christopher Perry, and Bessel van der Kolk 1989 Childhood Trauma in Borderline Personality Disorder. *American Journal of Psychiatry* 146: 490–495.

Holland, Dorothy and Naomi Quinn, eds. 1987 *Cultural Models in Language and Thought*. New York: Cambridge University Press.

Horowitz, Mardi J. 1987 *States of Mind: Configurational Analysis of Individual Psychology*. 2nd ed. New York: Plenum.

Johnson, Marcia K., Jung K. Kim, and Gail Risse 1985 Do Alcoholic Korsakoff's Syndrome Patients Acquire Affective Reactions? *Journal of Experimental Psychology: Learning, Memory, and Cognition* 11: 22–36.

Kernberg, Otto 1975 *Borderline Conditions and Pathological Narcissism*. New York: Jason Aronson.

1984 *Severe Personality Disorders*. New Haven, CT: Yale University Press.

Kohut, Heinz 1971 *The Analysis of the Self: A Systematic Approach to the Treatment of Narcissistic Personality Disorders*. New York: International Universities Press.

1977 *The Restoration of the Self*. New York: International Universities Press.

Kuhn, Thomas S. 1970 *The Structure of Scientific Revolutions*. 2nd ed. Chicago, IL: University of Chicago Press.

LeVine, Robert A. 1982 *Culture, Behavior, and Personality*. 2nd ed. Chicago, IL: Aldine.

Lichtenberg, Joseph D. 1989 *Psychoanalysis and Motivation*. Hillsdale, NJ: Analytic Press.

Mathews, Holly F. 1992 The Directive Force of Morality Tales in a Mexican Community. In *Human Motives and Cultural Models*, R. G. D'Andrade and C. Strauss, eds. New York: Cambridge University Press. Pp. 127–162.

McClelland, David, Richard Koestner, and Joel Weinberger 1989 How Do Self-Attributed and Implicit Motives Differ? *Psychological Review* 96: 690–702.

McWilliams, Nancy 1998 Relationship, Subjectivity, and Inference in Diagnosis. In *Making Diagnosis Meaningful*, J. Barron, ed. Washington, DC: American Psychological Association Press. Pp. 197–226.

1956 The Magical Number Seven, Plus or Minus Two: Some Limits on Our Capacity for Processing Information. *Psychological Review* 63: 81–97.

Mitchell, Stephen 1988 *Relational Concepts in Psychoanalysis*. Cambridge, MA: Harvard University Press.

Newell, Alan and Herbert Simon 1972 *Human Problem Solving*. Englewood Cliffs, NJ: Prentice-Hall.

Nisbett, Richard and Timothy Wilson 1977 Telling More Than We Can Know: Verbal Reports on Mental Processes. *Psychological Review* 84: 231–259.

Pascual-Leone, Alvaro, Angel Cammarota, Eric Wasserman, and Joaquim Brasil-Neto 1993 Modulation of Motor Cortical Outputs to the Reading Hand of Braille Readers. *Annals of Neurology* 34: 33–37.

Read, Stephen, Eric J. Vanman, and Lynn C. Miller 1997 Connectionism, Parallel Constraint Satisfaction Processes, and Gestalt Principles: (Re)introducing Cognitive Dynamics to Social Psychology. *Personality and Social Psychology Review* 1: 26–53.

Reber, Arthur S. 1992 The Cognitive Unconscious: An Evolutionary Perspective. *Consciousness and Cognition* 1: 93–133.

Redl, Fritz and David Wineman 1951 *Children Who Hate*. Glencoe, IL: Free Press.

Robins, Richard and Kenneth Craik 1994 A More Appropriate Test of the Kuhnian Displacement Thesis. *American Psychologist* 49: 815–816.

Roediger, Henry L. 1990 Implicit Memory: Retention Without Remembering. *American Psychologist* 45: 1043–1056.

Rumelhart, David E., James L. McClelland, and the PDP Research Group 1986 *Parallel Distributed Processing: Explorations in the Microstructure of Cognition*. vol. I: *Foundations*. Cambridge, MA: MIT Press.

Schacter, Daniel L. 1992 Understanding Implicit Memory: A Cognitive Neuroscience Approach. *American Psychologist* 47: 559–569.

Schacter, Daniel and Randy L. Buckner 1998 Priming and the Brain. *Neuron* 20: 185–195.

Shore, Bradd 1996 *Culture in Mind: Cognition, Culture, and the Problem of Meaning*. New York: Oxford University Press.

Singer, Jerome and Peter Salovey 1991 Organized Knowledge Structures and Personality: Person Schemas, Self-Schemas, Prototypes, and Scripts. In *Person Schemas and Maladaptive Interpersonal Behavior Patterns*, Mardi Horowitz, ed. Chicago, IL: University of Chicago Press. Pp. 33–79.

Smith, Elliot R. 1998 Mental Representation and Memory. In *Handbook of Social Psychology*, vol. I, D. T. Gilbert, S. T. Fiske, and G. Lindzey, eds. New York: McGraw-Hill. Pp. 391–445.

Sperling, George 1960 The Information Available in Brief Visual Presentations. *Psychological Monographs* 74: 1–29.

Spiro, Melford E. 1965 Religious Systems as Culturally Constituted Defense Mechanisms. In *Context and Meaning in Cultural Anthropology*, M. E. Spiro, ed. New York: Free Press. Pp. 100–113.

    1987 Collective Representations and Mental Representations in Religious Symbol Systems. In *Culture and Human Nature: Theoretical Papers of Melford E. Spiro*, B. Kilborne and L. L. Langness, eds. Chicago, IL: University Of Chicago Press. Pp. 161–184 (originally published 1982).

Squire, Larry R. 1986 Mechanisms of Memory. *Science* 232: 1612–1619.

Squire, Larry R. and Stuart Zola-Morgan 1991 The Medial Temporal Lobe Memory System. *Science* 253: 1380–1386.

Strauss, Claudia 1992 Models and Motives. In *Human Motives and Cultural Models*, R. G. D'Andrade and C. Strauss, eds. New York: Cambridge University Press. Pp. 1–20.

Strauss, Claudia and Naomi Quinn 1997 *A Cognitive Theory of Cultural Meaning*. Cambridge: Cambridge University Press.

Sullivan, Harry S. 1953 *The Interpersonal Theory of Psychiatry*. New York: Norton.

Tolman, Edward 1948 Cognitive Maps in Rats and Men. *Psychological Review* 55: 189–208.

Tulving, Endel 1972 Episodic and Semantic Memory. In *Organization of Memory*, E. Tulving and W. Donaldson, eds. New York: Academic Press. Pp. 381–403.

Tulving, Endel, Daniel Schacter, and Heather A. Stark 1982 Priming Effects in Word-fragment Completion are Independent of Recognition Memory. *Journal of Experimental Psychology: Learning, Memory, and Cognition* 8: 336–342.

Vaillant, George 1977 *Adaptation to Life*. Boston, MA: Little, Brown.

Vaillant, George, ed. 1992 *Ego Mechanisms of Defense: A Guide for Clinicians and Researchers*. Washington, DC: American Psychiatric Association Press.

Wegner, Daniel 1992 You Can't Always Think What You Want: Problems in the Suppression of Unwanted Thoughts. *Advances in Experimental Social Psychology* 25: 193–225.

Westen, Drew 1985 *Self and Society: Narcissism, Collectivism, and the Development of Morals*. New York: Cambridge University Press.

1991 Social Cognition and Object Relations. *Psychological Bulletin* 109: 429–455.

1994 Toward an Integrative Model of Affect Regulation: Applications to Social-Psychological Research. *Journal of Personality* 62: 641–647.

1995 A Clinical-Empirical Model Of Personality: Life After the Mischelian Ice Age and the Neo-Lithic Era. *Journal of Personality* 63: 495–524.

1997 Toward an Empirically and Clinically Sound Theory of Motivation. *International Journal of Psycho-Analysis* 78: 521–548.

1998a Case Formulation and Personality Diagnosis: Two Processes or One? In *Making Diagnosis Meaningful*, J. Barron, ed. Washington, DC: American Psychological Association Press. Pp. 111–138.

1998b The Scientific Legacy of Sigmund Freud: Toward a Psychodynamically Informed Psychological Science. *Psychological Bulletin* 124: 333–371.

1999 Psychodynamic Theory and Technique in Relation to Research on Cognition and Emotion: Mutual Implications. In *Handbook of Cognition and Emotion*, T. Dalgleish and M. J. Power, eds. New York: Wiley. Pp. 727–746.

Westen, Drew and Glen Gabbard 1999 Psychoanalytic Approaches to Personality. In *Handbook of Personality: Theory and Research*, 2nd ed., L. Pervin and O. P. John, eds. New York: Guilford. Pp. 57–101.

Westen, Drew, Pamela Ludolph, Barbara Misle, Stephen Ruffins, and M. Judith Block 1990 Physical and Sexual Abuse in Adolescent Girls with Borderline Personality Disorder. *American Journal of Orthopsychiatry* 60: 55–66.

White, Robert 1960 Competence and the Psychosexual Stages of Development. In *Nebraska Symposium on Development*, Ned Jones, ed. Lincoln, NB: University of Nebraska Press.

Wong, Philip, Howard Shevrin, and William J. Williams 1994 Conscious and Nonconscious Processes: An ERP Index of an Anticipatory Response in a Conditioning Paradigm Using Visually Masked Stimuli. *Psychophysiology* 31: 87–101.

Douglas Hollan

In this chapter I review recent developments in person-centered ethnography. I first define person-centered ethnography, briefly trace the historical development of this line of anthropological research, and then discuss contemporary examples, focusing especially on the advantages and disadvantages of conducting person-centered ethnography in particular ways. Given space limitations, I focus on general trends and new directions in the field, rather than examine or refer to the details of particular studies.[1] In the final section, I discuss how person-centered ethnography has contributed to the development of theory in psychocultural anthropology, and then conclude with some general observations on developments within the field.

What is person-centered ethnography?

Person-centered ethnography is a term used by Robert LeVine (1982) to refer to anthropological attempts to develop experience-near ways of describing and analyzing human behavior, subjective experience, and psychological processes. A primary focus of person-centered ethnographies is on the individual and on how the individual's psychology and subjective experience both shapes, and is shaped by, social and cultural processes. Indeed, to the extent that these studies focus on the individual as a locus of psychocultural processes and subjective experience, rather than on "the person" – the definition of which usually emphasizes the *moral* qualities that distinguish a human being, either living or dead,[2] from other beings or things – they are more appropriately termed "individual" or "subject"[3] centered ethnographies. However, because the term "person-centered ethnography" has gained recognition in the anthropological literature, I continue to use it here.

In contrast to standard ethnography which, according to LeVine, "produces a cultural description analogous to a map or aerial photograph of a community," person-centered ethnography "tells us what it is like to live there – what features are salient to its inhabitants" (1982: 293). An effort is made to represent human behavior and subjective experience from the point of view of the acting, intending, and attentive subject, to actively explore the emotional saliency and motivational force of cultural beliefs and symbols (rather than to assume such saliency and force), and to avoid unnecessary reliance on overly abstract, experience-distant constructs. The distinction drawn between relatively "experience-near" and relatively "experience-distant" descriptive and analytical constructs is borrowed from Kohut (1971, 1977) who used it to distinguish his own (experience-near) efforts to ground psychoanalytic theory in the language and subjective experience of the analysand from the more abstract (experience-distant), metapsychological theorizing of Freud.[4] Many person-centered ethnographers would ask, along with Robert Paul (1990: 436), for example: "What . . . does it add to the statement that 'John desires Mary very much' to say that this is an expression of his libidinal drive? What have we gained by translating a clear fact into this language of putative force?"

It is important to note here that while person-centered ethnographers wish to avoid constructs that take us away from, rather than closer to, the experience of our subjects, most are not adverse to cross-cultural comparison and analysis. Indeed, for many, this is a primary goal of the work. They simply feel that the categories of comparison should emerge from the experiential lives of our subjects and informants, rather than be imposed by the anthropologist without close reference to that experience. The point is to ensure that we end up comparing apples with apples, rather than with some other type of fruit. If we are developing a theory of human aggression, for example, it is important to know whether the overt, behavioral displays of aggression we observe are linked to individuals' perceptions of external threat, their reactions to narcissistic injury, or to inner "drives" that seem beyond their conscious awareness and control (Hollan 1996). Likewise, theories of human grief and bereavement must be able to specify different types and intensities of grief experiences and how those experiences are correlated with the formation and maintenance of different types of deeply felt attachments (Hollan 1995).

In either case, finely tuned theories must begin with the careful specification and description of human subjectivity. Only later can one begin to discriminate among these subjectivities, either within or among cultures, and understand how they are related to other variables in some systematic way. Hollan and Wellenkamp (1994: 217–222), for example, have used this bottom-up, comparative approach to specify the ways in which the Toraja emphasis on social harmony and nonaggression that coexists with interpersonal cautiousness and mistrust is both similar to and yet different from patterns of behavior and subjectivity found in other face-to-face communities around the world, including Africa, Polynesia, Mexico, and the Mediterranean. Csordas (1994) has used it to begin to delineate how the efficacy of Charismatic healing is related to other forms of symbolic healing and transformation. And Levy (1990) has used his own corpus of person-centered ethnography to suggest the ways in which patterns of subjectivity in face-to-face communities like Tahiti *systematically* differ from those found in "archaic" cities like Bhaktapur in Nepal. I return to a discussion of the ways in which person-centered ethnography has contributed to the development of theory in psychocultural anthropology in the final section.

Although this inductive, person-centered approach lends itself more readily to the development of limited generalizations than to the cross-cultural testing of grand theory, "it represents the conviction that greater ambitions cannot be fulfilled without data of better quality" (LeVine 1982: 293).

Historical roots

Person-centered ethnographers' mistrust of overly abstract and reified analytical constructs and their corresponding desire to move closer to the actual experience of actors has relatively deep roots in American anthropology. Over seventy years ago, Edward Sapir wrote a series of articles elucidating the relationship between cultural anthropology and psychiatry in which he pointed out the dangers of taking highly abstract concepts – such as "culture" – too seriously. The "complete, 'impersonalized' culture of the anthropologist," he reminded us,

can really be little more than an assembly or mass of loosely overlapping idea and action systems which, through verbal habit, can be made to assume a closed system of behavior. What tends to be forgotten is that the functioning of such a system, if it can be said to have any function at all, is due to the specific functioning and interplays of the idea and action systems which have actually grown up in the minds of given individuals. (Sapir 1958a: 594)

Accordingly,

The true locus of culture is in the interactions of specific individuals and, on the subjective side, in the world of meanings which each one of these individuals may unconsciously abstract for himself from his participation in these interactions. (Sapir 1958b: 515)

In a related article Sapir asked,

Have we not the right . . . [to] advance the position that any statement . . . which can be made about culture needs the supporting testimony of a tangible person or persons, to whom such a statement is of real value in his system of interrelationship with other beings? . . . Instead, therefore, of arguing from a supposed objectivity of culture to the problem of individual variation, we shall . . . have to proceed in the opposite direction. We shall have to operate as though we knew nothing about culture but were interested in analyzing as well as we could what a given number of human beings accustomed to live with each other actually think and do in their day to day relationships. . . . (Sapir 1958c: 574)

Thirty years after Sapir but forty years before the present, Hallowell was promoting similar ideas. In his widely cited article, "The Self and Its Behavioral Environment," he notes that:

The traditional approach of cultural anthropology . . . has not been directly concerned with the behavior of individuals. It has been culture-centered, rather than behavior-centered. . . . No matter how reliable such data are, or whatever their value for comparative and analytic studies of *culture*, of necessity the material is presented from the standpoint of the outside observer. Presented to us in this form, these cultural data do not easily permit us to apprehend, in an integral fashion, the most significant and meaningful aspects of the world of the individual as experienced by him and in terms of which he thinks, is motivated to act, and satisfies his needs. (Hallowell 1955: 88)

To understand the latter, Hallowell argues, we must actively explore how the actor perceives his or her world from the inside out.

Contemporary developments

In this chapter, I focus on person-centered ethnographies published subsequent to those examined by LeVine in 1982 (LeVine 1982). In that earlier review, LeVine identifies four major approaches in the cross-cultural study of human psychological and subjective experience: (1) ethnopsychology research – the description of indigenous concepts of the person, self, life span, and behavior and mental function in normality and deviance; (2) in-depth case study research of individual adults observed and interviewed over an extended period of time in the course of anthropological fieldwork; (3) studies of transference and countertransference in the anthropologist–subject relationship; and (4) ethnographies of communication – descriptions of indigenous conventions for disclosing, concealing, and disguising personal information in interpersonal communication.

For my purposes here, I wish to map the terrain of person-centered ethnography in a way that cross-cuts some of the topical areas of research identified by LeVine. As I read the contemporary literature, many person-centered ethnographers seem to be asking one of three questions and collecting data accordingly: (1) what do people *say* about their subjective experience? That is, what can they verbally report to us about their experience? (2) what do people *do* that enacts or reveals behaviorally their subjective experience? and (3) how do people *embody* their subjective experience, or conversely, how do the senses of the body, culturally elaborated in different ways, give rise to the sense of oneself and others? Of course verbal reports about subjective experience are themselves a type of behavior or enactment. I separate them here from other types of behaviors, however, because many of those found in ethnographies are elicited within the context of an interview setting, and so may be distinguished from behaviors that arise in more naturally occurring situations.

Obviously, I simplify here for the purposes of analysis. Some, if not most, person-centered ethnographers ask all of these questions at some point during their fieldwork. And one can find verbal reports, observations of actual behavior, and accounts of bodily experience or "experience embodied" in almost any person-centered ethnography. But I think it *is* fair to say that many ethnographers tend to ask one of these questions more frequently than the others and that as a result, they tend to privilege and report certain kinds of data and interpretations more so than others. For example, although those who emphasize an embodiment approach do observe people's behavior and record verbal accounts of subjective experience, they tend to collect such data not as ends in themselves, but rather, in order to draw inferences about the relationship among body, senses, and experience. Similarly, Wellenkamp and I (Hollan and Wellenkamp 1994, 1996) report extensive data on Toraja day-to-day activities and somatic experience in our efforts to analyze and interpret a large body of interview material, but we have emphasized the latter in our work thus far.

Let me outline, then, these different approaches, focusing especially on the strengths and limitations of each. I highlight sets of concepts, theoretical orientations, and assumptions that studies within each approach have in common, rather than discuss specific examples, because it is difficult to identify single studies that truly exemplify an entire approach. Rather than obscure this diversity within approaches, my characterizations remain at a more general level of analysis.

What do people *say*?

Historically as well as currently, many person-centered ethnographers have relied quite heavily on what people *say* about their subjective experience. Verbal reports or accounts of subjective experience have been used to identify and analyze cognitive schemas (e.g., D'Andrade and Strauss 1992, Holland and Quinn 1987, Strauss and Quinn 1997); to reveal the narrative structure and shaping of experience (e.g., Bruner 1988, Peacock 1988), including its socially constructed and intersubjective aspects (e.g., Good 1994); to identify vocabularies of thought and emotion and how those vocabularies vary cross-culturally (e.g., Heider 1991); to provide at least indirect evidence of psychodynamic conflict and processes of transference and countertransference (e.g., Herdt and Stoller 1990), and other aspects of unconscious motivation (e.g., Obeyesekere 1990); to examine the personal and cultural significance of dreams (e.g., Kracke 1987); to illuminate the constitutive relationship between language use and personhood (e.g., Cain 1991, Ochs and Schieffelin 1984, Stromberg 1993); and to describe and analyze – in a fairly straightforward way – subjects' phenomenology and their sense of being in the world (e.g., Hollan and Wellenkamp 1994, 1996, Levy 1990, Parish 1994, 1996). Interviewees are asked to reflect and comment on life experiences of their own choosing or on those of interest to the interviewer. While none of these studies assumes that language gives direct, unambiguous access to subjective experience, most of them do assume that it is certainly one primary means by which people communicate their experience to others, even if only imperfectly.

How do these person-centered studies of what people say about their subjective experience differ from more traditional psychoanalytic approaches, if at all? To the extent that both person-centered ethnographers and psychoanalysts engage interviewees as "respondents" (that is, as objects of systematic study and observation in themselves), rather than merely as "informants" (that is, as knowledgeable people who can talk *about* behavior, motivation, and subjective experience),[5] the two approaches can be quite similar. For example, both ethnographer and analyst may attempt to examine how wish and desire may reinforce or contradict moral conscience; the extent to which interviewees are consciously aware of conflicting desires or goals; the ways in which interviewees avoid some topics of discussion but actively promote others; who or what interviewees identify with and who or what they are repelled by; the extent to which interviewees assume responsibility for different aspects of their behavior, and so include them within the scope of their conscious "selves," or attribute such responsibility to beings or forces outside their conscious control; and so on.

Yet there are some important differences between these two listening stances as well. Most person-centered ethnographers are interested in examining the relationship between subjective experience and the larger social, cultural, and political economic contexts from which it emerges, including the extent to which it is affected by the context of the interview setting itself (Lutz 1992). While person-centered ethnographers do not necessarily presume that human subjectivity will vary significantly cross-culturally, neither do they rule out this possibility. A primary goal of the work is to examine this issue of variability as explicitly and empirically as possible and to listen to accounts of subjective experience with an ear toward how subjectivity has been influenced by the social surround.

Most psychoanalysts, on the other hand, tend to examine human sub-jectivity as a more purely intrapsychic phenomenon.[6] Observation and theoretical explanation is much more narrowly focused on the interview dyad itself and on the thoughts and feelings that are troubling the self-selected interviewee. Social, cultural, political, and economic influences on subjectivity are not usually closely examined. If anything, many psychoan-alysts often assume that such influences are secondary to more existential factors in human life, such as the always powerful influence of caretakers on the developing psyche of the infant or the inevitable conflict between individual desire and the requirements of social life.

Further, psychoanalysts, as part of their therapeutic goals, are explicitly concerned with *changing* interviewees' subjectivity. They do this, in part, by deliberately and self-consciously reflecting interviewees' interpersonal reac-tivity and behavior back to them in the hopes of generating what Bateson (1972) referred to as third-order learning. Person-centered ethnographers, on the other hand, do not wish to change interviewees' subjectivity – indeed, this would come into conflict with their more humanistic and scien-tific, not therapeutic, goals – but rather to observe and render it as faithfully and consistently as possible. Person-centered ethnographers' active engage-ment with interviewees as respondents does, of course, change the latter's subjectivity to some extent. How could this not be the case, given the inter-subjective nature of the interviewing process? But such change is an unin-tended, rather than intended, outcome of the work and is minimized as much as possible.

Person-centered ethnographers have relied so heavily upon the verbal report, I believe, because it is still the only means we have for "directly" sampling a phenomenon that is so inherently elusive and difficult to study. The great advantage that a person-centered ethnographer has over an archaeologist or a primatologist is that we can *ask* our subjects about their experience, not simply infer it from their artifacts or behavior.

But of course this sampling is not really so direct after all (see, e.g., Besnier 1994, Bruner 1990, Desjarlais 1994). Most of us now realize that the relationship between verbal utterance and subjective experience is an extremely complicated one, affected by conventions of narrating and telling, by the social context of who is telling what to whom and under what circumstances, by the difficulty of expressing certain types of experiences – especially dreams and other types of imaginal phenomena – in the relatively linear and discursive structure of verbal language, and so on. For all of these reasons and others, some contemporary person-centered ethnogra-phers have turned to other ways of exploring subjective and psychological experience.

What do people *do*?

Partly as a result of some of the problems with verbal reports just discussed, and partly as a result of the growing popularity of practice theory in anthropology (Bourdieu 1977, Ortner 1984), some person-centered ethnographers are currently emphasizing the importance of grounding our discussions of human experience in the compelling concerns of our subjects' everyday lives. Because the flow of experience is contested, indeterminate, and emergent, we must follow our subjects through time and space, and across different cultural domains, and in so doing, discover what is at stake for them in the course of their daily lives (e.g., Jackson 1989, Kleinman and Kleinman 1991, Wikan 1990). We must fully acknowledge, from this point of view, that actions not only can but usually *do* speak louder than words; that perhaps the best way of capturing – or even comprehending – our subjects' most salient thoughts, feelings, and intentions, is through carefully observing and recording their multiple enactments in and involvements with the world. This is essentially a call for a return to fine-grained, participatory ethnographic work, only this time the focus of attention is on real people as they live their lives, rather than on "culture" or "social structure" or "ritual" – or for that matter, on "emotions," or "cognitive schemas," or "the self."

I find myself in sympathy with this approach. The advantage of the ethnographer over the psychoanalyst is that the ethnographer does not have to guess so much about what part of someone's subjective experience is a projection or extension of his or her own intrapsychic drama and what part is deeply embedded in, if not determined by, the demands and expectations of the social surround. The ethnographer can observe the social surround and can make some assessment of these different dimensions and determinants of experience; the analyst cannot.

However, to paraphrase Edward Bruner (1988), life as lived is not life as experienced. No matter how much we know about the concrete details of a person's life, we can never really know how this person experiences a particular event or aspect of life without *asking* him or her about it.[7] Among the Toraja of South Sulawesi, Indonesia, for example, most adult men appear to be deeply involved in the competitive slaughter of water buffalo at elaborate funeral ceremonies, this being one important means by which they maintain or enhance their status and prestige within the community. Based on my observations of his public behavior, Nene'na Tandi, one of my most important collaborators and respondents, appeared to be as committed to this pursuit as anyone else. He was always in attendance at local funerals. He always carefully monitored the distribution of meat at these funerals to make certain that he would not be humiliated by receiving less than his own fair share or by allowing others to receive more than their status warranted. And he always attempted to associate himself with the high status individuals in attendance, thereby publicly demonstrating to others that he was worthy of acknowledgment and respect.

Yet during the course of my extended open-ended interviews with him (see Hollan and Wellenkamp 1994, 1996), it became apparent that he was more ambivalent about his involvement in slaughtering activities than his outward behavior had indicated. As a man of commoner birth and the owner of limited rice land, and as the stepfather of only one daughter, he had neither the wealth nor the extended family support to pursue slaughtering activities as successfully as other men in the community. As a result, he had become envious and resentful of these other men and contemptuous of the whole meat dividing process:

Why should we get angry [about the politics of meat]? This meat – indeed people call it meat, but I think of it as shit! Shit. Once we eat it, it becomes shit, right? It doesn't increase our wealth. After eating it, we sleep, and the next morning we go to the edge of the village and defecate. If it's like that, why get upset about it? *But some people say it's the most important* . . . Those are people who try to be big. Rich people. For one day [the day of the slaughtering], they can be rich. But they don't stay rich. Those who stay rich, ah, they sell pigs, they have nice houses. Ah, those are the happy ones. [Those are the ones] who are truly rich. But those who are rich for only an hour or two . . . I look at them [and think], they're all stupid.

Here we see how complicated the relationship between overt behavior and experience can be and why it can be so hazardous to make inferences about the latter based solely on observations of the former. So while I agree that good person-centered ethnography must begin with close observations of ongoing behavior in different social contexts and cultural domains, I would argue that it must eventually end with some more active engagement with our subjects in which we take advantage of their human capacity to reflect upon themselves and their experience.

What do people *embody*?

A third approach in contemporary person-centered ethnography asks how subjective experience is "embodied" or how the senses and perceptions of the body are culturally elaborated into the experience of self and other. This emphasis on the body and how it is both constitutive of and a constraint upon subjective experience includes formal phenomenological studies of how perception and consciousness are created and maintained (e.g., Csordas 1990, 1994), more qualitative studies of how bodily senses become culturally elaborated in different ways in different places (e.g.,

Classen 1993, Howes 1991, Stoller 1989), and studies in which bodies, including the body of the anthropologist, are used as a way of gaining privileged access to aspects of subjective experience that are otherwise unknowable or unspoken (e.g., Brown 1991, Daniel 1984, Desjarlais 1992). While there are significant differences within this approach, many of its practitioners agree that the body and its perceptions and senses have been neglected too long as a subject of serious study within anthropology and that traditional ethnography – with its emphasis on talk and linear, discursive, cognized forms of data collection and representation – misses, or has not been used to render,[8] important aspects of human experience that are more tacit, visceral, imaginal, and "preobjective" (Csordas 1994: 8).

Anthropologists working in this vein identify quite accurately, I believe, some of the major shortcomings of more traditional ethnography, especially the tendency to assume that minds can be studied apart from the bodies from which they emerge and in which they are embedded. However, if there is one thing that may be more problematic and difficult to study than the relationship between verbal utterance and subjective experience, it is probably the relationship between the body and experience. Just because the phenomena we seek to describe and represent are so tacit, visceral, and unspeakable, how do we convince our audiences that the senses, perceptions, and bodily experiences that we have discovered among a group of people are really those of our subjects – and so likely to be found by another anthropologist – and not our own physiological, sensual, and perceptual projections or preoccupations? Could not our newfound interest in the body itself be the product of a particular moment in the history of anthropology and the social sciences when it becomes important to reexamine (and collapse) the relationship between mind and body?

Even the use of our own bodies to gain access to the visceral experiences of others – through extended apprenticeships, for example (see especially Desjarlais 1992: 3–35) – though potentially of help to us here, is fraught with interpretive pitfalls. Although I think I greatly enriched my understanding of Toraja talk about suffering when I joined them in harvesting rice, the fact is that such work was even more backbreaking and exhausting for me than for them – since I was much taller than the average Toraja (and so found it very hard to stoop and bend for hours) and because I was not used to working so strenuously at high altitudes. Such work also brought back to me memories of childhood summers spent on my grandmother's farm in south Texas where I would stand in a trailer at the back of a cotton stripper – exhausted and covered from head to toe in dust and fiber – and desperately attempt to pitch an ever growing mound of cotton into the back of the trailer before it piled up and fell out the front.

Do such visceral sensations and emotionally charged memories from south Texas, triggered by my agricultural work in Toraja, help me to apprehend the subjective experiences of my Toraja subjects? Perhaps. But they may also, perhaps, lead me away from such experiences and set ablaze a chain of associations and bodily reactions that are peculiar to my own life.[9]

Discussion and examples

I mentioned at the outset of this chapter that for many person-centered ethnographers, inductive, cross-cultural comparison and theory building is a primary goal of their work. Now that I have sketched out some of the advantages and disadvantages of conducting person-centered ethnography in particular ways, let me discuss further a few examples of the ways in which person-centered ethnography has been used to develop and to refine psychocultural theory. I must underscore that almost all of the studies I cite here have made important theoretical contributions to our understanding of human behavior and experience. These contributions are many and varied and cross-cut the three investigative strategies I have outlined. Here, I can do no more than encourage the reader to explore these contributions further by bringing to their attention single examples from within each style of person-centered ethnography.

One of the perennial questions in psychocultural anthropology has been, does the organization of the human mind and psychological process vary by social and cultural context, and if so, how and in what ways? While this question has generated much heated debate, dating back at least as far as the contributions of Levy-Bruhl (1975) and Boas (1939), and has led to assertions of both strong universalism (e.g., Spiro 1984) and strong particularism (e.g., Rosaldo 1984), we have had very few grounded studies of the operation of specific minds in context that would help us answer this question definitively. One notable exception has been the work of Robert Levy.

In two books (Levy 1973, 1990) and in a series of articles (see especially 1984, 1989, 1996), almost all based on extensive open-ended interviews collected first in Tahiti and then among the Newars of Nepal (*what do people say?*), Levy has attempted to specify some of the aspects of human mental and emotional organization that do appear to vary by context, as well as those that do not. In *Tahitians: Mind and Experience in the Society Islands* (1973), Levy demonstrates through rich description of cultural and psychological forms that certain aspects of Tahitian learning and moral awareness appear to be deeply rooted in the face-to-face community organization of Tahitian village life. In *Tahitians* and elsewhere, he shows how this particular type of community organization shapes certain aspects of emotional experiences like grief and guilt as well, especially their felt intensity, but only after indicating that the *"qualitative* character" of many emotional feelings "probably has the same shape, the same initial stimulus characteristics" in any culture or society (Levy 1984: 223, emphasis in original).

In more recent work, Levy explicitly contrasts certain Tahitian states of mind and experience with those found among the Newars of Bhaktapur in Nepal. He argues that unlike Tahitian society where "culturally shaped common sense used to interpret culturally shaped face-to-face interactions and observations provides the core of community integration" (Levy 1990: 26), the Newars of Bhaktapur inhabit a dense, "archaic" urban environment "where multiple points of view are not only possible but forced on people," where citizens cannot escape "an epistemological crisis, forced to the understanding that external reality, as well as the self, is constructed, and in some sense illusory" (Levy 1990: 31), arbitrary, and contradictory. In such a place, integration of person and community is characterized not by a reliance on direct sensory experience of the concrete world, as in Tahiti, but by the efflorescence of, and commitment to, emotionally charged "marked" symbols – "objects or events that use some device to call attention to themselves and to set themselves off as being extraordinary, as *not* belonging to – or as being something *more* than – the ordinary banal world" (Levy 1990: 27, emphasis in original).

Levy's person-centered ethnography challenges us to think seriously about whether aspects of mind and experience vary *systematically* not so much by particular culture but by type of community organization, ranging from face-to-face villages to "archaic" cities like Bhaktapur to vast urban centers like contemporary Los Angeles or Jakarta. He asks us to consider how the dance of culture (Levy 1990: 28) in a particular type of community may be contingent upon, and constituent of, a particular type of dancer and conversely how certain types of cultural dancers may both require and construct certain types of communities.[10]

Psychocultural anthropologists also have long wished to better understand the origins and persistence of various forms of emotional distress and suffering, and have long pondered whether one can distinguish normal from abnormal or pathological states of mind (see Benedict 1934). Is depression, for example, a readily identifiable disease grounded in human genetics and biology that can be found in all cultures and historical periods, even if expressed in different ways? Or is it a socially constructed, culture-bound syndrome that has become reified in Western psychiatric nosology?

Arthur Kleinman, a strong advocate of grounding the study of human suffering in the compelling concerns and enactments of people's everday lives (*what do people do?*), has used person-centered ethnography to critique aspects of both biomedical and social science theory. In a number of publications (e.g., 1986, 1988), he has shown how Western psychiatric theory perpetuates a false dichotomy between mind and body and too readily reconstitutes experiences of pain and dysphoria arising out of complex interrelationships among mind, body, and culture into biological disease processes. He and Joan Kleinman have suggested, for example, that a psychosomatic interpretation of the bodily symptoms and complaints of a Chinese man falsely accused of a political crime during the Cultural Revolution would only poorly render the sense of shame and historical injustice that is at the true core of his suffering. Indeed, such an interpretation "would turn Huang Zhenyi into a passive object, a caricature unworthy of the tragic tale he had told . . . and of the moral significance it held for him . . ." (Kleinman and Kleinman 1991: 284).

But Kleinman has used the ethnography of experience to suggest the limits of social science theory and concepts as well. In studies of chronic pain in the United States and in China, he argues that while the concept of "resistance" helps to illuminate certain aspects of the pain experience – for example, expression of symptoms as a "rhetoric of complaint aimed at negotiating improvements in life situations" (Kleinman 1992: 175) – it obscures others. The intersubjective experience of pain, he suggests, "is so various, so multileveled, so open to original inventions that interpreting it solely as . . . disguised critique of dominant ideology, notwithstanding all the moral resonance" of that focus, "is inadequate" (Kleinman 1992: 190). Pain, he argues, has an emergent, novel, indeterminate aspect to it that eludes our contemporary conceptual and theoretical models.

Kleinman concludes that psychocultural theories of pain and suffering, whether they favor biomedical or social science explanations, must "fasten onto the overriding practical relevance of experience for those who engage in it, for whom something crucial is almost always at stake" (Kleinman 1992: 190). They must avoid mischaracterizing "the felt flow of experience through professional deconstructions that are totalistic and thereby claim an absolute, unpositioned knowledge of determinants and effects" (Kleinman 1992: 190). The theoretical (as well as ethnographic) challenge, then, is to "describe the processual elaboration of the undergoing, the enduring, the bearing of pain (or loss or other tribulation) in the vital flow of intersubjective engagements in a particular moral world" (Kleinman 1992: 190).

A third area that has intrigued psychocultural anthropologists is that of ritual and symbolic healing (Hollan 1994). How do various cultures help individuals to come to terms with, if not transcend or resolve, conflict, suffering, and misfortune in human life? Is symbolic healing, ritual or otherwise, truly efficacious? If so, why? If not, why not?

Thomas Csordas in his book, *The Sacred Self: A Cultural Phenomenology of Charismatic Healing* (1994), develops a comprehensive theory of ritual and symbolic healing. He uses the phenomenological approach of Merleau-Ponty (*what do people embody?*) in an attempt to specify when and under what conditions ritual healing becomes efficacious. His goal is to move beyond mere description of Charismatic healing's unique features and the experience of its participants to "identify features in it that are comparatively and cross-culturally relevant, and . . . to analyze it with theoretical constructs that are themselves valid for comparative study" (Csordas 1994: ix).

For my purposes here, let me draw attention to just one aspect of Csordas's extensive and complex work. Csordas points out that one of the weaknesses of earlier anthropological studies of symbolic healing is that they focus too narrowly on descriptions of ritual events and on the activities and behavior of the healer, but only rarely examine the ongoing experience of the patient or supplicant in a systematic way (Csordas 1994: 3). As a result, these earlier studies cannot delineate the experiential specificity of effect in healing and tend to attribute too much therapeutic efficacy and definitive outcome to vague, nonspecific mechanisms of global transformation such as trance, catharsis, placebo effect, or suggestion, thought to occur within the boundaries of the healing ritual or event itself.

Csordas points out, however, that when we shift our attention to the experience of the patient or supplicant and carefully investigate how the imaginal and self-transformative processes initiated in, or perpetuated by, the healing event may (or may not) remain active in the mind and experience of the patient after the healing event is concluded, we begin to see that the therapeutic process, when it occurs and is efficacious, "transcends the boundaries of particular sessions and permeates the pursuit of everyday life concerns" (Csordas 1994: 140). Thus, symbolic transformation and healing is not usually instantaneous, global, and definitive in nature, but rather gradual, partial, and incremental, and cannot be understood apart from the patient's or supplicant's life experience that both proceeds and then overflows the event or ritual of healing itself.

Csordas's work, with its detailed description and analysis of the supplicant's or patient's phenomenology, gives us a way of thinking about why symbolic healing is efficacious, when it is, and challenges us to *specify* the processes and mechanisms of therapeutic change for given individuals.

Conclusion

I conclude this brief review with four, more general observations:

First: I am heartened by both the quantity and quality of person-centered ethnography that is being produced today, and in fact, I think the two are related. Current advances have come about, in part, because – in contrast to other historical periods – we now have a critical mass of person-centered ethnographers who are reacting to one another and pushing the work in new directions.

Second: However, as in contemporary psychoanalysis where some of the followers of Kohut rapidly produced a language and theory that was at least as abstract and experience-distant as the metapsychology of drives and instincts they sought to replace, so in contemporary person-centered ethnography one can begin to see the creeping – perhaps inexorable? – reification of emerging terms and concepts such as "embodiment," "enactment," "habitus," and so on, none of which, of course, are completely transparent or without their own theoretical and conceptual incrustations. Let us hope that we can spare ourselves some of the irony that the psychoanalytic self psychologists have inflicted on themselves by keeping our concepts and descriptions of human subjectivity as experience-near as possible – if that is, in fact, the kind of work we claim to be doing.

Third: While most person-centered ethnographers would agree – at least theoretically – that human lives and subjective experience are complex and that it is unlikely that we will ever discover a *single* approach that would allow us to capture this complexity in its entirety, there is nevertheless a tendency among some person-centered ethnographers to conduct research in a particular way – either because of their own limitations (for example, limited mastery of the local language) or because of their own strong preferences (for example, a fascination with life history or sound or narrative or embodiment) – but then to report the research as if this were the only way it could or even *should* have been done.

But as I have suggested here, no one has yet (at least) cornered the market on ways of conducting person-centered ethnography. Each of the approaches outlined here entail clear disadvantages as well as advantages – as is true of any strategy in any scientific endeavor. Rather than ignore these disadvantages, we should attempt to control for them. As individual ethnographers we might, for example, begin or continue to experiment with ways of combining different styles and approaches. Or we might begin to engage one another more extensively in collaborative research, allowing the conceptual and methodological expertise of our colleagues to counterbalance the weaknesses of our own approaches and vice versa.

Fourth: Person-centered ethnography has persisted and will continue to develop not because it lends itself to the study of certain narrow, particular, historically and culturally bound issues, but because it offers a powerful way of grounding social, psychological, and even biological theories of human behavior in the lived experience of real people. For that reason, it behooves us to encourage its growth and refinement, and to carefully examine its results.

Acknowledgments

A shorter version of this paper was originally presented at the Fourth Biennial Meeting of the Society for Psychological Anthropology in San Juan, Puerto Rico, October 6–8, 1995. Sections of it also appear in *Transcultural Psychiatry* (1997) 34: 219–234 under the title, "The Relevance of Person-Centered Ethnography to Cross-Cultural Psychiatry." I am grateful to the editors, Carmella Moore and Holly Mathews, and to two anonymous reviewers for a number of helpful comments and suggestions.

NOTES

1 Further, I have not attempted to make an exhaustive review of the literature. Rather, I have cited references that in my opinion are representative of major trends in the field of person-centered ethnography.

2 Hallowell (1955) emphasizes that some nonliving beings, such as ancestral spirits, must be considered "persons" to the extent that they are thought to share the moral and behavioral attributes of human beings.

3 I am grateful to Alison Hamilton for suggesting this term to me after she read an earlier draft of this paper.

4 There are, of course, only "relatively" experience-near concepts. Any description of a concept is necessarily a level of abstraction away from the thing described or conceptualized. But person-centered descriptions and concepts do attempt to stay as close to the subject's experience as possible.

5 For further discussion of the distinction between *respondent* and *informant* in person-centered ethnography, see Levy and Wellenkamp (1989) and Levy and Hollan (1998).

6 From an anthropological or cross-cultural point of view, this (usually unexamined) assumption of the insularity of intrapsychic phenomena is a hazardous one and can (and does) lead to theorizing about human subjectivity that is culture-bound and ethnocentric.

7 Bruner (1988: 7), of course, makes a further distinction between life as experienced and life as told:

   A life as experienced consists of the images, feelings, sentiments, desires, thoughts, and meanings known to the person whose life it is. One can never know directly what another individual is experiencing, although we all interpret clues and make inferences about the experiences of others. A life as told, a life history, is a narrative, influenced by the cultural conventions of telling, by the audience, and by the social context.

8 Csordas (1994) demonstrates how interview materials and observational data *could be* used to study embodiment issues, but one of his central points is that they often are not so used.

9 This issue of whether observers' subjective and bodily experience helps or hinders their understanding others is widely debated within psychoanalysis as well.

10 Levy (1990: 28) alludes to Yeats' poem, *Among School Children*: O body swayed to music, O brightening glance, How can we know the dancer from the dance?

REFERENCES

Bateson, Gregory 1972 The Logical Categories of Learning and Communication. In *Steps to an Ecology of Mind*. New York: Ballantine Books. Pp. 279–308.

Benedict, Ruth 1934 Anthropology and the Abnormal. *Journal of General Psychology* 10: 59–82.

Besnier, Niko 1994 The Evidence From Discourse. In *Handbook of Psychological Anthropology*, P. K. Bock, ed. Westport, CT: Praeger Publishers. Pp. 197–210.

Boas, Franz 1939 *The Mind of Primitive Man*. New York: Macmillan.

Bourdieu, Pierre 1977 *Outline of a Theory of Practice*, trans. R. Nice. Cambridge: Cambridge University Press.

Brown, Karen M. 1991 *Mama Lola: A Vodou Priestess in Brooklyn*. Berkeley, CA: University of California Press.

Bruner, Edward M. 1988 The Opening Up of Anthropology. In *Text, Play and Story: The Construction and Reconstruction of Self and Society*, E. M. Bruner, ed. Prospect Heights, IL: Waveland Press. Pp. 1–16.

Bruner, Jerome S. 1990 *Acts of Meaning*. Cambridge, MA: Harvard University Press.

Cain, Carole 1991 Personal Stories: Identity Acquisition and Self-Understanding in Alcoholics Anonymous. *Ethos* 19: 210–253.

Classen, Constance 1993 *Worlds of Sense: Exploring the Senses in History and Across Cultures*. New York: Routledge.

Csordas, Thomas J. 1990 Embodiment as a Paradigm for Anthropology. *Ethos* 18: 5–47.

1994 *The Sacred Self: A Cultural Phenomenology of Charismatic Healing*. Berkeley, CA: University of California Press.

D'Andrade, Roy G. and Claudia Strauss, eds. 1992 *Human Motives and Cultural Models*. New York: Cambridge University Press.

Daniel, E. Valentine 1984 *Fluid Signs: Being a Person the Tamil Way*. Berkeley, CA: University of California Press.

Desjarlais, Robert R. 1992 *Body and Emotion: The Aesthetics of Illness and Healing in the Nepal Himalayas*. Philadelphia, PA: University of Pennsylvania Press.

1994 The Possibilities for Experience Among the Homeless Mentally Ill. *American Anthropologist* 96: 886–901.

Good, Byron. 1994 *Medicine, Rationality, and Culture*. New York: Cambridge University Press.

Hallowell, A. I. 1955 *Culture and Experience*. Philadelphia, PA: University of Pennsylvania Press.

Heider, Karl G. 1991 *Landscapes of Emotion: Mapping Three Cultures of Emotion in Indonesia*. Cambridge: Cambridge University Press.

Herdt, Gilbert and Robert J. Stoller 1990 *Intimate Communications: Erotics and the Study of Culture*. New York: Columbia University Press.

Hollan, Douglas 1994 Suffering and the Work of Culture: A Case of Magical Poisoning in Toraja. *American Ethnologist* 21: 74–87.

1995 To the Afterworld and Back: Mourning and Dreams of the Dead Among the Toraja. *Ethos* 23: 424–436.

1996 Conflict Avoidance and Resolution Among the Toraja of South Sulawesi, Indonesia. In *Cultural Variation in Conflict Resolution: Alternatives for Reduc-*

ing Violence, K. Bjorkqvist and D. Fry, eds. Mahwah, NJ: Lawrence Erlbaum Publishers. Pp. 59–68.

Hollan, Douglas W. and Jane C. Wellenkamp 1994 *Contentment and Suffering: Culture and Experience in Toraja*. New York: Columbia University Press.

1996 *The Thread of Life: Toraja Reflections on the Life Cycle*. Honolulu, HI: University of Hawaii Press.

Holland, Dorothy and Naomi Quinn, eds. 1987 *Cultural Models in Language and Thought*. New York: Cambridge University Press.

Howes, David, ed. 1991 *The Varieties of Sensory Experience: A Sourcebook in the Anthropology of the Senses*. Toronto: University of Toronto Press.

Jackson, Michael 1989 *Paths Toward a Clearing: Radical Empiricism and Ethnographic Inquiry*. Bloomington, IN: Indiana University Press.

Kleinman, Arthur 1986 *Social Origins of Distress and Disease: Neurasthenia, Pain, and Depression in Modern China*. New Haven, CT: Yale University Press.

1988 *The Illness Narratives: Suffering, Healing and the Human Condition*. New York: Basic Books.

1992 Pain and Resistance: The Delegitimation and Relegitimation of Local Worlds. In *Pain as Human Experience: An Anthropological Perspective*, M. Delvecchio Good, P. E. Brodwin, B. J. Good, and A. Kleinman, eds. Berkeley, CA: University of California Press. Pp. 169–197.

Kleinman, Arthur and Joan Kleinman 1991 Suffering and its Professional Transformation: Toward an Ethnography of Interpersonal Experience. *Culture, Medicine, and Psychiatry* 15: 275–301.

Kohut, Heinz 1971 *The Analysis of the Self*. New York: International Universities Press.

1977 *The Restoration of the Self*. New York: International Universities Press.

Kracke, Waud 1987 Myths in Dreams, Thoughts in Images: An Amazonian Contribution to the Psychoanalytic Theory of Primary Process. In *Dreaming: Anthropological and Psychological Interpretations*, B. Tedlock, ed. New York: Cambridge University Press. Pp. 31–54.

LeVine, Robert A. 1982 *Culture, Behavior, and Personality: An Introduction to the Comparative Study of Psycho-Social Adaptation*. 2nd ed. New York: Aldine.

Levy, Robert I. 1973 *Tahitians: Mind and Experience in the Society Islands*. Chicago, IL: University of Chicago Press.

1984 Emotion, Knowing, and Culture. In *Culture Theory: Essays on Mind, Self, and Emotion*, R. A. Shweder and R. A. LeVine, eds. Cambridge: Cambridge University Press. Pp. 214–237.

1989 The Quest for Mind in Different Times and Different Places. In *Social History and Issues in Human Consciousness: Some Interdisciplinary Connections*, A. E. Barnes and P. N. Stearns, eds. New York: New York University Press. Pp. 3–40.

1990 *Mesocosm: Hinduism and the Organization of a Traditional Newar City in Nepal*. Berkeley, CA: University of California Press.

1996 Essential Contrasts: Differences in Parental Ideas about Learners and Teaching in Tahiti and Nepal. In *Parents' Cultural Belief Systems: Their Origins, Expressions, and Consequences*, S. Harkness and C. Super, eds. New York: Guilford Publications. Pp. 123–142.

Levy, Robert I. and Douglas W. Hollan 1998 Person-Centered Interviewing and

Observation in Anthropology. In *Handbook of Methods in Cultural Anthropology*, H. R. Bernard, ed. Walnut Creek, CA: Altamira Press. Pp. 333–364.

Levy, Robert I. and Jane C. Wellenkamp 1989 Methodology in the Anthropological Study of Emotion. In *Emotion: Theory, Research, and Experience*, vol. 4: *The Measurement of Emotions*, R. Plutchik and H. Kellerman, eds. New York: Academic Press. Pp. 205–232.

Levy-Bruhl, Lucien 1975 *The Notebooks on Primitive Mentality*, trans. P. Riviere. New York: Harper and Row.

Lutz, Catherine 1992 Motivated Models. In *Human Motives and Cultural Models*, R. G. D'Andrade and C. Strauss, eds. New York: Cambridge University Press. Pp. 181–195.

Obeyesekere, Gananath 1990 *The Work of Culture*. Chicago, IL: University of Chicago Press.

Ochs, Elinor and Bambi B. Schieffelin 1984 Language Acquisition and Socialization: Three Developmental Stories and Their Implications. In *Culture Theory: Essays on Mind, Self, and Emotion*, R. A. Shweder and R. A. LeVine, eds. Cambridge: Cambridge University Press. Pp. 276–320.

Ortner, Sherry B. 1984 Theory in Anthropology Since the Sixties. *Comparative Studies in Society and History* 26: 126–166.

Parish, Steven M. 1994 *Moral Knowing in a Hindu Sacred City: An Exploration of Mind, Emotion, and Self.* New York: Columbia University Press.

   1996 *Hierarchy and Its Discontents: Culture and the Politics of Consciousness in Caste Society*. Philadelphia, PA: University of Pennsylvania Press.

Paul, Robert A. 1990 What Does Anybody Want? Desire, Purpose, and the Acting Subject in the Study of Culture. *Cultural Anthropology* 5: 431–451.

Peacock, James. 1988 Religion and Life History: An Exploration in Cultural Psychology. In *Text, Play, and Story: The Construction and Reconstruction of Self and Society*, E. M. Bruner, ed. Prospect Heights, IL: Waveland Press. Pp. 94–116.

Rosaldo, Michelle Z. 1984 Toward an Anthropology of Self and Feeling. In *Culture Theory: Essays on Mind, Self, and Emotion*, R. A. Shweder and R. A. LeVine, eds. Cambridge: Cambridge University Press. Pp. 137–157.

Sapir, Edward 1958a The Emergence of the Concept of Personality in a Study of Cultures. In *Selected Writings of Edward Sapir*, D. G. Mandelbaum, ed. Berkeley, CA: University of California Press. Pp. 590–597 (originally published 1934).

   1958b Cultural Anthropology and Psychiatry. In *Selected Writings of Edward Sapir*, D. G. Mandelbaum, ed. Berkeley, CA: University of California Press. Pp. 509–521 (originally published 1932).

   1958c Why Cultural Anthropology Needs the Psychiatrist. In *Selected Writings of Edward Sapir*, D. G. Mandelbaum, ed. Berkeley, CA: University of California Press. Pp. 569–577 (originally published 1938).

Spiro, Melford E. 1984 Some Reflections on Cultural Determinism and Relativism with Special Reference to Emotion and Reason. In *Culture Theory: Essays on Mind, Self, and Emotion*, R. A. Shweder and R. A. LeVine, eds, Cambridge: Cambridge University Press. Pp. 323–346.

Strauss, Claudia and Naomi Quinn 1997 *A Cognitive Theory of Cultural Meaning.* New York: Cambridge University Press.

Stoller, Paul 1989 *The Taste of Ethnographic Things: The Senses in Anthropology.* Philadelphia, PA: University of Pennsylvania Press.

Stromberg, Peter G. 1993 *Language and Self-Transformation: A Study of the Christian Conversion Narrative.* Cambridge: Cambridge University Press.

Wikan, Unni 1990 *Managing Turbulent Hearts: A Balinese Formula for Living.* Chicago, IL: University of Chicago Press.

3   Activity theory and cultural psychology

Carl Ratner

The theoretical and empirical direction that cultural psychology takes is greatly influenced by the manner in which culture is conceptualized. One's definition of culture determines which social influences on psychology will be researched, the manner in which culture is seen as affecting psychological processes, the kinds of cultural characteristics of psychological phenomena one investigates, the reciprocal effects which psychological phenomena can have on culture, and the methodological procedures which cultural psychologists employ.

In this chapter I shall review an approach to culture which differs from the common conception of culture as shared concepts and meanings. The alternative that I wish to describe construes culture as fundamentally consisting of socially organized practical activities. In this latter view, what is most basic to culture are the normative, institutionalized ways of working, schooling, playing, governing, treating disease, adjudicating disputes, arranging family life, owning, controlling, and distributing resources.

This conception of culture as practical activity is unusual in the field of cultural psychology. Most scholarship in cultural psychology construes culture as shared concepts and understandings of things. These social concepts are seen as molding psychological processes. From this perspective, both culture and psychological processes are mental. The relationship between culture and psychology is an interaction of mental processes. This viewpoint dominates works in cultural psychology such as Harre (1986), Kleinman and Good (1985), Lutz (1988), Shweder (1990), Shweder and LeVine (1984), and Shweder and Sullivan (1993).

For example, in his defining paper "Cultural Psychology – What Is It?" Shweder (1990) places the search for meaning – or "intentionality" – at the core of culture. He says that "a sociocultural environment is an intentional world" (pp. 2, 25, 26). Culture is essentially a world of meanings that humans bestow on things. Accordingly, "cultural psychology is a return to the study of mental representations . . ." (p. 24). Shweder illustrates this conception of cultural psychology in an analysis of sleeping arrangements. He argues that cultural arrangements for sleeping are generated by moral concepts: "the praxis [of sleeping] is an expression of [people's] preferences and not a by-product of a resource constraint" (Shweder 1996: 30).

This mentalistic approach to cultural psychology has been vitally important for explaining the formative impact of cultural concepts on psychological phenomena. However, the mentalistic view overlooks other important aspects of culture that bear on psychological phenomena. Cultural psychologists generally do not discuss the concrete social structures in which meanings are formed (cf. Ratner 1993, 1997a: 93–122, 1997b, 1999). These authors may believe that social structures condition concepts but they rarely articulate this fact. In the field of cultural psychology it is exceedingly rare to find a concrete discussion of culture that describes the principles of ownership, production, and distribution of resources; the class structure; the division of labor among activities; or the principles that govern action in specific social institutions. It is even less usual to find cultural psychologists connecting these features of a social system in a meaningful way to psychological phenomena.

Cultural psychologists have been correct to emphasize that cultural concepts about things, people, and life in general stimulate and organize psychological phenomena. However, this is only one half of the story. These concepts are usually grounded in practical, socially organized activities.

Culture as practical activity

The dependence of psychological phenomena on practical social activity is known as *praxis*, or *Tatigkeit* in German, or *deyatelnost* in Russian. This concept has a long intellectual history. Marx and Engels developed it as a major principle of their materialistic world view. The premises from which Marx and Engels began their system are "real individuals, their activity, and the material conditions under which they live, both those which they find already existing and those produced by their activity" (Marx and Engels 1964: 31). Marx and Engels argued that forms of consciousness are grounded in particular social activities. Emphasizing the centrality of productive activities for consciousness, the authors stated: "men, developing their material production and their material intercourse, alter along with this . . . their thinking and the products of their thinking" (Marx and Engels 1964: 38). Noneconomic activities, such as education and family interactions, would be related to psychology in a similar fashion.

Grounding consciousness in practical activity is important for several reasons. It explains the origins of consciousness in a new fashion. Plus it has crucial implications for promoting psychological change. If consciousness is rooted in social activity, then the latter must be transformed in order to alter and improve psychological functions. Marx and Engels strenuously criticized intellectualist views of consciousness that misconstrued mental phenomena as autonomous creations independent of practical activity. They particularly objected to suggestions that consciousness could be changed by itself without changing social institutions. In a famous statement, Marx proclaimed that, "The abolition of religion as the *illusory* happiness of men is a demand for their *real* happiness. The call to abandon their illusions about their condition is a *call to abandon a condition which requires illusions*" (1975: 176, emphasis in original).

Other scholars have emphasized the importance of practical activity for psychological functions. Dewey (1902: 219–220) espoused this position when he said,

Apperceptive masses and associational tracts of necessity conform to the dominant activities. The occupations determine the chief modes of satisfaction, the standards of success and failure. Hence they furnish the working classifications and definitions of value; they control the desire processes. Moreover, they decide the sets of objects and relations that are important, and thereby provide the content or material of attention, and the qualities that are interestingly significant. The directions given to mental life thereby extend to emotional and intellectual characteristics. So fundamental and pervasive is the group of occupational activities that it affords the scheme or pattern of the structural organization of mental traits. Occupations integrate special elements into a functioning whole.

The conception of mental activity as inspired by practical social activity has also been espoused by Vygotsky, Luria, Leont'ev, and other Russian and German psychologists (Ratner 1998a, 1998b). While these activity theorists are by no means unified in a single outlook (Van der Veer and Valsiner 1991: 185–186, 289–292), they agree that the social organization of an activity, and the cultural instruments that are utilized to carry it out, stimulate and organize psychological phenomena. Thus, Leont'ev stated that "the structure of man's consciousness is linked in a regular way with the structure of his activity" (1981: 231). Luria expressed the thrust of activity theory in similar terms:

Cognitive processes (such as perception and memory, abstraction and generalization, reasoning and problem-solving) are not independent and unchanging "abilities" or "functions" of human consciousness; they are processes occurring in concrete, practical activities and are formed within the limits of this activity. (Luria 1971: 266)

As Minick shows in an excellent article, Vygotsky maintained that various activities such as science, schooling, art, and reading stimulate unique kinds of thinking. Activities do not express preformed, natural cognitive, emotional, or personality characteristics of the individual. On the contrary, artistic, literary, scientific, and educational activities *generate* psychological functions. The concrete social relations and cultural technologies that are germane to the activities organize the individual's psychological processes (1990: 167).

Within cognitive anthropology, there has been a long-standing tradition, dating from the school of ethnoscience to more applied research today, to focus on the study of cognitive processes like decision-making, problem-solving, and inference making in natural settings (cf. Geoghegan 1973, Gladwin 1975, Hutchins 1980, Mathews 1983, Quinn 1978, and Young 1981). Some of this research emphasizes the importance of life activities for structuring cognitive processes. For example, Lave (1988) has investigated the manner in which different life activities shape mathematical thinking. She found that in everyday life people employ mathematical operations differently from the manner in which they do in school.

Lave reports that many people use more sophisticated mathematical operations in activities such as shopping, preparing meals, and working at various jobs than they did while in school (Lave 1988: 56, 66–67). In other situations, however, the procedures employed were less sophisticated (Lave 1988: 65, 128–129, 154, 165). For example, in preparing meals, one man faced the problem of calculating three-fourths of two-thirds of a cup of cottage cheese. He used a measuring cup to get the two-thirds of a cup. Then he dumped it out on a cutting board, patted it into a circle, marked a cross on it, and scooped away one quadrant of the circle. Such a procedure circumvented the mathematical operation of multiplying 2/3 x 3/4. Lave's conclusion is that "'the same' activity in different situations derives structuring from, and provides structuring resources for, other activities" (1988: 122).

Mistry and Rogoff (1994: 140) apply activity theory to memory. They explain that memory processes are remembering skills that "develop for the purpose of solving practical problems and they are tied to the familiar tasks and practices in which remembering takes place." Memory is not a mechanical process that retrieves information according to natural mechanisms. Rather, "Remembering is an activity that is defined in terms of the meaning of a task and its materials to the people remembering, and in terms of its function in the social and cultural system" (Mistry and Rogoff 1994: 141).

For instance, Dube (1982) found that the cultural activity of telling and listening to stories primes memory to recall episodes from oral stories. Thus, Botswana individuals (from a culture with a strong story-telling tradition) recalled more episodes from stories that were told to them than did Americans (with little experience of listening to long stories). Interestingly, the Botswanans recalled more episodes from both African *and* European stories than Americans did. This result led Dube to conclude that the activity of story-telling stimulates a general ability to recall orally presented material.

Another series of experiments has demonstrated that memory of colors depends upon the way that colors can be communicated interpersonally. Colors that can be accurately communicated in verbal descriptions are recalled better than colors that are difficult to communicate. The activity of interpersonal communication affects individuals' ability to remember colors in their own minds (Garro 1986, Lantz and Stefflre 1964, Lucy and Shweder 1979, Stefflre, Vales, and Morley 1966).

Along these lines, Cordua, McGraw, and Drabman (1979) demonstrated that children's memory of gender roles that are described in stories depends upon the consistency of these roles with the normative gender division of labor in society. Normative gender roles in the story (e.g., a male doctor and female nurse) are recalled more accurately than gender roles that contradict the usual sexual division of labor in society (e.g., female doctor and male nurse).

Activity theory is important to cultural psychology because it expands culture from being a realm of concepts to being activity which is organized in a specific social-technological system. It is this kind of activity that cultivates psychological phenomena. Unfortunately, activity theorists do not always adhere to this conception of activity. Activities are often mentioned in general terms with no indication that these activities and psychological functions are organized differently in different social systems. In addition, activity theorists often fail to identify the manner in which activity influences thinking.

For example, the aforementioned research on memory and activity treats story-telling and interpersonal communication in general terms. There is no discussion of the specific ways that story-telling and interpersonal communication are conducted and how this style, or form, affects the operations of memory. Activity is often so ill-defined as to be synonymous with experience.

Lave's 1988 work exemplifies these problems. Although she repeatedly emphasizes the point that situations and activities structure mental operations such as mathematics, she fails to consider the concrete social organization of the activities she describes. She is silent about the enormous culture of commercialism and consumerism that structures shopping inside and outside the store. She never considers the fact that people are primed by a fantastic assortment of inducements long before they enter the store as well as during their stay inside it. Advertising works to stimulate desire, to reduce rational and critical thinking, to encourage conformity, and to structure a self-concept that depends upon material consumption for confidence and personal satisfaction. Inside the store, commercial practices similarly structure shopping activity. Lighting is manipulated to make fruits and vegetables appear more succulent than they really are. The entire layout of the store channels the shopper into areas he/she might not normally visit. Products are displayed to entice extra buying of expensive brand names. Loss leaders mislead the shopper into believing that the prices are generally low.

This commercial system affects the purchasing decisions shoppers make. Encouraged to buy impulsively according to packaging, brand names, and product display, and confronted by difficult price comparisons which are deliberately created by a complex variety of measurement systems (pounds and grams; pints, one and one-half quarts, and fluid ounces) and pricing systems (e.g., 2 for 85¢), shoppers routinely forsake price comparisons altogether or else use inadequate shorthand methods for estimating the best price.

Lave ignores the full commercial organization of shopping and this makes it impossible for her to elucidate the specific character of mathematical thinking that shoppers employ. Lave is only able to discover that shoppers replace genuine mathematical reckoning with a variety of substitutes. However, she does not demonstrate the ways in which these substitutes reflect the specific character of shopping activity.[1] Ascertaining the specific character of mental processes requires knowing the social organization of activity and recognizing its reflection in mental processes.

Cole is another eminent activity theorist whose conception of cultural activity is abstract. In a recent publication, Cole (1995) states that culture is constructed of human artifacts – symbolic and material – that mediate and constrain our interaction with people and the natural world. This highly general statement is obvious and uninformative. Cole fails to indicate any concrete societal basis or character to artifacts. His description of culture is confined to trite examples of how parents symbolically project a probable future for their children.

Cole then enthusiastically describes a program he designed for teaching reading which is based upon activity theory. Although the program is couched in the terminology of activity theory – reading is mediated by artifacts and social relations – and although it is diagrammed in complicated schematics, it really consists of a very mundane procedure. The students who had reading difficulties were first presented with cards which specified roles which they were to adopt while reading a text. The roles were "a person who asks about words that are hard to say," "a person who asks about words that are hard to understand," "a person who says what the main idea is," "a person who asks about what is going to happen next," and "a person who picks the person to answer questions asked by others." Students then read a text with their assigned roles in mind and acted out these roles in a group discussion of the text.

Cole's procedure simply involved giving each student something to think about in order to focus attention while re ding. Unfortunately, the artifacts, cultural mediation, structured medium, and role-playing activity that Cole introduced were devoid of any concrete cultural considerations.

A pertinent discussion of these factors that influence reading would describe the content and availability of educational materials such as books, audio tapes, movies, and artistic supplies; the architectural structure and condition of the school buildings; the form, quality, and arrangement of the desks; the educational system, including the educational budget, teacher training, teacher salaries; the students' family lives; their parents' occupations and the social and economic rewards that accompany them (i.e., class position); the content of media that the children watch; and potential educational and occupational opportunities that might affect their motivation to read. In contrast, Cole's conception of activity was limited to having students focus on difficult words in the text. He never mentions concrete cultural activities that affect reading. Cole's neglect of this larger systemic influence is surprising given the extensive attention paid to the effects of the larger sociocultural system of schooling in America by educational anthropologists and practice theorists (cf. Holland and Eisenhart 1990, Luttrell 1989, Ogbu 1978).

The failure of activity theorists to identify the concrete social organization of activity can be traced back to Vygotsky and Luria. For all their stated emphasis on the sociohistorical nature of psychology, Vygotsky and Luria typically did not consider the ways in which concrete social systems bear on psychological functions. They discussed the general importance of language and schooling for psychological functioning; however, they failed to examine the real social systems in which these activities occur (Ratner 1998b, Van der Veer and Valsiner 1991: 155–180).

This omission is evident in Vygotsky's "Experimental Study of Concept Formation." Here, Vygotsky stated that social life is important for the development of conceptual thinking in adolescence. However, instead of analyzing the social demands and activities that occur during adolescence, he postulated that a new abstract use of words during adolescence generates concept formation (Vygotsky 1987: 131, 160). Vygotsky never indicated the social basis for this new use of words. His social analysis thus reduced to a semiotic analysis, which overlooked the real world of social praxis.

Luria's (1976) report of cross-cultural research in Uzbekistan similarly fails to mention any societal reasons for the obtained psychological differences among his ethnic groups. For example, he found that Uzbekistani peasants perceived certain colors as dissimilar (not classifiable together) whereas administrators and teachers perceived those colors as similar. Luria's explanation was that the two groups had a different conception of color. The peasants regarded color as intrinsically tied to objects whereas the teachers regarded color as an abstract property. The peasants perceived the color "pig's dung" as different from "cow's dung" because the two objects in which the colors inhered were different. The teachers abstracted the brown color from the objects and categorized the two shades of brown together (1976: 26–30). While Luria's analysis is interesting as far as it goes, it does not ground the concepts or the psychological functions in a particular social system of practical activities.

When researchers do consider the concrete social features of activity, they are able to elucidate the cultural character of psychological phenomena. Such research demonstrates that personality traits of men and women derive much of their character from the activities which men and women carry out in society. Where gender roles are distinctive, masculine and feminine personality traits diverge accordingly. For example, the severe gender division of labor during Victorian times led many middle-class urban men to become practical, ambitious, and assertive in many areas of life, while their female counterparts were generally diffident, indirect (suggestive), dependent, and solicitous. In societies where men and women engage in similar activities they often come to demonstrate similar personality traits. Furthermore, when men engage in activities that a society typically allocates to women, they may adopt the personality traits which are characteristic of women in that society (Ratner 1991: 156–157, 214–217). Tavris (1992:63) concluded that "New studies find that the behavior we link to gender depends more on what an individual is doing and needs to do than on his or her biological sex."

An excellent example of personality adapting to gender activities is found among the Luo people in southwestern Kenya. They assign some boys to engage in female tasks, especially when a family lacks a girl of the appropriate age. Ember (1973) compared the social behavior of boys who were assigned female tasks with boys who engaged in masculine tasks and also with girls who performed female tasks. Boys who participated in female social activities, especially household chores like tending children, cleaning house, serving food, and cooking, behaved socially more like girls than boys who did not engage in female tasks. The boys in cross-gender roles were less egoistic, aggressive, and dominant and more prosocial than boys fulfilling traditional male gender activities. Since the boys were assigned female roles on the basis of family need rather than according to personality characteristics the boys themselves displayed, Ember concludes that role assignment determined personality.

Emotions are also constructed in, and sustain, cultural activities (Ratner 2000a). We learn to cultivate (experience) and express different kinds of emotions in different activities such as interacting with family members or friends, studying in school, working, and attending religious services. In our society it is appropriate to express anger with relatives or friends, however this is not appropriate at work. Stearns (1989: 249) reports that a deliberate effort was made by industrial managers to channel anger in conformity to bourgeois work norms: "Middle-class personnel specialists like Frederick Taylor or Elton Mayo were truly appalled by the amount of open anger they found among workers . . . They therefore amended their own original agendas . . . to build in explicit attempts to banish anger from the workplace." This deliberate social organization of anger established norms of emotional expression, rewards for complying with the norms, and sanctions for disobeying. Emotional expression was also integrated into the power relations of work since managers remained free to express anger toward employees although the reverse was prohibited.

Jealousy is another emotion that reflects (and fortifies) cultural activities. Norms, rights, values, and sanctions which govern economic and family activity generate jealousy. Specifically, individual control of property, products, and people fosters possessiveness which is the basis of jealousy. Jealousy motivates us to maintain an exclusive relationship with things and people. It energizes us to combat threats to this exclusive relationship. In contrast, collective ownership and sharing minimize possessiveness and jealousy since exclusive possession is nonfunctional. Thus, the expression of jealousy is rare among the Nyinba people of Nepal who practice polyandry, where one woman marries all the brothers of another family. According to contemporary anthropological research (Ingoldsby 1995, Levine 1988), the brothers all have intimate relations with the common wife without feeling jealousy toward each other over her. Indeed, jealousy would subvert the group marriage which is a functional adaptation to economic pressures. The land is infertile and a great deal of labor is required to make it productive. Multiple husbands help in this regard. In addition, men are often away from home on trading expeditions, and the presence of other husbands provides the wife with continuing support. Polyandrous marriage also helps to reduce the birth rate in this resource-poor region because one wife's pregnancy deprives several men of reproductive outlets. The emotional acceptance of multiple intimate relationships fortifies the family practice of polyandry which is functional to the Nyinba's economic system.

Conclusion

I hope to have demonstrated that psychological phenomena have a basis in concrete, practical social activity. They are formed as people participate in social activities, they embody features of this activity, and they normally reinforce this activity although they can initiate change in activity.

The critique of the mentalistic tendency in cultural psychology is not meant to devalue this approach. Cultural psychologists of this persuasion are to be praised for correcting the prevailing bias in psychology that regards psychological phenomena as originating in intra-individual processes. However, culture is more than shared concepts about the meaning of things. A revised conception of cultural psychology should explore the relationship between psychology, practical cultural activity, and cultural concepts (Ratner 1999).

The contrasting views of culture held by mentalists and activity theorists not only affect the course of cultural psychology. They lead to different political directions as well. From the mentalistic view of culture, concepts and psychological phenomena appear to be divorced from practical matters. They seem not to be conditioned by social relationships, social dynamics, material, technological, and intellectual resources. The practical effect of this intellectualist viewpoint is to advocate psychological change apart from socioeconomic and political change. Psychological change can be accomplished by simply changing one's concepts or outlook. There is no need to alter social institutions or conditions since these are unrelated to cultural psychological phenomena. In contrast, the view of culture as practical activity leads to tying psychological change to societal change. Since concepts and psychological phenomena are grounded in practical activity, significant psychological change requires corresponding changes in the organization of social life (Ratner 2000b). The practical political implications of activity theory have great value in these troubled times. Activity theory is therefore noteworthy because it has political as well as scientific merit.

NOTES

1 It seems that Lave and other activity theorists do not believe that mental processes are structured by activity at all. Activity seems to be some innovative action that an individual takes in order to deal with situations rather than being socially organized behavior that is integral to a social system (cf. Nardi 1996). Many activity theorists champion the autonomy of the individual from social influences. They reject the idea that mental processes are truly organized by social factors. They disparage social causation as smacking of reification and mechanism. For example, Lave disparages school-based math as reified and she lauds individuals for spontaneously devising alternative ways of calculating prices.

REFERENCES

Cole, Michael 1995 Culture and Cognitive Development: From Cross-cultural Research to Creating Systems of Cultural Mediation. *Culture and Psychology* 1: 25–54.

Cordua, Glenn D., Kenneth O. McGraw, and Ronald S. Drabman 1979 Doctor or Nurse: Children's Perception of Sex-typed Occupations. *Child Development* 50: 590–593.

Dewey, John 1902 Interpretation of the Savage Mind. *Psychological Review* 9: 217–230.

Dube, Ernest F. 1982 Literacy, Cultural Familiarity, and "Intelligence" as Determinants of Story Recall. In *Memory Observed: Remembering in Natural Contexts*, U. Neisser, ed. New York: Freeman. Pp. 274–292.

Ember, Carol 1973 Feminine Task Assignment and the Social Behavior of Boys. *Ethos* 1: 424–439.

Garro, Linda C. 1986 Language, Memory and Focality: A Re-examination. *American Anthropologist* 88: 128–136.

Geoghegan, William 1973 *Natural Information Processing Rules: Formal Theory and Applications to Ethnography*. Monograph of the Language-Behavior Research Laboratory, No. 3. Berkeley, CA: University of California Language Research Laboratory.

Gladwin, Christina 1975 A Model of the Supply of Smoked Fish from Cape Coast to Kumsi. In *Formal Methods in Economic Anthropology*, S. Plattner, ed. Washington, DC: American Anthropological Association. Pp. 77–127.

Harre, Rom, ed. 1986 *The Social Construction of Emotions*. New York: Blackwell.

Holland, Dorothy C. and Margaret A. Eisenhart 1990 *Educated in Romance: Women, Achievement, and College Culture*. Chicago, IL: University of Chicago Press.

Hutchins, Edwin 1980 *Culture and Inference: A Trobriand Case Study*. Cambridge, MA: Harvard University Press.

Ingoldsby, Byron B. 1995 Marital Structure. In *Families in Multicultural Perspective*, B. B. Ingoldsby and S. Smith, eds. New York: Guilford Press. Pp. 117–137.

Kleinman, Arthur and Byron Good, eds. 1985 *Culture and Depression: Studies in the Anthropology and Cross-cultural Psychiatry of Affect and Disorder*. Berkeley, CA: University of California Press.

Lantz, DeLee and Volney Stefflre 1964 Language and Cognition Revisited. *Journal of Abnormal and Social Psychology* 69: 472–481.

Lave, Jean 1988 *Cognition in Practice: Mind, Mathematics, and Culture in Everyday Life*. New York: Cambridge University Press.

Leont'ev, Aleksei N. 1979 The Problem of Activity in Psychology. In *The Concept of Activity in Soviet Psychology*, J. Wertsch, ed. Armonk, NY: Sharpe Publishers. Pp. 37–71.

        1981 *Problems of the Development of the Mind*. Moscow: Progress.

Levine, Nancy E. 1988 *The Dynamics of Polyandry*. Chicago, IL: University of Chicago Press.

Lucy, John and Richard A. Shweder 1979 Whorf and His Critics: Linguistic and Nonlinguistic Influences on Color Memory. *American Anthropologist* 81: 581–615.

Luria, Aleksandr R. 1971 Towards the Problem of the Historical Nature of Psychological Processes. *International Journal of Psychology* 6: 259–272.

        1976 *Cognitive Development: Its Cultural and Social Foundations*. M. Lopez-Morillas and L. Solotaroff, trans., M. Cole, ed. Cambridge, MA: Harvard University Press.

Luttrell, Wendy 1989 Working-class Women's Ways of Knowing: Effects of Gender, Race, and Class. *Sociology of Education* 62: 33–46.

Lutz, Catherine 1988 *Unnatural Emotions: Everyday Sentiments on a Micronesian*

Atoll and Their Challenge to Western Theory. Chicago, IL: University of Chicago Press.

Marx, Karl 1975 The Critique of Hegel's Philosophy of Law: Introduction. In Karl Marx and Friedrich Engels, *Collected Works.* New York: International Publishers, vol. 3, pp. 175–187 (originally published 1844).

Marx, Karl and Friedrich Engels 1964 *The German Ideology.* Moscow: Progress (originally published 1846).

Mathews, Holly F. 1983 Context-specific Variation in Humoral Classification. *American Anthropologist* 85: 826–847.

Minick, Norris 1990 Mind and Activity in Vygotsky's Work: An Expanded Frame of Reference. *Cultural Dynamics* 2: 162–187.

Mistry, JayanthI and Barbara Rogoff 1994 Remembering in Cultural Context. In *Psychology and Culture*, W. Lonner and R. Malpass, eds. Boston, MA: Allyn and Bacon. Pp. 139–144.

Nardi, Bonnie A. 1996 Studying Context: A Comparison of Activity Theory, Situated Action Models, and Distributed Cognition. In *Context and Consciousness: Activity Theory and Human–Computer Interaction*, B. A. Nardi, ed. Cambridge, MA: MIT Press. Pp. 69–102.

Ogbu, John U. 1978 *Minority Education and Caste: The American System in Cross-Cultural Perspective.* New York: Academic Press.

Quinn, Naomi 1978 Do Mfantse Fish Sellers Estimate Probabilities in Their Heads? *American Ethnologist* 5: 206–226.

Ratner, Carl 1991 *Vygotsky's Sociohistorical Psychology and its Contemporary Applications.* New York: Plenum.

1993 Review of D'Andrade and Strauss, *Human Motives and Cultural Models. Journal of Mind and Behavior* 14: 89–94.

1997a *Cultural Psychology and Qualitative Methodology: Theoretical and Empirical Considerations.* New York: Plenum.

1997b In Defense of Activity Theory. *Culture and Psychology* 3: 211–223.

1998a Prologue to *Vygotsky's Collected Works*, vol. 5. New York: Plenum.

1998b The Historical and Contemporary Significance of Vygotsky's Sociohistorical Psychology. In *Psychology: Theoretical-Historical Perspectives*, 2nd edn., R. Rieber and K. Salzinger, eds. Washington, DC: American Psychological Association. Pp. 455–473.

1999 Three Approaches to Cultural Psychology: A Critique. *Cultural Dynamics* 11: 7–31.

2000a A Cultural-Psychological Analysis of Emotions. *Culture and Psychology* 6:5–39.

2000b Agency and Culture. *Journal for the Theory of Social Behavior* 30:413–434.

Shweder, Richard A. 1990 Cultural Psychology – What Is It? In *Cultural Psychology: Essays on Comparative Human Development*, J. Stigler, R. Shweder, and G. Herdt, eds. New York: Cambridge University Press. Pp. 1–43.

1996 True Ethnography: The Lore, The Law, and The Lure. In *Ethnography and Human Development*, R. Jessor, A. Colby, and R. Shweder, eds. New York: Cambridge University Press. Pp. 15–52.

Shweder, Richard A. and Robert A. LeVine, eds. 1984 *Culture Theory: Essays on Mind, Self, and Emotion.* New York: Cambridge University Press.

Shweder, Richard A. and Maria A. Sullivan 1993 Cultural Psychology: Who Needs It? *Annual Review of Psychology* 44: 497–523.

Stearns, Peter N. 1989 Suppressing Unpleasant Emotions: The Development of a Twentieth-century American Style. In *Social History and Issues in Human Consciousness*, A. E. Barnes and P. E. Stearns, eds. New York: New York University Press. Pp. 230–261.

Stefflre, Volney, Victor C. Vales, and Linda Morley 1966 Language and Cognition in Yucatan: A Cross-Cultural Replication. *Journal of Personality and Social Psychology* 4: 112–115.

Tavris, Carol 1992 *The Mismeasure of Woman*. New York: Simon and Schuster.

Van der Veer, Rene and Jaan Valsiner 1991 *Understanding Vygotsky: A Quest for Synthesis*. Cambridge, MA: Blackwell.

Vygotsky, Lev S. 1987 *Collected Works*, vol. I. *Problems of General Psychology*. R. Rieber and A. S. Carton, eds. New York: Plenum.

Young, James C. 1981 *Medical Choice in a Mexican Village*. New Brunswick, NJ: Rutgers University Press.

Part II

Acquiring, modifying, and transmitting culture

4 The infant's acquisition of culture: early attachment reexamined in anthropological perspective

Robert A. LeVine and Karin Norman

The child's acquisition of culture, or enculturation, is both a long-standing interest and a controversial issue in psychological anthropology. That individuals acquire the local culture of the community in which they grow up as inevitably as they acquire its language is a generally accepted assumption, but the questions of when they acquire it and with what psychological consequences, continue to divide us. Does enculturation begin during infancy? That was the explicit claim of earlier studies, as articulated by Ralph Linton in his influential book of 1936, *The Study of Man*: "Conditioning to social life begins so early that much of the groundwork of personality is laid before such extra-family agencies can be brought into play" (Linton 1936: 155). After a brief review of cultural variation in infant care practices, Linton (1936: 473) said:

The foregoing shows how different can be the influences which culture exerts upon the individual even during his first few months. Psychologists have written a good deal about the presumed effects of infantile experience upon the adult personality. It would seem that a study of individuals from societies with markedly different patterns of infant care could provide proof or disproof of many current theories, but this work has barely begun.

Margaret Mead (1930) initiated this line of research in her study of the Manus in Melanesia, and the field studies by John W. M. Whiting (1941) among the Kwoma of New Guinea and by Gregory Bateson and Mead (1942) among the Balinese reflected a similar interest in cultural learning during the first years of life. Decades later, William Caudill's comparative study of Japanese and Americans (Caudill and Weinstein 1969) introduced systematic observation into research on infant enculturation; other observational studies followed, including LeVine *et al.*'s (1994) recent work on the Gusii of Kenya.

Some anthropologists, including Riesman (1983, 1993) and Shweder (1979, 1991), have been skeptical of infant enculturation or have rejected it outright. Minoura (1992) claims to have discovered in her study of Japanese children residing in the United States that the years from 8 to 15

83

are a sensitive period for enculturation, and she casts doubt on the permanence of earlier acquisitions. There is, furthermore, the problem raised by Ewing (1992) that what anthropological observers identify as culturally divergent patterns of development might involve only overt social behavior while the (covert) intrapsychic experience that actually drives psychological development could be similar across apparently different cultures. There are thus several issues about early enculturation waiting to be resolved by future research.

In this chapter we propose that there is a stronger case for enculturation during infancy and early childhood than has been recognized in the literature of psychological anthropology. We interpret findings from infant psychology and related fields as indicating specific ways in which the interpersonal responsiveness of young children can be shaped by their social environments, and we present evidence from Germany and elsewhere to suggest that the parental behaviors involved in early attachment are influenced by cultural models of interpersonal relations. Our hypothesis is that parents of a particular culture tend to promote infant behaviors they see as consistent with their culture's model of virtue, and further, that they are successful enough on average that their children manifest selected behaviors at a "precociously" early age by the standards of other cultures with different concepts of virtue. Subsequent development is not simply or wholly determined by culturally promoted precocity in early childhood any more than infant nutrition by itself determines the later growth and health of the child. The enculturation of young children, however, gives them a head start on becoming virtuous by local standards, particularly in relational dimensions that are psychologically significant: attachment, preferred social distance, sensitivity to the feelings of others, conversational exchange. This cultural interpretation of early social development, although recognizing species-typical features and constraints, departs from universalist models (Bowlby 1969, 1988, Papousek and Papousek 1987, Trevarthen 1988), as enculturation replaces the attempt to define a single norm of optimal development for all humans and its concomitant tendency to pathologize variations.

Implications of infant research

The field of infant psychology has made great strides since 1960 (Osofsky 1987), providing an unprecedented empirical basis for understanding experience and development during the first years of life. The portrait emerging is of an infant far more open to culturally organized experience and participation in cultural activities than anyone had dreamt of earlier. More specifically, we now know the following:

1. Infants are born not as a bundle of reflexes but with a full complement of sensory and cognitive capacities for processing experience. There are immature but functional capacities for vision, hearing, tactile and olfactory sensation, perception and memory, state regulation, motor response, and learning. Neonatal research denies the portrait of a "blooming, buzzing confusion," and there is no reason to assume a delay in the newborn's readiness to appraise and participate in its environment.

2. Children in the first months of life are particularly sensitive to human faces and to facial expressions of emotion as well as to the sound qualities of the human voice. These sensitivities strongly suggest a preparedness for communicative interaction from the start rather than through a preliminary period of oral satisfaction or cognitive stimulation as the basis for the experience of social relationships. The crying of young infants can be, and routinely is, conditioned by consistent forms of caregiver response so as to amplify or diminish the amount of crying. By five months, infants show definite expectations of the conditions that consistently bring them comfort.

3. By the second half of the first year, that is before 12 months of age, babies form attachments to the mother and to others who consistently respond to them. The attachment research initiated by Mary Ainsworth (1967, 1977), beginning with her work in Uganda, has established unambiguously the development of social attachment as a universal of infant development and has demonstrated that it need not be linked to feeding.

4. During the second and third years of life, particularly from 18 to 36 months, children acquire basic competence in the primary language of those around them, and with it the culture-specific conventions of speaking: speech pragmatics and paralinguistic norms of gestures, facial expressions, and prosody. Mastery of syntax is involved but is only one component of emerging communicative competence in the young child (Schieffelin and Ochs 1986).

All of this means that there is reason to suppose infants are acquiring culture from the start, that enculturation affecting social interaction and relationships occurs during the first year of life, and that its impact on interpersonal communication should be apparent to anyone before a child is three years old. How early enculturation takes place, in what domains of behavior and subjective meaning, and with what short-term and long-range effects on the child's psychological development, are questions that can only be answered through field research in diverse cultural settings.

German infant care and attachment: a cultural view

If infant psychology provides grounds for assuming that enculturation begins during infancy, how is it that a cultural perspective is so rare among developmental psychologists? Psychologists have generally been as immune to a cultural approach as anthropologists are to "psychologizing." Psychologists tend to be interested in finding universals of development with which to understand individual differences; thus they are concerned with what is common to all humans and what differentiates one individual from another, leaving out the intervening level of populations, communities, or societies. Since that is the level at which anthropologists work, it is no wonder that the disciplinary perspectives fail to connect on the topic of infant enculturation (LeVine 1990). The study of attachment theoretically formulated by John Bowlby and translated into research by Mary Ainsworth is a perfect if somewhat perverse example: perfect in illustrating the jump from human universals to individual differences without considering cultural variations between populations; perverse because, though the first developmental study of attachment was carried out by Ainsworth (1967, 1977) in Africa (among the Ganda in Uganda), it gave rise to an approach as blind to culture as any other in psychology.

Attachment research using Bowlby's theoretical model and Ainsworth's assessment methods has been the dominant psychological approach to the "social development" of the infant, that is the formation of early social relationships, since the late 1970s. Much of its appeal to psychologists is due to its evolutionary rationale, its convenient and reliable assessment procedure (the videotaped Strange Situation), and its clinically interpretable categories (secure–insecure, optimal–suboptimal, sensitive–insensitive) – all features that are problematic from an anthropological point of view. Given its status as a leading theoretical paradigm in child development research, and its claims to have identified the biopsychological basis of social relations in the human lifespan, attachment theory deserves the attention of anthropologists.

The critical examination of attachment theory in this chapter begins with "anomalous" findings concerning infant–mother attachment in Germany (Grossmann *et al.* 1985), which are then reinterpreted from the perspective of ethnographic research in a German community (Norman 1991). Focusing on cultural ideas and practices of infant care, this population-level analysis makes sense of unexplained findings from cross-cultural studies of infant–mother attachment in the Strange Situation. In our view, the behavior patterns involved in assessing attachment and its hypothetical determinants are interpretable in terms of pathways for enculturation institutionalized in a particular population, specifically its norms of social distance and interpersonal responsiveness.

The Bowlby–Ainsworth model of attachment posits species universals in the optimal pattern of attachment and has no explicit place for cultural variations other than as "suboptimal," maladaptive, or pathogenic. Bowlby argued that the proximity-seeking behavior of infants to their mothers was selected for in hominid evolution by the predation of animals that killed straying infants and toddlers; those surviving (from whom we are all descended) had a genetically transmitted attachment system connecting their emotional responses such as crying to the proximity of those caregivers who responded to their signals. All human infants become attached to the mother or another caregiver during the first year, but they become "securely" or "insecurely" attached according to the sensitivity of their caregivers. Sensitive response to infant signals leads to secure attachment, insensitive caregiving in this sense leads to one of two kinds of insecure attachment, "avoidant" and "resistant."

In the Strange Situation (SS), a 12-month-old infant is temporarily separated from the mother in a home-like laboratory setting, and videotaped; when the mother returns, if the child avoids contact with her ("anxious–avoidant," class A) or is inconsolably distressed as the mother tries to comfort him ("anxious–resistant," class C), the child is considered insecurely attached to the mother. The securely attached child (class B) is distressed by the mother's brief absence but consoled by her comforting when they are reunited. (Although the letters were intended to avoid the appearance of an evaluative scale by putting secure attachment, B, in the middle, rather than calling it A, it has always been clear that security of attachment was supposed to indicate superior mental health and adaptation.) This assessment procedure was developed by Ainsworth in the course of a comprehensive longitudinal study of normal infants, including naturalistic observations at home, in Baltimore, Maryland (Ainsworth et al. 1978). The experimentally induced separation and reunion in the laboratory was intended to simulate the conditions of Ainsworth's observations in Uganda, where mothers left their infants with others in order to go to work in the fields and markets several times a day. Since separations and reunions were not as regular in the homes of the Baltimore sample, Ainsworth created the laboratory procedure to assess the infant's emotional reactions under such conditions. As it turned out, the child's behavior on being reunited with the mother (rather than in the separation episodes) showed the best correlations with the mother's sensitivity to infant signals (observed at home) and was taken as the primary criterion for security of attachment using the A, B, C classification.

The Strange Situation can be rapidly applied and recorded on videotape and reliably coded into the three classes (with some additions later). It became widely adopted by child psychologists not only as a standard assessment of the quality of attachment for a particular child but as the primary instrument for investigating social and emotional development during the transition from infancy to early childhood. Bowlby (1988) hailed it as the basis for a "developmental psychiatry." Here is his summary (Bowlby 1988: 166–167):

Three principal patterns of attachment present during the early years are now reliably identified, together with the family conditions that promote them. One of these patterns is consistent with the child's developing healthily, and two are predictive of disturbed development. Which pattern any one individual develops during these years is found to be profoundly influenced by the way his parents (or other parent-type figures) treat him . . .

The pattern of attachment consistent with healthy development is that of secure attachment, in which the individual is confident that his parent (or parent-figure) will be available, responsive and helpful should he encounter adverse or frightening situations. With this assurance, he feels bold in his explorations of the world and also competent in dealing with it. This pattern is found to be promoted by a parent in the early years especially by mother being readily available, sensitive to her child's signals, and lovingly responsive when he seeks protection and/or comfort and/or assistance.

A second pattern is that of anxious resistant attachment in which the individual is uncertain whether his parent will be available or responsive or helpful when called upon. Because of this uncertainty he is always prone to separation anxiety, tends to be clinging, and is anxious about exploring the world. This pattern is promoted by a parent being available and helpful on some occasions but not on others, by separations, and, later, especially by threats of abandonment used as a means of control.

A third pattern is that of anxious avoidant attachment in which the individual has no confidence that, when he seeks care, he will be responded to helpfully; on the contrary, he expects to be rebuffed. Such an individual attempts to live his life without the love and support of others. This pattern is the result of the individual's mother constantly rebuffing him when he approaches her for comfort or protection. The most extreme cases result from repeated rejection and ill-treatment, or prolonged institutionalization. Clinical evidence suggests that, if it persists, this pattern leads to a variety of personality disorders from compulsive self-sufficiency to persistent delinquency.

In the first American research, including the original Baltimore study and three other small studies (Ainsworth *et al.* 1978), 106 infants underwent the Strange Situation, and 65 percent were classified as securely attached (B), 20 percent as anxious-avoidant (A), and 13 percent as anxious-resistant (C). Subsequent studies in the United States showed roughly similar distributions in which the A category usually accounted for 20–26 percent of the sample (Van IJzendoorn and Kroonenberg 1988).

It was perhaps inevitable that the Strange Situation would be used in culturally diverse populations, producing results interpretable as questioning the universality of the American attachment profile or as indicating that some populations are suboptimal in their infant care practices. It might have been anticipated that such problematic evidence would come from Asia or Africa, but it emerged instead from Western Europe, specifically the town of Bielefeld in northern Germany, where Klaus and Karin Grossmann conducted a longitudinal study of fifty-four infants and their parents in a carefully executed replication of the Baltimore research (Grossmann and Grossmann 1981, Grossmann *et al.* 1985, Grossmann and Grossmann 1991).

In the Bielefeld study, 49 percent of the infants were classified as A, "anxious-avoidant," on the basis of their reunion behavior in the Strange Situation. This was a striking finding in contrast with the American evidence, and meant that, together with the children classified as C, two-thirds of the Bielefeld infants were "insecurely attached" (compared with about 35 percent in the Baltimore studies). The Grossmanns explained the results in terms of cultural patterns of infant care. They stated:

[T]here are strong demands for self-reliance on German infants, in the sense that mobile infants are discouraged from staying too close to the mother . . . Such demands have not been documented for US infants, and US researchers have not found it necessary to create a special category to describe such parental requests . . . (1985: 235)

[T]he pattern termed B3 (the largest of the eight subgroups identified by Ainsworth) is considered to index optimal security . . . [T]he B3 pattern would be judged by many German parents as that of a spoiled or immature toddler. (1985: 236)

The mothers never failed to comment upon their children's ability to play by themselves, and upon whether they were satisfied with the extent to which their babies were able to play alone. It was a reason for complaining if their infants always needed company or wanted to be entertained. Many mothers were concerned that they would spoil their infants if they reacted to every cry of his or hers, but they usually made sure that nothing "serious" was the matter. Crying for company was not considered "serious." (1991: 30)

An important feature of the ecology of our sample is the generally accepted practice by German parents to leave the infant alone at home in his or her bed for a short period of time particularly in the evenings. Eighty percent of the parents (39 out of 49) in our sample did so. This is considered part of the training for self-reliance, which seems to be important to the parents. (1991: 30)

The Grossmanns found in their home observations that the Bielefeld mothers were much less frequently "affectionate" than their Baltimore counterparts, but the extent of the differences may have been exaggerated by different conditions of observation. Perhaps more important is evidence from home observations that by 10 months of age, the Bielefeld infants showed clear signs of expecting less interactive attention from their mothers than their Baltimore counterparts:

Bielefeld infants communicated less than Baltimore infants. They cried less when their mother left the room and greeted her less often when she reentered. Bielefeld infants responded less often, either positively or negatively, to being picked up and put down, and they initiated pickup less often. (1985: 245)

Citing other German studies, the Grossmanns state:

[I]n German families the notion of obedience is still somewhat biased toward a concept of discipline and not, as with the obedient children in the Ainsworth Baltimore sample . . . toward a concept of compliance. . . . In our own work we use the terms *gehorchen* and *einwilligen* for the two kinds of obedience. . . . In the case of *einwilligen* (compliance), the child obeys directions because they have become part of a secure relationship. The child's compliance in this case implies an easy coopera-tion between the child and its mother or father on the basis of a well-developed, inti-mate and mainly preverbal communication. In the case of *gehorchen* (discipline), directions are not necessarily part of the pattern of a secure and intimate relation-ship. Rather, by being associated with negative consequences (threat, punishment, etc.) the disciplinary directions may create a stress on the relationship – at least tem-porarily. It may be, then, that our Bielefeld parents behave to some degree as Main describes mothers of avoidant infants in the United States; that is, to produce self-reliant and obedient infants, they may limit affective communication and reject infant bids for proximity. Perhaps the parent, rather than behaving as an intimate of the child, puts himself or herself at a distance like a teacher in the interests of *gehor-chen.* (1981: 696–697)

The Grossmanns emphasize that though there are cultural differences between the Bielefeld and US samples, the same relationships between maternal sensitivity variables and infant attachment variables hold within each sample, indicating that their evidence does not threaten the validity of attachment theory. It remains true, however, that insecure attachment, par-ticularly the A classification in the SS, is widely regarded by attachment researchers as an indication of risk to mental health, so there is a problem of interpreting the Bielefeld evidence within the confines of the Bowlby–Ainsworth model of attachment. Some attachment researchers see the dominant Bielefeld pattern as a secondary override of normal or "primary" attachment reactions (Main 1990) or "a temporary disturbance of relationship patterns" (Grossmann and Grossmann 1981: 697) – not necessarily pathogenic but far from optimal. The possibility that there is a multiplicity of optimal patterns for humans has been discussed largely in an evolutionary perspective that sees avoidant attachment as adaptive when fertility is very high and resources for children are scarce (Chisholm 1996, Main 1990). Given the facts that West Germany in the 1970s had one of the lowest fertility rates in human history under conditions of abundant resources for children, this evolutionary speculation does not help explain the Bielefeld case. A more satisfactory account is at hand which takes cross-population variation as a human species characteristic and makes the analysis of cultural ideas and practices a primary instrument of analysis.

The German case reconsidered

To explore the cultural side of this problem, we examined the ethnographic evidence on infant care practices from an anthropological study of socialization of the child (but which was not focused on infancy), conducted by Karin Norman in a small town pseudonymously called "Linden" near Frankfurt (Norman 1991). Although Linden is not in the same part of Germany as Bielefeld, similar infant care practices were observed there and local cultural interpretations were obtained from parents that are consistent with those from Bielefeld. We have concluded from this evidence that Linden mothers draw some of their ideas about child rearing and development from concepts of moral virtue and interpersonal relations that have roots in German cultural traditions, that these ideas guide the ways in which they design the environments of their infants and their interactions with them, and that the practices involved can plausibly be interpreted as determinants of A classifications in the SS. Figure 4.1 summarizes the argument and the evidence.

At the most general level, represented by the first box, the parents in Linden have inherited a cultural ideology, encoded in the German language, from which they draw concepts of moral virtue and interpersonal relations toward which the behavioral development of children should be moving, as well as models of the parental role in promoting these goals for child development. Beginning with the second of these, Linden parents believe in *erziehung*, which translates as "upbringing" or "education" but is interpreted to mean that parents must take an active role in promoting the goals they seek in their children's behavioral development. They reject the view that babies could become *Lebensfähig*, "fit for life," naturally; it requires parental intervention. The goals they see as fitting the child for life include *Selbständigkeit*, "self-reliance," an adult virtue for which children must acquire the capacity as rapidly as possible, and *Ordnungsliebe*, "love of order," which means both self-control and learning to comply with the demands of existing regimes of schedule and discipline first in the family and then in other institutions as the child grows older.

From this general ideology, Linden mothers draw their specific ideas about the needs of children and the demands of infant care, shown in the second box of Figure 4.1. They view the infant's needs for physical and social care as important but emphasize attention to satisfying those needs without disturbing family routines too much, and they are also concerned

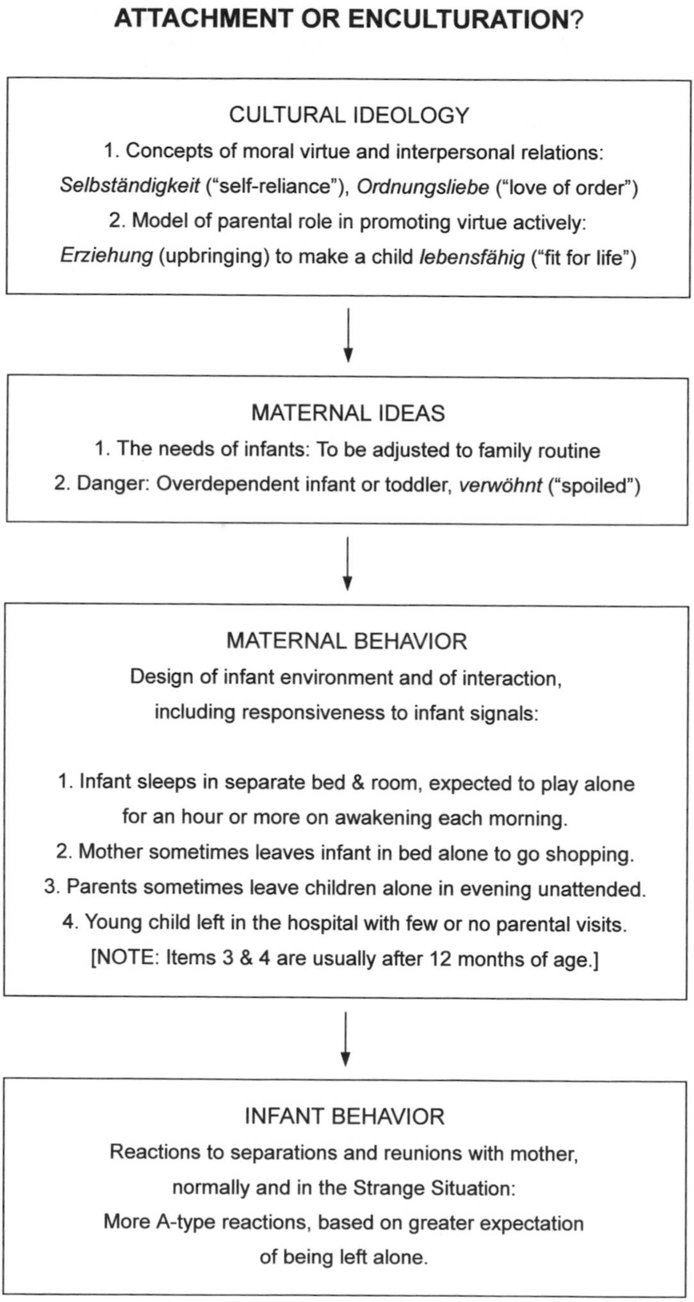

ATTACHMENT OR ENCULTURATION?

CULTURAL IDEOLOGY

1. Concepts of moral virtue and interpersonal relations:
Selbständigkeit ("self-reliance"), *Ordnungsliebe* ("love of order")
2. Model of parental role in promoting virtue actively:
Erziehung (upbringing) to make a child *lebensfähig* ("fit for life")

↓

MATERNAL IDEAS

1. The needs of infants: To be adjusted to family routine
2. Danger: Overdependent infant or toddler, *verwöhnt* ("spoiled")

↓

MATERNAL BEHAVIOR

Design of infant environment and of interaction,
including responsiveness to infant signals:

1. Infant sleeps in separate bed & room, expected to play alone
for an hour or more on awakening each morning.
2. Mother sometimes leaves infant in bed alone to go shopping.
3. Parents sometimes leave children alone in evening unattended.
4. Young child left in the hospital with few or no parental visits.
[NOTE: Items 3 & 4 are usually after 12 months of age.]

↓

INFANT BEHAVIOR

Reactions to separations and reunions with mother,
normally and in the Strange Situation:
More A-type reactions, based on greater expectation
of being left alone.

Figure 4.1 How the social development of infants can be culturally shaped

about the danger that a young child will become "spoiled," *verwöhnt*, by excessive attention and too much accommodation to its needs and demands. These German mothers make explicit a general characteristic of infant care customs – they are combining a concern for the child's moral development with considerations of parental convenience and logistics, particularly the mother's allocation of time and energy. At the same time, however, their explicit view that accommodation to parental routines is good for the baby as well as the family differs from the contemporary child-centered rhetoric of middle-class Americans and Swedes.

These ideas influence maternal behavior, specifically the way mothers design the infant's environment and organize their interaction, as shown in the third box of Figure 4.1. In Linden, this means not only that the baby sleeps in its own bed in a separate room but also that mothers tend not to go into the baby's room when the child wakes up in the morning but to leave the child for a while without outside intervention. Here is a vignette from KN's field notes:

Little Karl is almost two years old; he has no siblings yet and lives with his young parents in his maternal grandparent's house. One afternoon he accompanies his maternal uncle and his wife to friends for coffee and cake. Karl's parents are away on a two-week ski holiday. His *Oma* (grandmother) could not take care of him as she works outside the home, so he is staying with his aunt and uncle. "Oh, he's a good boy, but a bit fussy," his aunt says. They spend most of the visit talking about Karl, his habits, watching him, commenting on what he does, admonishing him, giving him food and drink. The aunt tells of how early he wakes up in the morning, at six o'clock, "but I'm not to take him out of bed, Sigrid (Karl's mother) said, he's to stay there until nine or he'll just get used to it and she won't have it; she's done that from when he was a baby." So Karl is kept in bed, he stays quiet, she doesn't know what he does, hears him move about in his bed, babbling to himself. Renate, her friend, thought it was expecting a bit too much of him, keeping him in bed that long: "an hour maybe, but three – that's too long!"

In this vignette, Sigrid is quoted as determined not to yield control to her young child by responding to him when he wakes up early in the morning, and she apparently trained him as an infant to comfort himself in his room alone. Sigrid considers herself entitled to have a child who is self-reliant at an early age so as not to interfere with her other activities. Renate's comment suggests that her expectations are familiar but somewhat excessive. Sigrid is an example of the kind of mother that Margret Schleidt (1991), a German ethologist, had in mind when she said, "The spontaneous reaction to calm the baby is often replaced by rational acting. Thus the baby is not picked up immediately 'because it should not be spoiled'" (1991: 24–25). Schleidt cites a German study showing that "a high percentage of [infant] crying (33 percent of the cases) is not reacted to at all or only answered after 10 to 30 minutes" (1991: 25).

It is socially acceptable in Linden for mothers to leave infants alone in the house when they go out shopping or are occupied with other tasks, and it seems to be a common practice, though we lack systematic data on its frequency. The difficulty in estimating how many infants are left alone for how long and how often is due partly to the fact that many mothers in Linden live near their own mothers, mothers-in-law, and other kin, creating a general sense that caregivers are accessible to infants. In fact, however, many infants may be left alone. Many women work at home sewing hats or handbags for local firms. While working in the basement, a woman will leave the infant sleeping upstairs in its bed and will not run up and down to check on it. The infant may be left alone for long periods so that the mother is less hampered in her tasks. One mother said she goes shopping while her baby is home alone, arguing that "He can't get out of bed, and he sleeps and is quiet anyway." Informants said a child must learn to be by itself. Babies are considered safe to leave alone since they cannot get out of their cribs and hurt themselves or get into mischief. When something does go wrong, particularly with slightly older children who cannot be kept in their cribs, neighbors blame the parents for not making sure that the child can handle the situation but do not criticize the practice of leaving a young child alone. Once neighbors heard a small child screaming for its mother when the parents were away at a party, and they criticized the parents for being so nonchalant and for forcing them to come to the aid of their child. Infants are felt not to understand or remember what happens to them, and leaving them is not being unkind. Should they awaken when mother is gone and start crying, nothing bad will really come of this, informants said, so long as the baby is fed and clean and the mother has seen to it that the child cannot hurt itself. Whatever anxiety the infant may feel is not considered to have serious consequences.

These first two items in the third box of Figure 4.1 suggest that the mothers' desire for a self-reliant baby leads them to condition the infant to expect *neither* interactive attention on awakening nor immediate comforting when distressed (on which we also lack estimates of frequency). These conditions alone could foster in the infant a high tolerance for separations from the mother and a low expectation of responsive attention from her. As indicated in the last section of Figure 4.1, this might help explain avoidant reactions in the SS.

We have also noted under Maternal Behavior that parents in Linden sometimes leave children unattended when they go out locally in the evening and that when young children are hospitalized (which happened quite often during KN's fieldwork, [Norman 1991]), parental visits tend not to be facilitated by the medical personnel or fully desired by parents, who think they might be more disturbing than helpful to the child. Although these tendencies might not have affected behavior in the SS at 12 months, they indicate the broad spectrum of maternal behaviors intended to promote and take advantage of the early development of self-reliance. They also indicate the extent of the difference from the contemporary United States, where leaving young children unattended is prohibited by criminal law in some states and where hospitals often make arrangements for parents to spend time with children being treated.

This analysis of the ethnographic data from Linden suggests that maternal theory and practice there have certain characteristics we identified in a study of infant care in a Kenya community: a moral direction, a pragmatic design, and conventional scripts for maternal responsiveness (LeVine *et al.* 1994). We believe the evidence from Linden is validly interpreted as a deliberate effort to socialize infants to a greater interpersonal distance and a lower level of maternal responsiveness than is typical of the United States samples studied in attachment research, in accordance with a different cultural ideology. We propose that insofar as the conditions observed in Linden are similar to those of Bielefeld, as they seem to be – or to have been at the time of both studies (the late 1970s) – then this deliberate socialization or enculturation process may explain the high proportion of A babies found in the Grossmanns' Bielefeld study (and in a more recent study in East Berlin by Ahnert *et al.* 2000).

Despite the Grossmanns' offer of a cultural interpretation of their findings (quoted above), their study has not initiated a general reexamination of evidence from the SS in cultural terms. Instead, attachment researchers (including, to some extent, the Grossmanns themselves) have attempted to explain away the Bielefeld results, to diminish their general significance. One argument is that the Grossmanns replicated the study in the town of Regensburg in the southern part of Germany and found a distribution of children into attachment categories much closer to the American profile than to Bielefeld, thus raising the possibility that the Bielefeld findings were particular to that locality, standing alone even in Germany. However, a study by Ahnert *et al.* (2000) of 38 infants in East Berlin in 1986 showed 42 percent classified as A, 45 percent as B, and 10 percent as C. The proportion of A is not quite as high as Bielefeld (49 percent) but is in the same general range and far higher than in American samples; furthermore, as in Bielefeld, the majority of East Berlin children are in the "insecurely attached" categories. The East Berlin study is also interesting because it took place in a population heavily exposed to the collectivist ideology of a Marxist state, and because in a reassessment of thirty-two of the children a few months later, after they had experienced state-sponsored day care, the proportion of the A patterns declined from 36 percent to 16 percent. This could be interpreted as meaning that the East Berlin mothers had retained "traditional" North German cultural models of interpersonal distance and responsiveness in early interactions at home, but that their "anxious-avoidant" children tended to switch to "securely attached" and "anxious-resistant" once they had been cared for in day care centers. If so, the impact of culturally designed environments on attachment as measured in the Strange Situation would have to be given far more weight than it has been in the Bowlby–Ainsworth theory. This is supported by a study in an Israeli kibbutz (Sagi *et al.* 1985) in which over 40 percent of infants assessed in the Strange Situation were found to be "insecurely attached" (higher in the C category) to both mother and *metapelet* (caregiver). Thus infant responses to the Strange Situation are not immune to the influence of interactive settings designed on the basis of cultural and political ideologies. The Bielefeld case should be seen as an example of this general phenomenon.

Another argument to diminish the significance of the Bielefeld study was the meta-analysis by Van IJzendoorn and Kroonenberg (1988) showing that in a large body of attachment studies intracultural variation is far greater than intercultural variation. However, their assumption that culture corresponds to nationality, so that differences among American samples, and other samples within nations, were classified as intracultural, biased their results in favor of the conclusion they found. In any event, a cultural theory of attachment would not predict that variance across culturally defined populations would necessarily exceed intrapopulation variance in attachment; it would depend on the distribution of environmental conditions within and between the populations being compared. But even a single case like Bielefeld raises fundamental questions about the universality of profiles like the American one, in which the majority of babies are securely attached and no more than one quarter is in the anxious-avoidant category.

Finally, there have been attempts, mentioned above, to deal with the Bielefeld findings theoretically, defending the Bowlby–Ainsworth model against the fact of cultural variation in Strange Situation results. The Grossmanns (in Grossmann *et al.* 1985) emphasize that maternal sensitivity correlates with attachment outcomes within the Bielefeld sample, as do Ahnert *et al.* (2000) for their East Berlin sample, and Main (1990) argues that security of attachment should be seen as a primary attachment strategy, with the insecure categories as secondary strategies that could be adaptive under certain conditions for a certain period of time. The Grossmanns (1990) also argue for a "wider concept of attachment" in which universal and culture-specific patterns are both taken into account, without, however, giving up the idea that secure attachment is more adaptive, and without directly confronting the fact that two-thirds of the Bielefeld children were classified as "insecurely attached." They say, "Bowlby's clinical and theoretical insights seem to hold true. Sensitive parenting and experienced security of the child are the foundations for healthy mental functioning" (1990: 45).

The major question that attachment researchers avoid is if security of attachment is the hallmark of mental health, and insecure attachment indicates risk of mental disturbance, then how should we understand a population like that of Bielefeld where two-thirds of infants exhibit this "risk factor" and almost half of the total fall into a category (A) that Bowlby (1988: 167) described as leading to "a variety of personality disorders from compulsive self-sufficiency to persistent delinquency"? More specifically, is the prevalence of personality disorders in Bielefeld, and other parts of Germany that resemble it in attachment patterns, actually higher than that of the United States and other places where a large majority of infants are securely attached? Or, given the absence of evidence bearing on this question, is it possible that "compulsive self-sufficiency" simply refers to a pattern of behavior that counts as moral virtue in some German communities but which is morally disapproved of by contemporary Anglo-Americans? If so, how do we distinguish between moral judgments about personality and the medical diagnoses of a developmental psychiatry? Attachment researchers can argue that they are investigating the patterns of psychosocial adjustment that correlate with attachment classification, in longitudinal studies of children who were assessed in the SS at 12 months (Sroufe 1983) and among adults whose attachment has been assessed by other methods (Main *et al.* 1985). In both cases there is evidence suggesting that securely attached persons are likely to be better adjusted, experience less emotional suffering and manifest less disruptive behavior. In no case, however, have these variations been shown, despite Bowlby's (1988) claims, to involve psychopathology as opposed to individual differences within a normal range. If this is so, then attachment research may legitimately be seen as imposing on the study of normal personality differences a form of moral evaluation framed in terms of mental health and psychopathology and claiming the authority of biomedical science for what are basically moral judgments. The moral dimension becomes more evident in comparisons of populations with differing normative standards of social distance and interpersonal responsiveness.

The infant enculturation hypothesis provides an alternative framework for interpreting attachment data from culturally diverse populations. From this perspective, the Bielefeld babies can be understood as precociously self-reliant in accordance with a culture-specific parental agenda for behavioral development, just as middle-class American toddlers are often precociously talkative, Gusii (of Kenya) toddlers precociously obedient (LeVine *et al.* 1994) and Japanese preschoolers often precociously adept at using indirect speech strategies (Clancy 1986, Kelly 1989). "Precocious" means simply that the behavior pattern emerges at an earlier age than in populations with a different agenda for early child development. Such an interpretation does not preclude a long-term impact on development, particularly since the parental agenda does not end in infancy but continues to be implemented during the preschool years and beyond. German parents expect more self-reliance of their children in the post-infancy years, building on the child's initial acquisition of a culturally appropriate sense of interpersonal distance and self-control.

Some critics, including Minoura (1992), would cast doubt on the "early experience hypothesis" in general, including *both* attachment and enculturation interpretations of the German evidence, and claim that early behavioral tendencies manifested by infants and toddlers vanish soon afterwards and do not affect later development. They invoke an irreversibility criterion, arguing that there is no evidence to support the notion that a child raised for the first three years in one culture and then moved to a different one would continue to differ from children raised from birth in the second culture. According to this view, the reversal of behavioral tendencies acquired in the first cultural environment by a radically different experience invalidates the hypothesis that early experience influences later behavior. But the influence of early experience need not entail irreversibility. A child raised in a totally Chinese-speaking environment for the first three years and then switched to an entirely English-speaking one will eventually lose the ability to speak Chinese, but the skill of the three-year-old child who is not switched facilitates further language acquisition and cultural learning in a Chinese context. Similarly, the child who acquires German norms of social distance and interpersonal responsiveness may lose these expectations if moved to an entirely Japanese or Puerto Rican environment, but for those who do not move, precocious self-reliance becomes the basis for their parents' expectations and for elaboration of their self-reliant behaviors during the next few years. Enculturation is not a simple cause–effect mechanism but a continuing interaction of person and environment. Although it can be disrupted by extreme discontinuities in experience, its normal progression of cumulative learning over time, with later lessons reinforcing and elaborating earlier ones, is a central feature of enculturation as social and psychological process. More evidence is needed on how this process works, but it does not depend on the irreversibility of early acquisitions.

An historical perspective

There was a time – from about 1920 to 1950 – when the infant care practices and attitudes of urban Americans resembled those of German parents of a more recent period. In that earlier time, American mothers were told by pediatricians and other experts, and often believed, that infant schedules and cleanliness were all-important, rapid response to crying would spoil a baby, and that it was essential for babies to play alone and control themselves as early as possible. This changed after World War II, particularly during the 1950s, as a new ideology of affectionate and emotionally responsive infant care spread among parents and professionals concerned with children. The humane care of children was redefined from the provision of hygiene and discipline to the fulfillment of children's emotional needs for love and affirmation.

A thorough history of this ideological shift has yet to be written, but its basic outlines are clear. In the first part of the century, child care was "medicalized" as protection from infectious disease, with pediatricians dispensing authoritative advice to mothers on the hygienic conditions under which infants should be raised, including inflexible routines for feeding, sleeping, and body contact. By the 1930s, this had begun to generate a backlash, which was given an intellectual form by psychoanalysts of the neo-Freudian school (Karen Horney, Erich Fromm, Harry Stack Sullivan, and Clara Thompson). Horney's best-selling book of 1937, *The Neurotic Personality of Our Time*, centered on the child's need for emotional security and the role of parents in promoting or preventing neurosis by their degree of responsiveness to that need. This was part of what might be called the "psychiatrization" of child care – the move from physical health to mental health as a goal of parental activity, which took hold among middle-class American and British parents after World War II. The primary advice-givers became psychiatrists, psychoanalysts, and above all the psychoanalytically trained pediatricians Benjamin Spock and D. W. Winnicott.

John Bowlby, a British psychiatrist and psychoanalyst, became a leader of this movement with his 1951 World Health Organization monograph, *Maternal Care and Mental Health*, his widely read popular book based on the monograph, *Child Care and the Growth of Love* (1953), and his activities in reforming British and North American institutions dealing with children. Like others in the reform movement, Bowlby formulated his ideas of what children need and how they should be treated partly in opposition to the normative British and American middle-class patterns of infant care at that time, which involved regimentation, emotional distance, and the prevention of infant dependence. These patterns are very similar to the patterns still observed in Germany more than twenty-five years later. But more than anyone else in those movements, Bowlby was determined to give this ideological turn a strong scientific basis and unequivocal moral authority. His early writings focused on "maternal deprivation," and he used observations of severely disturbed children who had experienced extreme conditions –

parental death and abandonment, wartime separations, crowded and uncaring institutions – as the basis for recommendations for mothering in ordinary stable households. He emphasized the power of maternal deprivation to block the child's capacity for stable relationships and moral behavior. Controversy over what constituted maternal deprivation, particularly the alleged dangers of temporary mother–child separation, led Bowlby to modify his warnings about the psychological harm done by separation between mother and child. As he turned to the integration of ethological evidence and evolutionary theory with clinical and experimental observations of humans for his three-volume synthesis, *Attachment, Separation and Loss* (Bowlby 1969, 1973, 1980), Mary D. S. Ainsworth – who had worked with him in the middle 1950s and jointly developed with him the theory of attachment – provided a research program designed to measure attachment in the child and the maternal behaviors that promote it, in a normal population of mothers and infants. Having linked his psychiatric clinical observations with biology on one side and psychometrics on the other, Bowlby (1988) was satisfied that a solid scientific basis for the humane treatment of children had been found.

But the problems of combining moral reform with science have been present in attachment research from the start and emerged into the open with the Bielefeld study. "Security of attachment" is not simply a behavioral category; it is a moral ideal, a concept of optimal development; "maternal sensitivity" is not simply a causal influence in the development of attachment, it is a judgment on the adequacy of a mother – a way of distinguishing good from bad mothers. The decision to retain this value-laden conceptual terminology in attachment research reveals the fact that despite its scientific credentials, the attachment model of early child development belongs to the ideological camp of child-centered freedom and equality against old-fashioned parentally imposed order and discipline. The Strange Situation is a weapon in this intergenerational battle of Anglo-American middle-class parents after 1950. (The dialectical opposition between freedom and constraint has deep roots in Western ideologies of child rearing, as the writings of Calvin, Rousseau, and Locke demonstrate; the mid-twentieth century "modernization" of infant care represents a recent swing of this ancient pendulum.) Furthermore, the attachment model holds – although attachment researchers do not speak with a single voice on this point – that insensitive mothering and insecure attachment lead to emotional disturbance. Bowlby believed it, and while the developmental research to prove it is still going on, the Strange Situation is already used in the United States as an instrument for the clinical diagnosis of emotional disturbance in young children. The Bielefeld findings, however, suggest that there is a wider range of pathways to normal emotional development than has been imagined in attachment theory, that the theory attempts to impose a framework of health and pathology on individual and population differences indicating not differential propensity for emotional disturbance but approximation to the ideals of modern (post-1950) middle-class Anglo-American culture. Bowlby's "developmental psychiatry" can be seen as a moral prescription for child care in a particular context rather than a universal science of emotional development.

Conclusions

In this chapter we have inquired into whether the child's acquisition of culture begins in infancy, through an examination of the conditions of infant–mother attachment in Germany. We find that enculturation does indeed begin in infancy, as the young child accommodates to, and learns to participate in, activities influenced by culture-specific norms of social distance, interpersonal responsiveness, and communicative performance, mediated by parents in situations of child care. The result of infant enculturation is observable "precocity," that is the emergence of locally desirable behavior patterns at an age that would be considered extremely early elsewhere. Thus German infants become capable of self-comforting at an early age (by American standards) in accordance with the developmental goal of self-reliance toward which the infant's toleration of isolation is the first step. We believe that each cultural group produces precocious behavior in their young children, reflecting their shared parental agenda for development, which in turn reflects broader cultural ideologies prevailing in their population. Parents of different cultures would disagree about what is desirable in early behavioral development. Many contemporary middle-class Americans, for example, would find the precocious self-reliance of German infants excessive and unnecessary and the maternal conditions promoting it immoral and even criminal. Conversely, German parents are likely to see babies raised according to contemporary American standards as "spoiled." Similar variations occur within the population of the United States, as Harwood, Miller, and Lucca-Irizarry (1995) have shown concerning the preferences for infant–mother behavior of Puerto Ricans and Anglos. These cases of contrasting standards for early interaction are no more than a small sample of the worldwide range of variation, but they argue for a pluralistic view of early social and emotional development.

The dominant view of early social and emotional development in developmental psychology, the Bowlby–Ainsworth theory of attachment, is not pluralist but universalist in its premises. It claims that the secure attachment pattern found in the majority of American one-year-olds is adaptive for all humans and that other patterns jeopardize the child's mental health. From this perspective, the findings from German samples in which a majority of infants are classified as insecurely attached could be interpreted as indicating that the majority of German parents are raising emotionally disturbed children. Attachment researchers have understandably refrained from that conclusion, but without offering a satisfactory alternative explanation of the results. We have argued in this chapter that these results can be understood as an outcome of infant enculturation, suggesting that many more patterns of early development are consistent with mental health than has been claimed by attachment theorists, and that their culture-bound theoretical position – despite its scientific rationale – is driven by commitment to an ideological movement to reform Anglo-American child care in the second half of the twentieth century.

REFERENCES

Ahnert, Liselotte, Tatyana Meischner, and Alfred Schmidt 2000 Maternal Sensitivity and Attachment in East German and Russian Family Networks. In *The Organization of Attachment Relationships: Maturation, Culture and Context*, P. M. Crittenden and A. H. Claussen, eds. New York: Cambridge University Press. Pp. 61–74.

Ainsworth, Mary D. Salter 1967 *Infancy in Uganda*. Baltimore, MD: Johns Hopkins University Press.

 1977 Infant Development and Mother-Infant Interaction among Ganda and American Families. In *Culture and Infancy*, P. H. Leiderman, S. R. Tulkin, and A. Rosenfield, eds. New York: Academic Press. Pp. 49–67.

Ainsworth, Mary D. Salter, Mary C. Blehar, Everett Waters, and Sally Wall 1978 *Patterns of Attachment: A Psychological Study of the Strange Situation*. Hillsdale, NJ: Erlbaum.

Bateson, Gregory and Margaret Mead 1942 *Balinese Character: A Photographic Analysis*. New York: New York Academy of Sciences.

Bowlby, John 1951 *Maternal Care and Mental Health*. Geneva: World Health Organization.

 1953 *Child Care and the Growth of Love*. London: Penguin.

 1969 *Attachment and Loss*, vol. I: *Attachment*. New York: Basic Books.

 1973 *Attachment and Loss*, vol. II: *Separation*. New York: Basic Books.

 1980 *Attachment and Loss*, vol. III: *Loss*. New York: Basic Books.

 1988 *A Secure Base*. New York: Basic Books.

Caudill, William and Helen Weinstein 1969 Maternal Care and Infant Behavior in Japan and America. *Psychiatry* 32: 12–43.

Chisholm, James S. 1996 The Evolutionary Ecology of Attachment Organization. *Human Nature* 7: 1–38.

Clancy, Patricia M. 1986 The Acquisition of Communicative Style in Japanese. In *Language Socialization Across Cultures*, B. Schieffelin and E. Ochs, eds. New York: Cambridge University Press. Pp. 213–250.

Ewing, Katherine P. 1992 Is Psychoanalysis Relevant for Anthropology? In *New Directions in Psychological Anthropology*, T. Schwartz, G. M. White and C. A. Lutz, eds. New York: Cambridge University Press. Pp. 251–268.

Grossmann, Karin and Klaus E. Grossmann 1991 Newborn Behavior, the Quality of Early Parenting and Later Toddler–Parent Relationships in a Group of German Infants. In *The Cultural Context of Infancy*, J. K. Nugent, B. M. Lester, and T. B. Brazelton, eds. vol. II. Norwood, NJ: Ablex. Pp. 3–38.

Grossmann, Karin, Klaus E. Grossmann, Gottfried Spangler, Gerhard Suess, and Lothar Unzner 1985 Maternal Sensitivity and Newborns' Orientation Responses as Related to Quality of Attachment in Northern Germany. In *Growing Points of Attachment: Theory and Research*, I. Bretherton and E. Waters, eds. Monographs of the Society for Research in Child Development. Chicago, IL: University of Chicago Press. vol. 50, nos. 1–2. Pp. 233–256.

Grossmann, Klaus E. and Karin Grossmann 1981 Parent-Infant Attachment Relationships in Bielefeld: A Research Note. In *Behavioral Development: The Bielefeld Interdisciplinary Project*, K. Immelman, G. Barlow, L. Petrovich, and M. Main, eds. New York: Cambridge University Press. Pp. 694–699.

1990 The Wider Concept of Attachment in Cross-Cultural Research. *Human Development* 33: 31–47.

Harwood, Robin L., Joan G. Miller, and Nydia Lucca-Irizarry 1995 *Culture and Attachment*. New York: Guilford Press.

Horney, Karen 1937 *The Neurotic Personality of Our Time*. New York: W. W. Norton.

Kelly, Victoria E. 1989 Peer Culture and Interactions Among Japanese Children. Ed. D. Dissertation. Cambridge, MA: Harvard University.

LeVine, Robert A. 1990 Enculturation: A Biosocial Perspective on the Development of Self. In *The Self in Transition: Infancy to Childhood*, D. Cicchetti and M. Beeghly, eds. Chicago, IL: University of Chicago Press. Pp. 99–117.

LeVine, Robert A., Suzanne Dixon, Sarah LeVine, Amy Richman, P. Herbert Leiderman, Constance H. Keefer, and T. Berry Brazelton 1994 *Child Care and Culture: Lessons from Africa*. New York: Cambridge University Press.

Linton, Ralph 1936 *The Study of Man*. New York: Appleton-Century-Crofts.

Main, Mary 1990 Cross-Cultural Studies of Attachment Organization: Recent Studies, Changing Methodologies, and the Concept of Conditional Strategies. *Human Development* 33: 48–61.

Main, Mary, Nancy Kaplan, and Jude Cassidy 1985 Security in Infancy, Childhood and Adulthood: A Move to the Level of Representation. In *Growing Points of Attachment: Theory and Research*, I. Bretherton and E. Waters, eds. Monographs of the Society for Research in Child Development. Chicago, IL: University of Chicago Press, vol. 50, nos. 1–2. Pp. 66–104.

Mead, Margaret 1930 *Growing Up in New Guinea*. New York: William Morrow.

Minoura, Yasuko 1992 Sensitive Period for the Incorporation of a Cultural Meaning System: A Study of Japanese Children Growing Up in the United States. *Ethos* 20: 304–339.

Norman, Karin 1991 A Sound Family Makes a Sound State: Ideology and Upbringing in a German Village. Stockholm: Department of Social Anthropology, University of Stockholm.

Osofsky, Joy D. ed. 1987 *Handbook of Infant Development*. 2nd ed. New York: Wiley.

Papousek, Hanus and Mechthild Papousek 1987 Intuitive Parenting. In *Handbook of Infant Development*, J. D. Osofsky, ed. New York: Wiley. Pp. 117–136.

Riesman, Paul 1983 On the Irrelevance of Child Rearing Practices for the

Formation of Personality: An Analysis of Childhood, Personality and Values in Two African Communities. *Culture, Medicine, and Psychiatry* 7: 103–129.

1993 *First Find Your Child a Good Mother: The Construction of Self in Two African Communities.* New Brunswick, NJ: Rutgers University Press.

Sagi, Abraham, Michael E. Lamb, Kathleen S. Lewkowicz, Ronit Shoham, Rachel Dvir, and David Estes 1985 Security of Infant–Mother, -Father, and -Metapelet Attachments among Kibbutz-Reared Israeli Children. In *Growing Points of Attachment: Theory and Research*, I. Bretherton and E. Waters, eds. Monographs of the Society for Research in Child Development. Chicago, IL: University of Chicago Press. vol. 50, nos. 1–2: 257–275.

Schieffelin, Bambi and Elinor Ochs 1986 Language Socialization. *Annual Review of Anthropology* 15: 163–191.

Schleidt, Margret 1991 An Ethological Perspective on Infant Development. In *Infant Development: Perspectives from German-Speaking Countries*, M. Lamb and H. Keller, eds., Hillsdale, NJ: Lawrence Erlbaum Associates. Pp. 15–34.

Shweder, Richard A. 1979 Rethinking Culture and Personality Theory, Part I. *Ethos* 7: 255–278.

1991 *Thinking Through Cultures.* Cambridge, MA: Harvard University Press.

Sroufe, L. Alan 1983 Infant–Caregiver Attachment and Patterns of Adaptation in Preschool: The Roots of Maladaptation and Competence. In *Minnesota Symposium on Child Psychology*, M. Perlmutter, ed. Hillsdale, NJ: Erlbaum. 16: 41–81.

Trevarthen, Colwyn 1988 Universal Cooperative Motives: How Infants Begin to Know the Language and Culture of Their Parents. In *Acquiring Culture: Cross-Cultural Studies in Child Development*, G. Jahoda and I. M. Lewis, eds. London: Croom Helm. Pp. 37–90.

Van IJzendoorn, Marinus H. and Pieter M. Kroonenberg 1988 Cross-Cultural Patterns of Attachment: A Meta-Analysis of the Strange Situation. *Child Development* 59: 147–156.

Whiting, John W. M. 1941 *Becoming a Kwoma.* New Haven, CT: Yale University Press.

5   The remembered past in a culturally meaningful life: remembering as cultural, social, and cognitive process

Linda C. Garro

Remembering and communicating the past are singularly human experiences. Only humans "travel back into the past in their own minds" in a conscious and reflexive way (Tulving 1983: 1; see also Nelson 1989) and share the remembered past with others. In contemporary psychology, a growing trend is the study of "everyday memory." Ulric Neisser, a renowned cognitive psychologist, noted in the late 1970s: "If X is an interesting or socially significant aspect of memory, then psychologists have hardly ever studied X" (1978: 4). He urged researchers to turn their attention to "how people use their own past experiences in meeting the present and the future . . . under natural conditions" with research questions "driven by the characteristics of ordinary human experience" (1978: 13). Neisser voiced the growing dissatisfaction among some researchers with the exclusivity of the dominant research paradigm of laboratory-based experiments under controlled conditions. His comments serve as a benchmark of increasing interest in studying memory in situations more closely approximating those of real life.

The issues addressed under the rubric of everyday memory are diverse,[1] but one avenue of inquiry attracting considerable attention is that of personal or autobiographical memory which broadly refers to the "capacity of individuals to recollect their lives" (Baddeley 1992: 26). In this chapter, using ethnographic examples and drawing on the predominantly cognitive psychology literature on memory and autobiographical memory, I explore remembering the past as a jointly cognitive, social, and cultural process. With reference to widely accepted concepts in contemporary psychological theory, such as schemas and reproduction versus (re)construction, I advance the claim that the study of remembering requires integrating what takes place in the world with what takes place in the mind. Remembering in everyday life cannot be understood apart from the social and cultural contexts in which it occurs. By this I mean more than a claim that the content of memory is culturally shaped or that the telling of memories is a social act which reflects culturally appropriate communicative forms. A basic premise is that cultural and social processes, in conjunction with cognitive processes, play a constitutive role in remembering. Cultural and social processes are integral not just to what we remember of the past but to how we remember as well. Remembering, even the remembering of personal experience, cannot be understood as solely an individual cognitive process. Attention to acts of remembering situated in everyday life serves to reveal the inseparability of cultural, social, and cognitive processes.

Among psychologists there are varying opinions as to which memories should be classified and studied as autobiographical memories, with some circumscribing the field more narrowly. A minimal or core definition of autobiographical or personal memory that no existing research paradigm would exclude from consideration is the following: "a recollection of a particular episode from an individual's past" (Brewer 1986: 34) "in which somehow, self was engaged" (Bruner and Feldman 1996: 292). While much work on autobiographical memory is consistent with this core meaning, some researchers find this definition too restrictive and see the field as a broader one with fuzzy boundaries. Some of the examples provided later in this chapter suggest a more encompassing conceptual framework. In this introduction, however, I will start with an example consistent with the core definition and use it to introduce several questions about remembering and the remembered past.

The example is taken from a study on cultural knowledge about illness in an Anishinaabe (Ojibwa) reserve community located in Manitoba, Canada, and was obtained during a series of biweekly visits to a set of families to ask about ongoing illness cases. This account is one of several relating to *ondjine*. *Ondjine* refers to illness or other misfortune that occurs for a reason, with the reason attributable to something someone did at some point in the past. Harming an animal is the prototypical and by far the most frequently encountered scenario, but the underlying causal framework is considerably more complex (Garro 1990). Remembering a relevant past event is an integral part of dealing with illness or misfortune of this nature. Often the person afflicted and person accountable are the same individual.

As background to this particular case, Arthur Roland's five-year-old daughter had, over several weeks, been suffering from a rash described as looking like "burn blisters."[2] During a previous visit to the family, it was reported that the girl was seen by a physician who prescribed an ointment. Her mother applied the ointment and soon the rash on the forehead receded, but it then surfaced on her cheek. After applying the ointment to her cheek, the rash reappeared on her forehead. The parents decided to seek the assistance of an Anishinaabe healer. In the following quote, Mr. Roland relates what happened on this visit to the healer:

So we went to see this medicine man. He started singing and he said, "You're a little boy, it's in the evening, the sun is going down and you're playing with fire. Try and remember what you did." Right away I remembered. I used to dig in the – there was an old barn there – and we used to dig in the manure, in the evening when the sun was going down. Cause the snakes don't go out after dark, they don't crawl around. We used to dig for these snakes and throw gasoline on them and they'd . . . you know. And I guess this snake burnt just on the head part and he crawled into a hole. But the snake looked at me and it is like the snake said to me "some day you're going to have someone you love and she's going to pay for this."

At the time he related this account, Arthur Roland was in his mid-thirties. Although the incident he remembers occurred some twenty-five years earlier, his telling still vividly conveys a sense of that moment in time. The place, the time of day, what occurred to a particular snake, his personal involvement, both in terms of what he did and the realization of possible future consequences are all included.[3] Mr. Roland provides a relatively concrete instance of how the reconstruction of a past event serves the needs of the present and future. The recollection of this incident provides the framework for the healer's treatment recommendations, with an integral component involving Mr. Roland taking steps to make amends for his past actions.

example

Beyond this, what does it mean to "travel back" and revisit one's past? What is involved in the process of remembering? Is Mr. Roland simply retrieving an essentially veridical record of an original event, faithfully capturing what actually transpired? And if so, what is to be made of the recollection of the threat of harm attributed to the snake? Another issue is why some past events become memories and others do not. Given the sheer magnitude of potentially memorable occurrences, there is a necessary selectivity in what is attended to, retained, and recalled. Vivid accounts of specific episodes, like the one provided by Mr. Roland, are more exceptional than commonplace. Why are some events more memorable? Within this Anishinaabe community there are cultural expectations that causing harm to an animal creates a predisposition for illness, if not for the responsible individual, then for his or her children or grandchildren. Moving back in time to when the remembered event is judged to have occurred, did cultural knowledge about this predisposition to illness or misfortune play a role in establishing what will be remembered later? Do such cultural expectations influence the form that the retelling takes? Finally, what about the social context in which the memory is recounted? In this specific instance, there are two contexts of note. The first is the treatment context where the earlier event was first recollected and relayed to the healer. What is the contribution of what the healer said to what Mr. Roland remembers? To what extent does Mr. Roland construct an account in response to what is suggested? The second context is the retelling of what happened in the treatment session. Is this narration shaped to be a persuasive account, to provide a convincing explanation for the daughter's illness and subsequent improvement and thereby also to validate the actions taken in response to the illness?

Questions similar to many of these (with the possible exception of those relating to cultural knowledge) motivate psychological research on how persons remember their past. And, there are points of convergence between the autobiographical memory literature and anthropological approaches to how persons remember and talk about their past which suggest the potential for work in either field to mutually inform the other. For example, issues comparable to those raised in the preceding paragraph also arise in Peacock and Holland's (1993) anthropologically oriented review of life history (or, as they prefer, life story) studies.[4] While Mr. Roland's recounting of this brief episode is, of course, quite different from the telling of a life story (e.g., Agar 1980, Linde 1993, Peacock and Holland 1993) or even a narrative covering a longer period of time, such as an illness narrative (e.g., Garro 1994), all three are alike in that processes involving remembering and narrating are integral to their production.[5] And the broader literature on narrative has informed anthropologists working with such accounts (Garro and Mattingly 2000, Peacock and Holland 1993) and researchers studying autobiographical memory (see Rubin 1996). Generally speaking, however, anthropologists working with life stories or other extended accounts have not drawn on the everyday memory or autobiographical memory literatures (see Bourguignon 1996: 374).[6] Thus, even though Peacock and Holland (1993: 373) promote a multidimensional approach which situates the telling of life stories "in processes crucial to human life," the process of remembering is not included among these (its addition would complement the other processes cited). Another area of shared interest, although not a frequent theme in the autobiographical memory literature, concerns the remembered past in relation to the construction of self (in anthropology, see Peacock and Holland 1993; in psychology, see review by Baddeley 1992; other examples include Barclay 1996, Bruner and Feldman 1996, Fitzgerald 1988, 1996, Fivush, Haden and Reese 1996, Nelson 1993, 1995, Kotre 1995).[7] Turning to psychology, it is pertinent to note that some psychologists and cognitive scientists acknowledge the cultural grounding of autobiographical memory (e.g., Barclay 1996, Bruner and Feldman 1996, Fitzgerald 1996, Nelson 1995, Robinson 1992, Schank 1990, Singer and Salovey 1993). Bruner and Feldman (1996: 292) declare: "Because autobiographical memory is, as it were, maximally situated in a culturally meaningful life, it is perhaps the most interesting form of memory a psychologist interested in naturalistic processes can find." At the same time, Bruner and Feldman express doubts about the adequacy of current understandings within psychology to deal with this complexity.

In recent years, explanations treating "everything cognitive as being *possessed* and residing *in the heads* of individuals" (Salomon 1993: xii, emphasis in original) have come under fire as fundamentally misguided (e.g., Hirst and Manier 1995, Middleton and Edwards 1990a, Resnick, Levine, and Teasley 1991, Salomon 1993, Lave and Wenger 1991, Shotter 1990). Within both psychology and anthropology, the prevailing implicit acceptance of the theoretical separation between the study of the mind and the study of culture has been increasingly challenged (e.g., Bruner 1990: 12, Cole and Engeström 1993, Hutchins 1995, Shore 1996, Strauss and Quinn 1994).[8] There is a growing interdisciplinary literature exploring how individuals "appear *to think in conjunction or partnership* with others and with the help of culturally provided tools and implements" (Salomon 1993: xiii, emphasis in original; see also Hirst and Manier 1996, Middleton and Edwards 1990b), with research attending to the patterning of socially and culturally distributed cognition (e.g., Cole and Engeström 1993, Hutchins 1995, Wegner 1987; cf. Schwartz 1978), and the situated nature of cognition (e.g., Hutchins 1995, Lave and Wenger 1991).

As stated earlier, in this chapter, using examples from my own research, I explore the implications of the claim that remembering the past is a jointly social and cultural process as well as a cognitive one.[9] Before turning to these examples, however, I will provide some background through a highly selective review of the psychological memory literature, with special attention to the burgeoning literature on autobiographical memory. A starting point is the seminal book *Remembering* (subtitled *A Study in Experimental and Social Psychology*) by Frederic Bartlett, published in 1932, which foreshadows the perspective to be developed here (much of what Bartlett refers to as "social" would be considered "cultural" by anthropologists). Although Bartlett initially intended to investigate perceiving and remembering as individual level cognitive activities, "it soon appeared that, in numerous cases, social factors were playing a large part" (1932: v). Bartlett strove to encompass both of these aspects within his theoretical model. While the bulk of his supporting data comes from experimental investigations carried out in England, Bartlett also traveled to southern Africa and he presents a series of observations suggestive of cultural influences on remembering.

Bartlett and remembering

Bartlett's perspective on the constructive nature of remembering was first considered to be peripheral to memory research, then virtually ignored during the heyday of behaviorism and verbal learning theory, but since the late 1960s has undergone a transformation from innovation to orthodoxy in contemporary cognitive theory (see Baddeley 1989, Brewer and Nakamura 1984). Nevertheless, almost completely overlooked, until quite recently, are Bartlett's views on remembering as developing in response to the challenges of everyday life, the way remembering reflects cultural and social influences, how "attitude" guides remembering, and how culture contributes to "attitudinal" frameworks and the schematic basis for constructive remembering.

Bartlett's principal objective, as signaled by his choice of title, was to develop a theoretical understanding of the complex process of remembering. A recurring theme throughout the book is that remembering "is a function of daily life, and must have developed so as to meet the demands of daily life" (1932: 16). Bartlett rejected the then prevailing approach to memory which attempted to control for meaning and prior experience by investigating the learning and forgetting of artificial nonsense syllables (exemplified by the work of Ebbinghaus 1964). Predating Neisser's avowal by nearly fifty years, Bartlett contended that this approach impeded an understanding of the nature of memory and claimed that remembering was more appropriately studied by using material, like simple pictures or meaningful stories, "of the type which every normal individual deals with constantly in his daily activities" (1932: v). When compared to some contemporary studies of everyday memory, Bartlett's use of specifically selected material and his laboratory-based experimental approach seem somewhat set apart from everyday life, but his approach was quite innovative for its time.

The focus on process in Bartlett's theory represents a significant shift away from the study of memory as mental structure (again, in contrast to Ebbinghaus 1964). According to Bartlett, memory cannot be considered analogous to a "storehouse," "a place where things are put in the hope that they may be found again when they are wanted exactly as they were when first stored away" (p. 200). He claimed that in "a world of constantly changing environment, literal recall is extraordinarily unimportant" (p. 204). Further, Bartlett asserted that remembering cannot be understood in isolation but only in relation to other mental processes: "in order to understand how and what we remember, we must set into relation to this how and what we perceive" (p. 15). Meaning is central to every cognitive activity, indeed cognition can be seen as "effort after meaning" (p. 44).

Bartlett introduced the theoretical concept of "schema," defining it as "an active organisation of past reactions, or of past experiences, which must always be supposed to be operating in any well-adapted organic response" (p. 201). Schemas (or schemata) are dynamic interpretive processes mediating our understanding of the world.[10] Schemas are not static, they are "living and developing" (p. 214) generic mental representations (or using Bartlett's wording "organised settings") which actively incorporate incoming information and are modified by new experiences. Schemas are integral to perceiving, recognizing, imaging, constructive thinking, and the "imaginative reconstruction called memory" (p. 296). Our understanding of new information is influenced by what we already know; interpretations are actively constructed to make sense in terms of prior knowledge and experience, with a bias towards "rationalisation" and transformation in the direction of the familiar. While these processes operate at an unconscious level (see pp. 20, 200), they can also be accessed through conscious strategy (see pp. 68, 87–89).

Bartlett presents several lines of evidence. The best known involves the recall of a *Kwakwaka'wakw* (or Kwakuitl) tale, entitled "The War of the Ghosts," that was collected and translated by Franz Boas. This story differs from conventional English folktales, both in structure and content. In recall, there was a pronounced tendency for individuals to either omit details and features that were unusual or to transform them, to be consistent with prior knowledge and expectations by adding information (see Rice 1980, Steffensen and Colker 1982 for follow-up studies which highlight the role of culturally based expectations in recall of prose). Thus, deviations from the original reflect the interaction of incoming material with what is already known. Through "rationalisation," the "relatively unfamiliar," such as the supernatural component in the story, became transformed into the "relatively familiar" (p. 89, for a clear illustration see pp. 67–70). In addition, the story when recalled became more conventional by setting up "definite, stated links of connexion [*sic*] between parts of material which are *prima facie* disconnected" (p. 85), with the resulting reconstruction taking on the form of an "orderly narration" (p. 86). Paving the way for his discussion of "social" influences on remembering later in the book, Bartlett (1932: 89) states that "rationalisation" serves: "to render material acceptable, understandable, comfortable, straightforward; to rob it of all puzzling elements. As such it is a powerful factor in all perceptual and in all reproductive processes. The forms it takes are often directly social in significance."

An often overlooked, but theoretically central ingredient of Bartlett's formulation is the concept of attitude. In part, this is because "attitude" is rather amorphously characterized as: "a complex psychological state or process which is very hard to describe in more elementary psychological terms" but which is "very largely a matter of feeling, or affect" (pp. 206–207). Attitude is an orienting and permeating characteristic of cognitive activity.[11] Motivation, interests and values all interact with attitude to "direct the course and determine the content" of cognitive activities (p. 33). An example of how this works comes from a task where individuals were asked to verbally describe a previously presented series of line drawings of faces. These reports often centered on the "affective attitude" aroused by a face with additional details constructed to be consistent with the attitude. Commenting more generally, Bartlett (1932: 207) wrote:

"when a subject is being asked to remember, very often the first thing that emerges is something of the nature of attitude. The recall is then a construction, made largely on the basis of this attitude, and its general effect is that of a justification of the attitude." The level of confidence in recall is also encompassed by attitude. While a confidently rendered account often included specific details, Bartlett found the degree of confidence (or its lack) to bear no relation to objective accuracy (p. 61).

Although Bartlett's work is most often cited as championing the role of schemas and the constructive nature of cognition, in developing his theory of remembering Bartlett was also concerned with the recall of specific memories and the role of nonschema details in this process. This aspect differentiates reconstructing from constructing (while perceiving is constructive, remembering can be constructive and/or reconstructive). In summarizing his observations of one recall task, Bartlett stated: "This constitutes yet another case of that curious preservation of the trivial, the odd, the disconnected, the unimportant detail to which I have already referred" (p. 184). The apparent retention of nonschema details, which are often "novel" (p. 107) or "striking" (p. 83), poses difficulties for a purely constructive approach to remembering. As incoming information is seen to merge with existing schemas, a purely constructive theory cannot account for the recollection of unique features of specific past occurrences. In proposing a resolution to this quandary, Bartlett's theory of remembering has been described as a "partially reconstructive position" involving both schemas and nonschema details (see Brewer 1986, Brewer and Nakamura 1984). According to Bartlett, the problem is to "find a way of individualising some of the characteristics of the total functioning mass of the moment" (p. 208; as human cognition is complex, "functioning mass" refers to the "cross-streams" of schemas that may be brought into play by cognitive activity, see p. 302). He notes:

But the immediate return of certain detail is common enough and it certainly looks very much like the direct re-excitation of certain traces. The need to remember becomes active, an attitude is set up; in the form of sensory images, or, just as often, of isolated words, some part of the event which has to be remembered recurs, and the event is then reconstructed on the basis of the relation of this specific bit of material to the general mass of relevant past experience or reactions, the latter functioning, after the manner of the "schema," as an active organised setting. (p. 209)

Attitude, in terms of interests, values and affect, enters into this "individualising" process and helps account for why some details stand out: "The traces that our evidence allows us to speak of are interest-determined, interest-carried traces. They live with our interests and with them they change" (p. 211; see also p. 210). Consciousness renders possible reconstruction of identified past events, allowing an individual to "turn round upon its own 'schemata' and to construct them afresh" (p. 206; see also pp. 301–303). This is a principal means through which human beings "escape from the complete sway of immediate circumstances" (p. 301) and "over-determination by the last preceding member of a given series" (p. 209). Reconstructing a specific past experience can be seen as an inferential process, building on "interest-carried" details and seemingly directed toward a tacit determination that: "This and this and this must have occurred, in order that my present state should be what it is" (p. 202).[12] In recognizing the interdependence of cognition, emotion, and motivation, Bartlett's schema concept is not dissimilar to more recent definitions, such as one from a cognitive anthropologist: "cognitive schemas are learned internalized patterns of thought-feeling that mediate both the interpretation of on-going experience and the reconstruction of memories" (Strauss 1992: 3).[13]

The second part of Bartlett's book, devoted to the "social psychology of remembering," has received scant notice. Not surprisingly, given Bartlett's repeated finding in the first part of the book that the "manner and the matter of recall are often predominantly determined by social influences" (p. 244), he expressed difficulty in demarcating "social psychology" as an independent field of study:

We seem forced to say that conduct springing directly from beliefs, conventions, customs, traditions and institutions characteristic of a group is material for social psychology. This is, theoretically speaking, rather troublesome, because it seems to mean that everything in psychology belongs to social psychology, except idiosyncrasies and such forms of reaction as are immediately and dominantly determined by physical stimuli. (Pp. 242–243)

Highlighted in the second part of the book are some field investigations carried out during a visit to southern Africa.[14] In one example, he reports the impressive, almost error-free, recall of details for a series of cattle transactions by a Swazi cow herder and relates this feat to the tremendous social importance of cows (noting that in other situations there was no evidence of superior memorial skills). Bartlett suggested that whenever there are "strong, preferred, persistent, specific, social tendencies, remembering is apt to appear direct," analogous to reading off a copy (p. 267). More generally, Bartlett acknowledged the integral relationship of cultural context and remembering, and how cultural influences awaken in the individual an "active tendency to notice, retain and construct specifically along certain directions" (p. 255). Children acquire these "predisposing tendencies" through interactions with others and, consistent with Bartlett's comments about "interest," they provide a means for organizing and highlighting (i.e., "individualising") past experiences which allow humans to break free from the press of present circumstances (see p. 210). Further, Bartlett writes:

Every social group is organised and held together by some specific psychological tendency or group of tendencies, which give the group a bias in its dealings with external circumstances. . . [and this] immediately settle[s] what the individual will observe in his environment and what he will connect from his past life with this direct response. It does this markedly in two ways. First, by providing that setting of interest, excitement and emotion which favours the development of specific images, and secondly, by providing a persistent framework of institutions and customs which acts as a schematic basis for constructive memory. (1932: 255)

Although Bartlett did not use these terms, he is clearly implying that remembering is influenced by cultural knowledge and expectations. Bartlett's comments foreshadow cognitive anthropological concerns with how cultural schemas (schemas which are generally shared in a particular setting) come to be constitutive of individual-level schemas.

Although much of Bartlett's work is concerned primarily with remembering at an individual level, he did discuss the process of "conventionalisation" in social groups (this is essentially rationalization extended to groups) to explain "how the established conventions of one group fare, when they are introduced to another group possessing different conventions" (p. 95) so that the "new material is assimilated to the persistent past of the group to which it comes" (p. 280). And, albeit very briefly, Bartlett notes one way incoming elements tend to become transformed is through the goals and activities of groups, with a new social form or group trend emerging through "unwitting modifications produced by practice" (p. 277).[15]

Autobiographical memory and the remembered past

As in Bartlett's work, autobiographical memory research seeks to understand memory in relation to everyday life. In the introduction to the first edited book devoted to autobiographical memory, Rubin (1986: 3; see also Rubin 1996: 1) outlines the challenges and breadth of this area of study:

A complete understanding of autobiographical memory would require: a knowledge of basic memory processes in the individual as well as of the influences of the society in which the individual lives; a knowledge of the memory processes in the individual at one age and time as well as the effects of changes in development and environment over a lifetime; a knowledge of the intact as well as of the impaired individual; a knowledge of cognition as well as affect.

Several edited collections provide good overviews of this diverse and expanding field (Conway *et al.* 1992, Neisser and Fivush 1994, Rubin 1986, 1996). In this section, although necessarily selective and attentive to remembering as a social and cultural process as well as a cognitive one, I review and comment on some of the key issues and emerging themes in what can be loosely referred to as the autobiographical memory literature.

A common thread throughout this literature is a focus on the consciously remembered past. Somewhat unexpected, however, is the penchant toward addressing the same issues as more conventional memory research. One consequence of this tendency, according to Fitzgerald (1996: 349), is that an understanding of remembering within daily life remains elusive:

> For all of its attempts to understand the mechanisms and/or structures of memory, psychology remains oddly bereft of an understanding or even a description of how memory behavior fits into the daily commerce of human behavior. Even those of us who study autobiographical memory, more often than not find ourselves drawn to classical questions in the study of memory such as accuracy, structural organization, and retention.[16]

Still, over the years, attention has repeatedly and ever-increasingly been drawn to the everyday uses of memory. This includes how the past is used to accomplish something in the present or to plan for the future (Neisser 1988a), how remembering enters into social life (e.g., Edwards, Potter, and Middleton 1992, Fivush, Haden, and Reese 1996, Miller 1995, Neisser 1988a, Wegner 1987), or how an understanding of the past helps individuals give meaning to their lives and the world (Bruner 1990; cf. Schank 1990, Schank and Abelson 1995). As Robinson (1986: 23) points out: "autobiographical memory is not only a record, it is a resource."

[handwritten margin note: some of the literature of everyday uses of memory]

In addition to the diversity of objectives in autobiographical memory research, there is considerable variability in methodology. In some studies, the targeted memories are specified quite precisely, such as stopping individuals on a college campus and requesting them to recall events of the previous summer (Barsalou 1988), or providing a common activity and/or mental state as a general cue to guide the recall of memories (Reiser, Black, and Kalamarides 1986), or asking undergraduate students to write down their three clearest, most vivid, autobiographical memories (Rubin and Kozin 1984) or memories of influential experiences occurring during their freshman year in college (Pillemer *et al.* 1996). As occurred in the two latter studies, participants may also rate various characteristics of their memories (e.g., vividness, intensity of emotion, level of surprise). Researchers have served as subjects as well, keeping diaries over extended time periods and then comparing memories with what was recorded (e.g., Linton 1975, 1986, Wagenaar 1986). One novel study (Brewer 1988) asked participants to record their thoughts and actions when a randomly programmed beeper sounded and later tested memory using these records and different types of foils. Although rather less common, some researchers have collected data in situations seen as more closely approximating to real life, such as legal testimony (e.g., Neisser 1981), individuals recounting narratives of their own past (e.g., Barclay 1993, 1996), members of an identifiable group relating a shared history either individually (Bruner and Feldman 1996) or collectively, such as family members retelling a past occasion (Hirst and Manier 1996), or individuals brought together to talk about a common experience (Middleton and Edwards 1990b). A number of studies on remembering involving children are based on actual observations, such as recording a child's monologues (e.g., Nelson 1989), or conversations of parents and children reminiscing about a shared past (e.g., Edwards and Middleton 1988, Fivush, Haden and Reese 1996). The heterogeneity of existing approaches is consistent with Rubin's (1996: 1) assertion that the study of autobiographical memory is "an area that mixes rigorous, controlled, laboratory methods and theory with everyday questions." Although some researchers acknowledge the potential of social class and/or culture to shape autobiographical remembering (e.g., Bruner and Feldman 1996, Fitzgerald 1996, Singer and Salovey 1993: 209), researchers almost exclusively rely on data obtained from middle-class participants living in North America or Europe. Like other areas of psychological inquiry, researchers typically seek to discover psychological principles, functions, or processes of general applicability.

As Bruner and Feldman (1996: 292) point out, how autobiographical memory is defined may vary across studies: "By autobiographical memory some mean any situated, real-life memory; others mean only personal memories, things, in which somehow, self was engaged. All would agree, though, while strictly autobiographical memory of this latter type is the prototype of this category, it is not all of it." Still, in practice, as mentioned in the introductory section of this chapter, much of the empirical work in cognitive psychology is implicitly, if not explicitly, oriented around this "prototype" or core meaning. Pillemer (1992: 238, emphasis in original; see also Brewer 1996) regards remembering distinctive personal circumstances as the "*defining* characteristic" differentiating personal or autobiographical memories from other kinds of knowledge in memory (e.g., autobiographical facts unaccompanied by recollection of personal circumstances or memories based on schemas abstracted from a series of past occurrences). Remarking that "most theorists still think of personal memory as if it were just a set of remembered concrete experiences" (Neisser 1988b: 356), Neisser advocates a broader view. He maintains: "Individual episodes have no privileged status in memory; it is at least as natural to remember extended situations or typical patterns" (1988b: 362). While Neisser's point is valid and, along with Bruner and Feldman, underscores the need for theories rich enough to account for "all" of autobiographical memory, attention to the "prototype" does provide a sharper focus and serves to highlight specific questions for research.

In the introduction to a recent book on autobiographical memory, Rubin (1996), a prominent researcher and the editor, pulls together diverse strands in the psychology literature in an attempt to more explicitly specify attributes of an autobiographical memory. "Minimal components" include verbal narrative, imagery, and emotion. The telling of autobiographical memories is usually a social act, typically verbally conveyed by means of a culturally based, learned narrative structure. Qualitative characteristics "include a 'reliving' of the individual's phenomenal experience of the original event, reports of visual imagery and less frequently of other forms of imagery, a belief that the remembered episode was personally experienced, and a belief that the remembered episode is a veridical record of the original event" (Rubin 1996: 1–2). Recollections grounded in specific, detailed imagery seem more accurate and believable, both to the person remembering and to an observer. And although the relationship is complex and not well understood, emotional engagement profoundly impacts on autobiographical memory. Consistent with Bartlett's legacy, a recurrent theme is that autobiographical memories are constructed. Rubin (1996: 4) notes: "this does not mean that they are either accurate or inaccurate, but that they are not encoded, stored and retrieved as wholes, but rather created at retrieval," with the potential for construction being guided by goals at the time of retrieval as well as by goals at encoding. It "is often more important that our memories seem real than that they be real" (Rubin 1986: 4), and it has been observed that we believe our own memories to be faithful even when we know from independent evidence that they are not (Brewer 1986, 1996, Rubin 1986, 1996).[17]

A substantial amount of research pertains to autobiographical memories as records of the personal past. While accuracy and completeness of memory (i.e., how well memories reflect past events) is a general issue, it acquires prominence in studies of autobiographical memory because of implications for legal testimony, survey research, and other tasks that rely on the recollective reports of participants. Some, however, like Bruner and Feldman (1996: 293), lament the "misguided emphasis in the current literature on accuracy of reference." Neisser has expressed concerns about a research climate that takes the "ideal of verity for granted" and that has "unanimously treated remembering as an individual activity focused on the past" (Neisser 1988a: 558).

Yet, as reports of what happened, autobiographical memories do relate the particularities of a past event. This characteristic has prompted a renewed theoretical interest in the relative importance of reproduction versus construction in memory (Winograd 1988: 14–15). As in Bartlett's work, the retention of nonschema details is seen as problematic for purely constructive accounts. Based on an extensive literature review of laboratory-based studies, Alba and Hasher (1983: 225) conclude: "we think it is clear that the stored record of any event is far more detailed than any prototypical schema theories imply." Extending Bartlett's "partially reconstructive position" to an understanding of autobiographical memory, Brewer

Some attributes of autobiographical memory

(1986: 44) proposes that "recent personal memories retain a large amount of specific details from the original event (e.g., location, point of view) but that with time, or under strong schema-based processes, the original experience can be reconstructed to produce a new nonveridical personal memory that retains most of the phenomenal characteristics of other personal memories (e.g., strong visual imagery, strong belief value)." An instructive case example comes from Neisser's (1981) study comparing a portion of John Dean's testimony of conversations held in Nixon's Oval Office as recorded in the "Watergate" hearings with the eventually obtained transcripts of the original conversations. John Dean prided himself on his "good memory" and his account of a critical conversation referred to "vivid" and specific details. Yet, Neisser finds that Dean is almost entirely wrong in terms of what actually occurred during that specific conversation. At another level, however, Neisser suggests that John Dean's testimony can be considered essentially correct, if appraised with regard to an underlying schema for the series of conversations. Dean's remembered account clearly shows the work of schema-based constructive processes, yet Dean was confident that he reported the essentials of what transpired in particular conversations.

Attending to the constructive processes in remembering shifts attention from meaning as a property of items and situations to meaning as integral to what a person brings to acting and being in the world.[18] Neisser (1981) discusses how Dean, throughout his testimony, consistently amplified the importance of his own role in the events reported and portrayed his own actions in a more favorable light than warranted. In another study, Linton (1986: 64) says, reflecting on some "remarkable shifts" occurring over her twelve years of diary writing, "one can see the internal historian beginning to exercise its prerogative – rewriting has begun to occur." A first meeting with a shy academic takes on new importance when Linton begins to date and decides to marry him. In both of these instances, the past is reflexively constructed in light of present understandings. A constructive perspective allows for the general expectation that "anything that alters the way a past experience is interpreted would alter what a person remembers from that experience" (Robinson 1996: 209). Although psychologists have tended to discuss meaning and changes in meaning at an individual level, the centrality of meaning within a constructive perspective presupposes, as Bartlett appreciated, the intrinsically social and cultural nature of remembering.

As mentioned previously, given the sheer magnitude of material available, there is a necessary selectivity in what is attended to, retained, and recollected. Bartlett highlighted the connection between perceiving and remembering. Although the contribution of constructive processes to what is remembered is generally acknowledged, the focus on accuracy means research is often directed to assessing the correspondence between what really happened and what is remembered rather than on the process of remembering. The research concentration on issues of retrieval tends "to de-emphasize research into encoding and how autobiographical knowledge is acquired in the first place" (Conway 1996: 85). But this situation appears to be changing. One area attracting considerable interest is emotion and autobiographical memory. Reviewing both laboratory-based studies and memory for real world happenings, Christianson and Safer (1996) find that events with strong emotional impact are more likely to be recalled than more neutral, commonplace events, and with the central details well retained. More generally, efforts to explain why particular points in time are remembered, have led some researchers to ask about the "real-world useful-ness or adaptive significance of memory mechanisms" (Bruce 1989: 45). Research addressing this question suggests that events which are novel, transitional, and/or deviate from schema-based expectations may be better remembered because of their potential usefulness as a resource in meeting future life challenges, providing a basis for predicting and explaining the world or directives for action (Pillemer 1992, Pillemer et al. 1996, Schank 1990).

While the importance of individual level goals, interests, and prior knowledge has long been recognized by cognitive psychologists (Robinson 1996), how culture contributes to and shapes what individuals pay atten-tion to, care about, and hence remember, is rarely acknowledged, despite Bartlett's efforts to bring such matters to the forefront. Similar to the way attention to and subsequent memory for details of cattle transactions may be attributed to the cultural importance of cows for the Swazi cow herder, cultural salience may help explain why some parts of the past become the remembered past, and others do not. In the example presented at the begin-ning of this chapter, what Arthur Roland remembered was a singular inci-dent involving a snake, a situation which is culturally marked in that it deviates from Anishinaabe expectations about proper relations between human beings and animals. Such incidents, as will be seen in other examples from the Anishinaabe community, are also culturally defined as potentially important in responding to future sickness or other misfortunes. Everyday life is a culturally meaningful life; the usefulness of the past in meeting the present and future is grounded in particular settings and is culturally vari-able. The personal past is a cultural past.[19]

Another outcome of the spotlight on the individual and the retrieval of personally experienced episodes as the "real" phenomenon of interest, is a relative lack of attention to social context and the ways autobiographical memory reflects interactions with others.[20] Recent legal cases alleging "false" memories for traumatic events have led to research examining how individuals may come to "honestly but falsely remember" (Belli and Loftus 1996: 159). In one of these studies (see Loftus 1993), after being provided with vague information by a trusted family member, an individual comes to construct, in quite specific detail, an autobiographical event which never occurred, such as being lost in a shopping mall as a child. This is a dramatic illustration of the combined potential of constructive processes and social interactions to guide what comes to be remembered. Yet, the theoretical implications of this work are only starting to become integrated with other work on autobiographical memory.[21]

In reminiscing, individuals may collaboratively reconstruct a shared past. Observations of joint reminiscing, often involving children and parents, illuminate how memories are constructed and negotiated (e.g., Fivush, Haden, and Reese 1996, Miller, Fung, and Mintz 1996). Miller (1995: 180), one of the few whose research involves cross-cultural comparisons (but see also Mullen 1994), surmises that cultural variability in "the different ways in which past experience gets collaboratively carved out and structured for the purposes of personal story-telling will be reflected in patterns of remembering." Further, she notes that "remembered events, as they get narrated and renarrated, will be shaped in systematic ways by the interests of the narrating participants who are inevitably socially positioned relative to one another" (Miller 1995: 181; cf. Edwards, Potter and Middleton 1992). Commenting on these social processes more generally, Middleton and Edwards (1990a: 7) suggest that in conversational remembering "what is recalled and commemorated extends beyond the sum of the participants' individual perspectives: it becomes the basis of future reminiscence. In the contest between varying accounts of shared experiences, people reinterpret and discover features of the past that become the context and content for what they will jointly recall and commemorate on future occasions" (cf. Halbwachs 1980, Hirst and Manier 1995: 113).

For Hirst and Manier (1996: 271) the act of remembering cannot be divorced from the act of communicating: "recollections arise not from the depths of a storehouse in the head, but from a desire to communicate with others about the personal past." Recounting past experiences not only conveys information about events in the world but also tells the listener something about the kind of person we are (Fivush, Haden, and Reese 1996: 341; for a comparison between Chinese and American communicative practices see Miller *et al.* 1996). Telling about a past event allows us to relay what matters to us and to impart how an event takes on meaning for us (Mattingly and Garro 1994: 772), to recreate an event so that the listener identifies with the teller's experience (Fivush, Haden, and Reese 1996: 354). In American culture, children learn to tell stories that "are studded with rich detail and emotional elaboration" (Fivush *et al.* 1996: 356). A study carried out in England based on conversations recorded while mothers and children looked at family photographs further underscores the communicative aspects of remembering:

The past was noted and recalled in terms of why and how it *mattered* to them. What mattered were their affective reactions to things, their personal involvement and actions, their personal identity and how this was presented or altered over time, their relationships with each other and with other depicted people, and, not least with rationales and explanations of events, of personal conduct and of affective reactions. (Edwards and Middleton 1988: 10, emphasis in original)[22]

Across disciplines, various authors have commented on the value of talking about one's past in establishing and maintaining social relationships (e.g., Connerton 1989, Fivush, Haden, and Reese 1996, Halbwachs 1980, Linde 1993, Neisser 1988a, Pillemer 1992), including a sense of group identity (Connerton 1989, Halbwachs 1980, Linde 1993, Mankowski and Rappaport 1995, Neisser 1988a).

From a communication perspective, remembering (and forgetting) can be viewed as "social action." Here, the key question becomes "what shapes this particular account or description, in this context: what is being *done* here, in this formulation of events" (Edwards, Potter, and Middleton 1992: 443, emphasis in original; cf. Gee 1992: 89–90). The explanatory locus is not cognition, but action or performance (Edwards, Potter, and Middleton 1992: 442). To refer back to an example provided earlier, a social action view suggests an alternate interpretation of Dean's testimony at the Watergate hearings as "*designed to accomplish* authenticity and accountability, rather than being man's best (but flawed) efforts at accurate recall" (Edwards, Potter, and Middleton 1992: 445, emphasis in original). Through his efforts to vividly convey past events, Dean's testimony became more persuasive. In a discussion of the functions of memory, Bruce maintains that persuasion is an "ultimate function of all story-telling memory mechanisms" (Bruce 1989: 50). Accounts of personal experiences are compelling, and elaboration makes this even more so (Pillemer 1992: 244–245). Still, there is no apparent reason why regarding Dean's testimony as social action is incompatible with the operation of schema-based memory processes. Remembering is a complex, multifaceted process.

The communicated past is a narrated past. This claim holds whether an account is judged to accurately represent the past or not, though, as the preceding discussion makes clear, an exclusive focus on accuracy misses much of what takes place in remembering. Narrative provides a framework for telling and understanding events. Thus, how a narrative is constructed provides a basis for interpreting it, including, if desired, interpretations of its accuracy (Bruner and Feldman 1996: 291). By themselves, the "facts" of the past "do not supply the patterning or schematic structure of narrated reports" (Bruner and Feldman 1996: 293). Bruner and Feldman (1996: 293) state that in order to be communicable, autobiographical memory "must be constructed of cultural material." They propose that autobiographical experiences "are constituted meaningfully into a public and communicable form" by drawing upon "narrative properties like genre and plot type that are widely shared with a culture, shared in a way that permits others to construe meaning the way the narrator has" (p. 293). Based on developmental studies, Fivush, Haden, and Reese (1996: 344) claim that through reminiscing with others about the past: "children are learning the skills of remembering and reminiscing, not the content of particular experiences." Thus, children are not learning what to recall, but how to recall, the culturally appropriate narrative forms for recounting the past.[23]

As mentioned earlier, psychologists interested in autobiographical memory generally have not expressed interest or been inspired to move outside of familiar cultural settings. In addition, as Fitzgerald (1996: 379) notes: "with few exceptions, autobiographical memory researchers have centered their attention on the individual independent of contextual factors." While anthropologists have collected narrative accounts of the past in diverse settings, they have generally not focused on an analysis of memory processes. Therefore much work needs to be done exploring the ways memory serves as "a meeting ground between individual and culture" (Teski 1995: 49). As suggested by this review, minimally this would involve integrating psychological insights about memory with attention to remembering in response to the demands of daily life – a daily life grounded in a culturally meaningful world and where remembering may grow out of social interactions.

The remembered past in daily life

In the remaining space, I will only attempt to sketch out some preliminary ideas using illness accounts obtained during the course of my fieldwork in an Anishinaabe (Ojibwa) reserve community in Canada. While not all illness conditions lead to retrospective assessments of the past, such assessments may accompany the search for meaning, explanation, and treatment occasioned by illness. In talking about illness conditions, whether one's own or another person's, individuals remember, drawing on their experiences and knowledge to link the remembered past with the present and to make projections into the future. In such instances, remembering is tied as much to current and future concerns as it is to the past.

Remembering, as Bartlett first proposed, is active and constructive. But remembering the past in relation to a present illness differs from the recall of stories or other material studied by Bartlett. Bartlett's experiments demonstrated that what is remembered in these instances is directed or shaped by what is already known, that remembering is organized in ways that make sense of prior knowledge and experience. Yet, in illness there are often multiple interpretive frameworks or alternative cultural schemas available. In addition, individuals may come into contact with new frameworks or new ways of applying preexisting frameworks to make sense of illness experience. These frameworks may come to play a constitutive role in a reorganization and reflexive reinterpretation of past experiences. Establishing a match between a recollected past experience and a culturally available interpretive framework is thus a generative process as well as a reflexive one (cf. Robinson 1986).[24] Through remembering, culturally available knowledge becomes situated knowledge (cf. Cain 1991, Mathews, Lannin, and Mitchell 1994). In the examples presented here, I explore how preexisting culturally based understandings and social interactions are integral to constructive processes involved in remembering and serve to guide this process.

The first example returns to the situation described at the beginning of the chapter, concerning Arthur Roland's daughter and an illness which persisted over several weeks despite being treated by a physician. In this community, when an illness is resistive to physicians' treatment or is judged to be "unusual," there is often recourse to Anishinaabe healers who are "gifted" and guided by spiritual beings (when speaking in English, such healers, who are generally males, are locally referred to as "medicine men"; see Garro 1990 for a more complete discussion of the interpretation and treatment of illness in this community). Their counsel is typically sought when there is uncertainty about the nature of illness. Although such healers treat a variety of illness conditions, often one or both of two possible, but distinct, explanatory frameworks are under active consideration by those seeking help. One of these, relating to *ondjine*, connects a present illness with inappropriate conduct at some point in the past. The other involves "bad medicine." Illness explained with reference to bad medicine is attributed to intentional, malevolent, and covert wielding of supernatural power by another person.

When Arthur Roland and his wife consulted the medicine man, they were open to a number of alternative interpretive possibilities. It was only through the healer's direction and validation that the remembering of the critical incident occurred. Remembering one's personal past helps both the accountable individual and others to give meaning to misfortune while setting the course for the response to illness in the present and future. In this instance, constructing a compatible account entails remembering an appropriate incident from the personal past. Only then can actions be taken to make amends for the past and prevent the possibility of other misfortune stemming from the same event. However, more than simply establishing a plausible connection between past and present is required. There must be an unreserved acceptance of the causal link. Failure to achieve a cure may be attributed to a lack of conviction on the part of those seeking help. Since the family judged the outcome of the visit to the medicine man as successful, Mr. Roland's account, grounded in this social context, is thus necessarily a confident one.

From a psychological perspective, the healer can be viewed as providing a goal at the time of retrieval which guides the construction of a compatible account. How remembering is guided by an Anishinaabe healer has parallels with the guidance of other treatment providers, like physicians.[25] The medicine man and the physician both provide a general, and culturally authorized, explanatory framework, but it is typically the afflicted person who reflexively and generatively evaluates the applicability of the framework within the context of their own life (the lack of fit between personal experience and an explanatory framework may also figure prominently in illness accounts, see Garro 1994).[26] This process of remembering is jointly cognitive, social, and cultural. Neither the goal nor its realization can be separated from social context and preexisting cultural schemas.

Consistent with the overview of the autobiographical memory literature, remembering the personal past is best described as "partially reconstructive," in which remembered detail and constructive processes intermingle. In telling his account, Arthur Roland seeks to reproduce what he remembered at the healing session. In his recollection of the long-ago event, remembered details from his childhood provide the foundation of what is recalled. In the preceding section the attributes of an autobiographical memory were described. While the relevant research comes from a limited cultural base and may also reflect characteristics of experimental tasks (e.g., ratings of imagery vividness), these attributes provide a useful starting point for examining how accounts are constructed, and constructed in a way which reflects cultural expectations as well as what is culturally salient. The "minimal components" listed by Rubin (1996) of verbal narrative, imagery, and emotion can all be seen in the quote from Mr. Roland. Both in structure and content, this telling of the past makes sense to Mr. Roland and to others in the community and his telling is shaped to reflect communicative goals. It conforms to culturally based narrative expectations about the facilitation of remembering through spiritual means while authorizing the linkage of identifiable past deeds of the protagonist with subsequent misfortune. The phenomenally experienced immediacy and sense of a veridically recollected past are convincingly conveyed through the recall of details that create an imaginal context. The remembered past is relived in the present. The vividness of his account serves to strengthen the conviction that this long-ago event is implicated in the present-day illness. The most distinctive aspect involves the injured snake. Although the snake did not actually speak, the portent attributed to the snake's menacing look sets the emotional tenor for this long-ago event.

Arthur Roland's comment about what the snake seemed to say to him imbues this incident with meaning and illustrates the interpenetration of cultural and constructive cognitive processes. His use of perceptual terms situates the emotional impact at the time of the original event, and is suggestive of the imprint of culture on perceptual processes which construct the event as an especially meaningful one. It is also plausible that a reconstruction of this episode became tagged as significant sometime during the interval between the original incident and its recall in the healing session. In addition to goals at the time of retrieval, goals at the time of encoding also figure in psychological theory. Although not expressed by Mr. Roland, in some other discussions of *ondjine*, individuals recalled that at the time of the original predisposing event they wondered if something would occur as a consequence of their actions. The following reminiscence from Laura Mason, a young woman in her early twenties, points to the potential of cultural schemas to shape such encounters and contribute to their salience in memory:

One time too, I was scared. I was a kid. At that time I guess I was 13 or something. I was at my mom's that time and our puppy got run over. I was scared to touch it because I was told never to touch a dog if it's suffering or something, even if you're trying to help it. But the puppy was crying and at that time what I did was I kept thinking in my mind, like nothing will happen. I just want to help this puppy. And I carried it back to the house. I always wonder if something could happen because of this.[27]

The feelings of anxiety and bewilderment reflect the impact of cultural proscriptions on determining a course of action at the time of this event. But the emotional atmosphere has less to do with the puppy's accident and injuries than with the possible aftermath of a decision to care for the puppy. Given the cultural potential for future misfortune to be explained and managed with reference to such incidents, it is not surprising that such occurrences become part of the remembered past. As Bartlett (1932: 255) noted, culture provides "that setting of interest, excitement and emotion which favours the development of specific images." The relationship between the affective aspects of remembering and how culture shapes what persons care about and hence remember warrants a fuller exploration than can be given here.

As stated earlier, the study of autobiographical memory encompasses more than the recall of particular episodes from an individual's past. The next example covers a longer period in the remembered past, yet the cultural and social nature of remembering can also be seen. This example also alludes to the interplay of constructive processes at the time of an original event with those involved when remembering. In the following quote, Jemina Fredette discusses the circumstances contributing to her two-month-old infant being born with a facial deformity involving the mouth. This account does not vividly depict the remembered past, but it is structured around what matters to her and the emotional consequences of the past. As in the other examples, this account is told from the perspective of the present and is constructed to reflect her current understanding of what caused the problem:

I was always worried about my baby. I was always scared something would, you know, be wrong. It always went back to when I was feeding these calves, and you know, helping my husband to deliver the calves and stuff like that. I used to always help him, you know, my hands are smaller and I could reach in and help pull the calf out. A lot of women used to tell me: "You shouldn't do that." They said: "If you ever have another baby, something is going to be wrong with it." Like *ondjine*. And then when I was pregnant I used to be always so worried. I know when they used to say that to me, and I'd think about all the work I did with the cows and stuff like that. I used to wonder how my baby . . . I always hoped I'd have a normal baby, that nothing would be wrong with it or anything. Sometimes I'd look at the calves when I was feeding them with the bottle, I'd be looking at their mouth, and you know, really staring at them and that was before I was pregnant. And then when I was pregnant, I always thought of that, what if my baby is born with something wrong, something wrong with my baby's mouth, and it really did happen.

The question of whether this account overstates the sense of foreboding during her pregnancy in light of what is now known cannot be answered. However, in some other statements she asserts that she worried "about a lot of things" that might be wrong with her infant (the involvement with the calves received by far the most discussion and elaboration) and listed a number of potential maladies. Unborn children are considered particularly vulnerable to *ondjine*. Mrs. Fredette did quit helping with the calves as soon as she became aware of this unplanned pregnancy to lessen the risk of repercussions for her unborn child.[28] Even prior to her pregnancy, Mrs. Fredette reports helping her husband only sporadically and somewhat reluctantly. As in the preceding examples, the quote conveys a heightened affective response associated with interactions with animals. In this case, her feelings of unease are reinforced by other women warning her of the possible consequences of her actions. The lack of vivid recall of her involvement with the calves is not critical here as the events of the past are recurrent ones and also widely known. The one concrete description of staring at the mouths of calves is best understood with reference to cultural expectations that misfortune can result from staring at an animal (in all of the cases I recorded, these animals are in somewhat abnormal situations and there is often a sense that the rivetting of attention occurs involuntarily).

Upon first seeing her infant, Mrs. Fredette says she immediately suspected the bottle feeding of the orphan calves.[29] This was subsequently confirmed by the medicine man consulted. Looking back she states: "It was from feeding the calves because the calves would die on me." Mrs. Fredette still worries that other problems could result in the future from her past dealings with the calves. She has refused her husband's recurring entreaties to return to assisting him with their livestock. While one past activity has been targeted, a heightened concern about this whole period continues. The potentiality exists for other unfortunate occurrences to be explained with reference to this part of her remembered past.

As individuals seek appropriate treatment and care for an illness, they may become exposed to and acquire new explanatory frameworks which are then used in reinterpreting past experiences. This reframing process may be elusive, it can occur without conscious awareness and may be undetectable unless different accounts are obtained at relevant points in time. In other instances, individuals are aware that their understanding of a situation has changed. In the following example, the account was obtained shortly after a visit to a medicine man. His advice radically altered this woman's earlier interpretation of a singular, emotionally charged, occurrence. In this quote, Emily McKay describes the event:

Well, it was just one night. Like I woke up. I didn't know if I was dreaming or something, but the way it was, I was lying on my stomach. Then it seemed like I woke up. I guess I had seen something. There was something behind me, like something black. And I kept trying to look back and I couldn't. I couldn't look back. I could see something out of the corner of my eye. But I couldn't – it's as if something was holding me, not letting me look back. I just couldn't look back. And then I felt like the bed was just moving. And then later the next morning, Frank [her husband] asked me if the bed was moving or something, and I told him yes, it felt like it was moving. Then I told him, I thought that was a dream, did you really feel the bed moving? He said yes. Well, then I got up and all that night I kept trying to think was this a dream or something, or did it happen? I couldn't sleep. I was scared after that, 'cause I thought what if this is the devil or something. Then I told my mom about it and then she told me that I should do something about it. She told me, it must mean something. And then I decided to see a medicine man.

Like the episodes recounted by Arthur Roland and Laura Mason, this recollection is richly elaborated. As in these other episodes, narrative, imagery, and emotion are constitutive. And while the meaning associated with the experience portrayed in the above quote changed when new information was acquired, the integral quality of the experience, including the sensation of being restrained and her impression of an ominous presence, remains constant. As will be seen in the subsequent discussion, this event is revisited a number of times. In psychological parlance, rehearsal occurs each time the past event is revisited or reinstated, increasing the likelihood that it will be remembered in the future (e.g., Nelson 1995). But, it is important to note that this event is revisited, because it becomes marked as culturally meaningful.

Emily McKay's marriage had been going through a tumultuous period of several months duration, but the couple of weeks preceding this incident had been particularly trying. In addition to ongoing family problems, her car had broken down several times. She had several spells of dizziness and debilitating headaches. Just prior to the start of these additional problems, Emily McKay had started a new job. The difficulties with the car and her health led her to suspect someone was trying to harm her with bad medicine. She speculated it was someone who was jealous of her employment and quite likely one of the unsuccessful applicants for her position. Noticing a change in demeanour on the part of one of these individuals, she became even more apprehensive. Taken together, this set of circumstances as narrated by Mrs. McKay – the car's breakdowns, impaired health, the new job, the perception of malice in a distrusted other – converge on a prototypical cultural scenario consistent with suspecting bad medicine. She was in a state of heightened awareness for detecting additional indicators that someone was trying to harm her in this manner. The night-time episode was seen as possibly confirming this fear, although she did wonder whether this was a product of her own imagination. Nevertheless, dream or not, at best it was a nightmare, at worst a premonition of impending danger.

Agreeing with her mother's assessment that "it must mean something," a medicine man was consulted. She described what happened during this visit:[30]

Then he started singing . . . I heard three voices. I know I heard a man's voice and two old women's voices, 'cause I was sitting there and he was singing. And I thought, oh no, what if someone's coming, while he's singing and all this, cause I heard someone. I kept looking and there was nobody, you know, I was just waiting for someone to come up the stairs and no one was coming. All through that time like my legs just felt weak and you know, I don't know how I felt, I just felt like I wanted to cry right there and then . . . Then, after he finished singing he told me that dream that I had was like a warning . . . it was the devil . . . it was sort of like he was trying to take my life. The spirits were giving me a warning through my dream for me to try and do something right away. The dream was meant for real, that I had to do something right away.

At first, unaware that the healer was in communication with spiritual beings, Emily McKay does not realize the three voices she hears are not those of other people coming to visit but rather her spirit protectors. But through the medicine man's guidance she comes to understand that they were also present at her "dream." As well, he presents an alternative scenario, one which still draws on cultural understandings (i.e., consistent with a culturally appropriate narrative form) but which rejects the more culturally common and predictable interpretation of bad medicine. In this alternative scenario, by restraining her movements, the spirit protectors shielded her from the presence of evil – the unseen black shape now confirmed as the devil. She came to see herself as especially vulnerable at this point in time. Emily McKay describes herself as someone who believes deeply in God and in what she refers to as "the tradition." But, due to the number of stressful events in her life, she was not living up to her spiritual commitments, she was "letting things go." Heeding this warning requires her to change her life. Phenomenally the description of this night-time encounter remains the same, but her interpretation is quite dramatically transformed. Mrs. McKay now considers herself blessed by the visitation, especially as the medicine man intimated that the visit bears the promise of future gifts. Through her interaction with the healer, Emily McKay has adopted an alternative explanation which allows her to reinterpret what has become a major transition point in her life.

My final example illustrates how even apparently unique illness accounts may draw upon shared understandings in the effort to use the past to give meaning to the present. This account comes from a larger study on understandings of high blood pressure (see Garro 1988). Mr. Hamilton was 58 years old when I spoke with him. He typically spoke in Anishinaabemowin but, for this interview, he chose to give his account in English. For Mr. Hamilton, dizziness and headaches indicate that his blood pressure is up and that he should take medication to bring it down. In his community, there is strong consensus that such symptoms reliably accompany "blood that rises," which is how the Anishinaabemowin term for high blood pressure translates into English. In the following quote he recounts his experiences of spraying chemicals on crops (referring to the chemical mixture several times as "stuff") and developing illness as a consequence:

When I was young, we never knew anybody who had that high blood pressure. We had a farm, and I usually use that stuff in there since it started bothering me. Had it for about twenty years and I stopped farming five years ago. Well I was getting sick already when I quit. I was kind of feeling dizzy, that's before when I was working with the stuff. Always I was down doing the spraying myself. I was alone, nobody to help me. So every time I sprayed, I had a little bit of headache. I was all the time kind of dizzy in the field there, early in July, I usually sprayed then. I've been working all along since I was fourteen, I've been working. I never had any trouble until I start farming, that's when it started bothering me. I should not have had a farm. Well, I never wear a mask, anything when I go out on the field there. Even when I was smoking, I usually roll my own cigarettes, so all that stuff on my hand, it just goes in my body.

In this account, the narrative patterning which organizes the "facts" of the past reflects shared cultural understandings about the potential causes of high blood pressure (see Garro 1988). As the facts of this case are drawn from habitual work activities, there is no basis for suggesting that these events were marked as significant at the time they occurred (i.e., at encoding). Unlike the other accounts, no distinctive emotional milieu is established. Rather, from the vantage point of the present, the events of the past provide the basis for situating the occurrence of illness within a particular life, for making sense of what has transpired. From a psychological perspective, the goals at the time of retrieval direct the narrative construction.

The symptoms of dizziness and headaches that Mr. Hamilton suffered when spraying chemicals in the past and the manifestation of these same symptoms when his blood pressure rises in the present provide a basis for constructing his illness account. The regularity of this association across repeated episodes helps to establish the connection. But, while important, the recollection of these past episodes is not the only knowledge he draws upon in constructing his account. His account is also based on shared cultural understandings about potential causes of bodily imbalance which can result in high blood pressure, understandings which are essentially available to all but are variably used by individuals in reconstructing and making sense of the past. These culturally shared understandings serve as resources which guide remembering, but not in a deterministic fashion (as is perhaps suggested in Bartlett's work). In the case of high blood pressure, there are a number of widely shared explanatory frameworks which can be used as a basis for constructing an account of illness.[31] Even though he does draw upon shared understandings, Mr. Hamilton's account is unique; out of twenty-six individuals interviewed with a diagnosis of high blood pressure, his was the only one where personal experiences with handling chemicals are linked to the development of illness. It was much more common, for example, for individuals to situate the development of high blood pressure within the context of stressful events in their lives.[32]

Within this community, high blood pressure is considered a "white man's illness," which indicates that it was not present "in the old days" (Mr. Hamilton starts by stating that when he was younger he didn't know anyone with high blood pressure). When talking about high blood pressure, individuals often talked about the chemicals sprayed on crops or used in processing store bought foods. Such statements are not typically linked to personal history, but to the community history, in order to account for the relatively recent emergence of high blood pressure and the substantial number of persons diagnosed with high blood pressure. Comments about "white man's sickness" can be seen as "a making sense of the past as a kind of collective autobiography" (Connerton 1989: 70); a means of asserting a collective memory about a past when the Anishinaabe were healthy. The presence of "white man's sicknesses" is seen by community members as but one manifestation of the disruption and destruction of the Anishinaabe way of life which has occurred and is still ongoing.

In Mr. Hamilton's account, this culturally available explanatory framework has become personal knowledge. The conceptual framework implicating chemicals in the development of high blood pressure can be seen as the generative link between the illness and symptoms he currently experiences with the headaches and dizziness experienced while farming in the past. Mr. Hamilton's account also provides evidence which strengthens the causal relationship of chemicals and white man's sickness and helps maintain its availability as a cultural resource for understanding illness experience. In the course of my fieldwork, several individuals told me about Mr. Hamilton when talking about how high blood pressure was related to chemical contaminants introduced by white men. A compelling account provides a resource that may help guide how others come to reconstruct their past (see also Cain 1991, Mankowski and Rappaport 1995). Hearing the remembered accounts of others augments the listener's "fund of cultural knowledge" with which to meet the future (Price 1987: 315). Such cultural resources are needed for persons to go beyond what merely happens to impart how events take on meaning for them, to situate the remembered past in a culturally meaningful life (cf. Bruner and Feldman 1996, Mattingly and Garro 1994).

Conclusion

In a history of cognitive science published in 1985, Gardner wrote:

Though mainstream cognitive scientists do not necessarily bear any animus against the affective realm, against the context that surrounds any action or thought, or against historical or cultural analyses, in practice they attempt to factor out these elements to the maximum extent possible. So even do anthropologists when wearing their cognitive science hats. This may be a question of practicality: if one were to take into account these individualizing and phenomenalistic elements, cognitive science might become impossible. In an effort to explain everything, one ends up explaining nothing. And so, at least provisionally, most cognitive scientists attempt to so define and investigate problems that an adequate account is given without resorting to these murky concepts. (1985: 41–42)

As discussed throughout this chapter, there are a growing number of challenges to the viewpoint expressed in Gardner's statement. The interest in everyday memory, including autobiographical memory, has led some researchers to pose and confront questions about the uses and purposes of human memory within the context of everyday life. In addition, there is a growing interdisciplinary dialogue promoting a "cultural theory of mind" (Cole and Engeström 1993: 42) grounded on the inseparability of cultural processes and cognitive processes and advancing the socially distributed and situated nature of cognition. Bartlett, however, can be seen as the first cognitive psychologist to recognize that an adequate account of remembering cannot ignore these "murky concepts." Culture, affect, meaning, narrative structure, and the specific contexts in which remembering occurs are all inextricably intertwined in Bartlett's theoretical perspective. Central to his perspective is an emphasis on remembering as process, rather than memory as content. Also fundamental is Bartlett's view of remembering developing to meet the demands of everyday life. In this chapter, I have built upon Bartlett's insights.

The perspective developed here also represents a shift away from the view of culture that has motivated much research in cognitive anthropology (see Quinn and Holland 1987: 4) and was first expressed by Goodenough (1957: 167) as: "whatever it is one must know in order to behave appropriately in any of the roles assumed by any member of a society." Hutchins (1995) has recently argued that this view of culture contributes to the marginalization of culture in cognitive science. In addition to Goodenough's statement, Hutchins cites a paper concerning the "cultural part" of cognition in which D'Andrade (1981) proposed an intellectual division of labor with psychologists responsible for the cognitive processes and anthropologists for the cognitive content. Although D'Andrade notes concerns about the neatness of this separation (1981: 193–194), Hutchins (1995: 353) decisively rejects the relegation of culture to "simply a pool of ideas that are operated on by cognitive processes." Rather than content, Hutchins (1995: 354) defines culture as process: "It is a human cognitive process that takes place both inside and outside the minds of people. It is the process in which our everyday cultural practices are enacted." It is a process occurring in the "everyday world, where human cognition adapts to its natural surroundings" (Hutchins 1995: xiv). While the realm of autobiographical remembering is quite removed from the types of activities Hutchins focuses on in his 1995 book, the view developed here that remembering is a multifaceted process is clearly in step with efforts to reconceptualize the role of culture in cognition as integral to process and not just simply content.

In summary, I have argued that remembering, even the remembering of personal experience, cannot be understood as solely an individual cognitive process. Remembering the personal past is jointly a cognitive, social, and cultural process. Remembering an event from the personal past involves cultural, social, and cognitive processes prior to the situation, during the situation, and during remembering, and potentially during the intervening time period. Remembering is not analogous to opening a window on the past, but is an activity occurring in the context of a culturally meaningful life and constructed using cultural materials as well as personal experience. Culturally available knowledge and interactions with others, including what is communicated as their remembered past, serve as guides in remembering. In everyday life, remembering is oriented to the present and future as much as to the past.

Acknowledgments

Foremost thanks are to those who shared their memories with me and to others in the Anishinaabe community who helped me with this research in many other ways. I am indebted to Holly Mathews for the suggestion that I write this chapter and who, along with Carmella Moore, provided encouragement, considerable guidance, and valuable insights. Robert Whitmore has read and constructively commented on several versions of this chapter. Writing this also provides me the opportunity to thank one of my significant mentors, David Rubin, who first introduced me to the study of autobiographical memory and the challenges of understanding memory in the context of everyday life. The research in the Anishinaabe community was supported by grants from the National Health Research and Development Program (6607–1402–43) and the Manitoba Health Research Council (6278).

NOTES

1 The interest in "everyday memory" has led to research on a wide variety of topics (Cohen 1989, Davies and Logie 1993, Poon, Rubin, and Wilson 1989 provide introductions to this varied field) and engendered sometimes impassioned debate over the value of different approaches to the psychological study of memory (e.g., naturalistic studies of memory versus laboratory methods of experimentation, see Banaji and Crowder 1989 and the subsequent series of replies and commentaries in the *American Psychologist*, 1991, vol. 46, pp. 16–48, the individual contributions of Conway, Crowder, and Baddeley in Davies and Logie 1993, and Hirst and Manier 1995). Despite some polemic statements, the situation cannot simply be characterized as researchers pitting laboratory methods against other approaches to studying memory. For example, as will be seen in the next section of this paper, Bartlett's (1932) laboratory-based studies provide the empirical basis for his novel insights about the workings of memory in the context of everyday life. As Landauer (1989: 124; see also Bruce 1989) states: "the real test of whether something is being studied in the right context is not whether the place of study is the laboratory or the field, but whether or not

the phenomenon being studied is a naturally important one." A critical concern for many advocating more naturalistic approaches to the study of memory is whether "the phenomenon studied under tightly controlled conditions is the *same* as the one encountered in real-life circumstances" (Salomon 1993: xii, emphasis in original).

2 All names used are pseudonyms. In interactions with individuals my own age or younger, we mutually referred to each other using either first names or nick-names. However, as a convention in this paper, I use either both first and last names or the surname with an appropriate title.

3 While Mr. Roland speaks English fluently and used English when speaking to me, he more commonly speaks in Anishinaabemowin and it is the language of his childhood. If the same account were to be related in Anishinaabemowin, the final sentence in the excerpt quoted would not specify the gender of the individual to be harmed as a consequence of his actions.

4 I focus on life story and extended narrative approaches because they are so common in anthropology and because of the apparent overlap in areas of interest with the autobiographical memory literature A more comprehensive discussion of the diverse anthropological literature on memory would range far beyond the scope of this paper. Such a review would cover cognitively oriented work (D'Andrade 1995 discusses a number of studies) but would also include, among others, Connerton (1989), Douglas (1986: 69–90), Battaglia (1992) and two recently edited collections (Antze and Lambek 1996, Teski and Climo 1995).

5 As all three types of accounts mentioned are often obtained in research settings, a relevant question is the extent to which they can be considered representative of "everyday" uses of memory. As this is a complex matter (and one that recurs later in this chapter with reference to the psychological literature), I will only make a few observations. As my discussion in the text of the quote from Mr. Roland indicates, I regard this example as illustrative of one way in which remembering is used in everyday life. It is not uncommon for accounts similar to the one presented here to be told in this community. Indeed, the hearing of such accounts is a principal means through which cultural knowledge about misfortune, including possible causes and appropriate responses, is acquired. The more general question is whether, and under what conditions, interview data can be considered representative of naturally occurring discourse. This issue has been addressed by Linde (1993), a linguist who relies on interview data in her own study of the life stories of middle-class Americans. She directs attention to the relation of what is obtained through interviews to spontaneous conversation: "In its strongest form, the question is whether the investigator may be inducing the speaker to produce a kind of speech unlike anything that would be produced under any other circumstances" (Linde 1993: 59). With regard to life stories, Linde (1993: 61) contends that in American culture interviews are an appropriate means of data collection because the life story "as a major means of self-presentation, occurs naturally in a wide variety of contexts (including interviews) and is thus quite robust." Similarly, I would maintain that the other examples from my own research presented later in this paper are comparable to accounts of illness told in other settings. Linde (1987: 345, emphasis in original;

see also Connerton 1989: 18–19), however, in a discussion of the life history approach within anthropology, raises the following caution:

> The life story in anthropology is usually presented as a form of autobiography of someone in another culture, a presentation of his or her experience and sense of self that is the collaborative product of the subject and the anthropologist. The major difference is that the presentation of self in this form may not be at all a natural discourse form for the subject; indeed, the whole notion of *self* present in the subject's culture may be quite different from that of the anthropologist.

To support this appraisal, Linde (1993: 47–48) reviews in some detail a paper by Rosaldo (1976) presenting the life story of Tukbaw, an Ilongot man. Tukbaw did not spontaneously offer "a deep and intricate life story":

> Rather, Tukbaw's account focused on his public self and public actions, but hardly touched on what Rosaldo considered a necessary description of his private self. To obtain such material, Rosaldo found himself eliciting narratives that his informant never would have produced on his own. Life story narratives were not familiar discourse types in his informant's culture. Narratives were familiar; so stories of hunting expeditions, raids, and fishing trips were easy to elicit. But narratives about the self – particularly what we would call intimate or revealing narratives – were simply not known. (Linde 1993: 47–48)

Rosaldo (1976: 122) describes the elicitation of Tukbaw's life history as "an exploration of a little known cultural domain."

While Rosaldo began with the assumption that "the life history is a natural and universal narrative form" (Rosaldo 1976: 145), an assumption he considered to be shared by most anthropologists working with life histories, he came to realize that the "narrative was profoundly shaped by the situation: the questions I asked, Tukbaw's intentions, our very relationship" (Rosaldo 1976: 146). Peacock and Holland (1993: 376) suggest that while anthropologists should acknowledge "the significance of the relationship between the researcher and the researched for the research," care must be taken not to overemphasize the influence of the ethnographer to the exclusion of other forces contributing to the narration.

6 Although not directly concerned with the process of remembering, papers by Cain (1991), Garro (1994) and Mathews, Lannin, and Mitchell (1994) do touch on memory in relation to narrative construction.

7 Based on their review, Peacock and Holland (1993: 374) conclude that: "life stories are likely important in self-formation and self-expression, though not perhaps in all cultures" (see Linde 1993: 220 for a somewhat different assessment). Although psychologists have typically concentrated on the cognitive mechanisms involved in recollecting the events of our lives, some psychologists have related work on autobiographical memory to the individual construction of a concept of self. Bruner and Feldman (1996: 292) posit a reflexive "self schema" which unlike other interpretive schemas is not a "self-contained procedure for interpreting text, but is itself constituted by those acts of interpretation." Others who relate autobiographical memory to personal identity are less cognitively oriented. A representative statement comes from Fitzgerald (1996: 369; see also Barclay 1996: 95) who states that "an essential part of identity

formation is the development of a self-narrative that consists of a collection of stories and their themes that brings [*sic*] an understandable order to the course of a person's life." Within the psychological literature, there is some explicit recognition that this may represent a culturally specific practice as well as being based on a particular cultural construction of the self. Fitzgerald (1996: 370) notes that members of contemporary Western cultures rely extensively on "narrative thinking as a means of knowing the self and others" (see also Singer and Salovey 1993).

8 Shore (1996) provides a thought-provoking analysis of the psychic unity "muddle" and its contribution to the schism between the study of mind and the study of culture. Approaching this issue from a different angle, Strauss and Quinn (1994: 295–6) contend that the rift between the study of mind and the study of culture has stymied the development of culture theory and conclude: "It is time to say that culture is both public and private, both in the world and in people's minds . . . [so] we can better account for what we have learned about culture so far and begin to develop a deeper understanding of the problems that still elude us."

9 Pointing to these three processes is not intended to exclude others; the list proposed is not seen as exhaustive, but simply the focus of this paper. Peacock and Holland's (1993) review is suggestive of other possibilities (see also Connerton 1989, Middleton and Edwards 1990a, Teski and Climo 1995). In addition, other psychological writings on remembering contain an individual differences component. For example, Bartlett (1932), whose theoretical perspective is reviewed in the next section, linked cognitive process with social and cultural influences. However, he also considered "temperament" and "character" to be significant factors contributing to what an individual remembers, giving memory its "characteristically *personal* flavor" (Bartlett 1932: 10, 213, emphasis in original; it is interesting to note that he also situated these factors in relation to cultural context, see p. 256). The authors of a recent book examining the relationship between memory, emotion, and personality, are particularly interested in what they call self-defining memories: "the memories that matter most to us and the role of these memories in identity and personality" (Singer and Salovey 1993: 9).

10 Shore's recent book, *Culture in Mind* (1996), came to my attention as I was completing the first draft of this chapter. Although this shared focus is unacknowledged by Shore (see citations to Bartlett on pages 45 and 326), central to both Bartlett's and Shore's theoretical perspective is the "vital human capacity" to make meaning out of experience (Shore 1996: 319). Shore's views on memory and preexisting models as essential to the process of "meaning construction" (Shore 1996, see especially chapter 13) correspond in broad outline with some aspects of Bartlett's position. Shore characterizes meaning construction as "the apprehension of novel experience as a kind of memory, through the active mapping of new experiences onto ready-made models" (1996: 339). Like Bartlett, Shore does not isolate memory from other cognitive processes, although, unlike Bartlett, Shore provides little elaboration about affective aspects of remembering specifically in relation to meaning construction. On the other hand, Shore's discussion of the contribution of culture to meaning construction is far better developed and more intricate than Bartlett's. For Shore, "culture is usefully conceived as a collection of models of great diversity" (p.

312) and this perspective opens onto an understanding of the "role of cultural forms in the creation of meaning" (1996: 316). However, Shore (1996: 46) also states that not all models are culturally mediated: "The human ability to create mental models as ways of dealing with reality has two distinct dimensions: personal and cultural." The argument I develop in this paper, building on the insights of Bartlett and others, addresses comparable concerns and provides a venue for exploring how the personal and the cultural are intrinsic to remembering one's past.

11 Writing about rationalisation, Bartlett commented it "is only partially – it might be said less only lazily – an intellectual process. . . . The end state is primarily affective" (p. 85).

12 This discussion provides a bridge for Bartlett to comment on the intimate relationship between remembering and the constructive nature of imagination and thinking (pp. 312–313).

13 The phrase "thought-feeling" comes from Wikan (e.g., Wikan 1989).

14 Omitted from my synopsis is a problematic section where Bartlett posits a distinct "low level" type of recall characterized by a temporally ordered rote recapitulation of events which he associates with "primitive" social organization (1932: 264–267).

15 Although one would expect that Bartlett would be sympathetic to other scholars interested in how memories relate to what is learned through social interactions, he seems to have misunderstood the work of Halbwachs (1980). Halbwachs, a student of Durkheim and contemporary of Bartlett, advanced the nonintuitive claim that purely individual memory did not exist as even "our most personal feelings and thoughts originate in definite social milieus and circumstances" (1980: 33). The apparent diversity of individual memories arises from a "combination of influences that are social in nature" (1980: 48). Although by the term "collective memory" Halbwachs was not proposing a superordinate "group memory," Bartlett (1932: 294–298) seems to have interpreted Halbwachs' work as a rather speculative and unsubstantiated commentary on the "literal memory *of* the group" (p. 298, emphasis in original). Although space does not permit, it is possible to point to numerous links between Halbwachs' highly original perspective and contemporary work, reviewed in the following section, exploring the cultural and social embedding of autobiographical memory.

16 For a cogent survey of theories about types of autobiographical knowledge see Brewer (1996). For reflections on the structural organization of autobiographical memory see Barsalou (1988), Conway (1996), Neisser (1988b), Reiser, Black, and Kalamarides (1986).

17 The relationship between the vividness and accuracy has been relatively well-studied in what are known as "flashbulb" memories. The original article on this topic defined flashbulb memories as "memories for the circumstances in which one first learned of a very surprising and consequential (or emotionally arousing) event" such as hearing about the shooting of President Kennedy (Brown and Kulik 1977: 73). Memories associated with hearing important public news are often vivid and richly detailed. Yet, as Winograd and Neisser (1992: viii, emphasis in original) note in a preface summarizing the general findings of a conference, such classical examples of flashbulb memories "may very well be *less* reliable than other kinds of emotional memories."

18 To quote Bartlett: "remembering is thus only one special form of the general problem of meaning, and occurs when the setting of a particular group of stimuli is treated and described as belonging to the past life of the remembering subject" (1932: 237).

19 Cole (1991: 412–413; see also Cole and Engeström 1993) provides an insightful example of the implicit use of culturally shared understandings to bring the past into present which contrasts with the more explicit examples of individuals revisiting their past examined in this paper. Cole reviews a study based on transcripts of comments made by parents upon first seeing their newborn child and discovering the child's sex: "using . . . information derived from their cultural past and assuming implicitly that there will be cultural stability, the parents projected a probable cultural future for the child: she will be sought after by boys, causing her father anxiety or she will not participate in a form of activity (rugby) requiring strength and agility that is the special preserve of boys." Cole concludes that: "only a culture-using human being can reach into the cultural past, project it into the future, and then carry that (purely conceptual) future into the present in the shape of beliefs that then materially constrain and organize the present sociocultural environment of the newcomer."

20 Commenting on this neglect, Larsen (1988: 330), a psychologist, suggests it reflects a guiding assumption of empiricism, seemingly embraced by contemporary cognitive psychology, that "all knowledge is acquired by immediate sensation." He continues:

> Only in more recent Continental philosophy (Marxism and French philosophy, e.g., Halbwachs, 1925) was another alternative developed – namely that knowledge may have a social origin, that it may be acquired from other people and social institutions. Mainstream cognitive psychology still seems peculiarly unaware of this possibility, in respect to exploring its theoretical implications as well as in choosing objects of research.

A notable exception to this general trend, as discussed later, are studies based on observations of parents and children reminiscing about the past.

21 The inclusion of a chapter by Belli and Loftus in Rubin's 1996 edited volume contrasts with his 1986 edited volume, where he lists the work on eyewitness testimony as one of the "paths not taken" (p. 8) in inviting chapter contributors.

22 Another quote from Bartlett (1932: 96) is germane for it shows he appreciated the difference between recall in psychological experiments, no matter how closely the material approximates that of everyday life, and remembering in everyday life:

> Definitely to ask a person for a representation is to depart from everyday conditions. The actions and reproductions of daily life come largely by the way, and are incidental to our main preoccupations. We discuss with other people what we have seen, in order that we may value or criticise, or compare our impressions with theirs. There is ordinarily no directed and laborious effort to secure accuracy. We mingle interpretation with description, interpolate things not originally present, transform without effort and without knowledge.

23 Fivush, Haden, and Reese (1996: 354–357) provide a cogent overview of three alternative conceptualizations of the relationship between language and

memory. On the basis of their research, they advance a strong claim about the relationship between learning culturally appropriate narrative forms and the organization of experience: "as children come to recount their past experiences to others in more narratively coherent ways, they also begin to represent their past experiences to themselves in more narratively coherent ways. In this way language becomes the medium both of recounting and of representing the past. Language is not a simple overlay on memory; language and memory are inextricably intertwined in experiencing, remembering and recounting events" (p. 344; see also Nelson 1993). According to Schank (1990: 138) narrating past events affects the memory representation profoundly: "memory tends to lose the original and keep the copy. The original events recede, and the new story takes its place."

24 As suggested earlier, Bartlett's somewhat sketchy theoretical statements about consciousness and the constructive human ability to "turn round" on its own schemas, as well as his views concerning the inseparability of remembering from other cognitive activities, are compatible with such reflexive and generative qualities.

25 Theoretical perspectives about socially distributed and situated cognition are relevant here. My use of culturally available knowledge (which is broader than and incorporates generally shared cultural knowledge) is intended to recognize intracultural variation (including idiosyncratic understandings) and the "social organization of diversity" (Wegner 1987: 206; cf. Schwartz 1978).

26 As suggested by the review of the psychological literature, anomalous and novel events deviating from schema-based expectations may be individually remembered. In a study carried out with support group members (Garro 1994), narratives of the past provided a vehicle for confronting contradictions between an individual's experience and expectations based on shared cultural models. In the examples involving interactions with animals, I have suggested that these events are more likely to be remembered because they fit cultural schemas and are seen as having the potential to lead to misfortune. Common to both of these is Schank's (1990: 12) observation that stories are told for "especially interesting prior experiences, ones that we learn from."

27 This recollection was prompted by a question that I asked: "Could *ondjine* occur because someone helped an animal?" In a visit to another household, I had just learned of an injury attributed to helping a suffering animal. This was surprising, as in all previous instances I had heard about, causing harm was central. In a separate conversation, another woman explained why seemingly helpful behavior was improper: "You're not supposed to feel sorry for an animal and you're not supposed to pity it."

28 Ceasing to help with the calves was mentioned a couple of times by Mrs. Fredette and brings to mind a parallel with the work of Price (1987). Many of the naturally occurring accounts of illness she recorded in Ecuador conveyed the implicit message that the caretaker, who was often the teller and the mother of an ill child, "did the right thing." Accounts of the past may be shaped to accomplish diverse communicative goals, including to convince the listener of the essential merit of the teller's point of view or to justify a moral position.

29 As in the cases involving Arthur Roland and Jemina Fredette, there is often, though not always, a homology between the past transgression and the ensuing affliction. For Mrs. Fredette, this is why, out of a number of possible explanations, bottle feeding the calves almost immediately became the most likely explanation upon seeing what was wrong with her infant. Thus, how misfortune manifests itself also guides remembering along certain lines.

30 This quote is considerably shortened from the original with significant deletions indicated by ellipses. Sections that have been taken out require additional contextual information and are not relevant to present purposes.

31 For other illness conditions, there may be a more marked tendency to construct accounts along specific explanatory frameworks. For example, a condition known as "twisted mouth" is almost always interpreted as indicating the involvement of "bad medicine" and the intent of one individual to harm another covertly through supernatural means. Even in this instance, however, it is possible for individuals to construct an account using an alternative framework (e.g., one person blamed a physical accident for a case of "twisted mouth" and sought the help of a physician, despite his family's assessment that it was due to "bad medicine"). In the high blood pressure interviews, although much less common, there were a couple of instances where individuals used explanatory frameworks which are generally not considered relevant to high blood pressure but which made sense to these individuals in terms of their personal experiences, while still being plausible in terms of culturally available frameworks for understanding illness experience (this refers to the distinction made in an earlier footnote differentiating between culturally shared and culturally available knowledge). While culturally shared models may predispose toward certain explanations, they are not deterministic. For example, one woman incorporated a past blood transfusion in her account of high blood pressure. Since she had heard on a television program that AIDS could come about because of a blood transfusion, the timing of onset for her high blood pressure seemed best to fit this interpretation of past events.

32 Mr. Hamilton also shared these understandings. In the course of the interview he related specific occasions of rising blood pressure to other commonly used explanatory frameworks (e.g., stress and alcohol). This more inclusive framework has also figured in actions taken in response to high blood pressure.

REFERENCES

Agar, Michael 1980 Stories, Background, Knowledge and Themes: Problems in the Analysis of Life History Narratives. *American Ethnologist* 7: 223–235.

Alba, Joseph W. and Lynn Hasher 1983 Is Memory Schematic? *Psychological Bulletin* 93: 203–231.

Antze, Paul and Michael Lambek, eds. 1996 *Tense Past: Cultural Essays on Trauma and Memory.* New York: Routledge.

Baddeley, Alan D. 1989 Finding the Bloody Horse. In *Everyday Cognition in Adulthood and Late Life*, L. W. Poon, D. C. Rubin, and B. A. Wilson, eds. Cambridge: Cambridge University Press. Pp. 104–115.

1992 What is Autobiographical Memory? In *Theoretical Perspectives on*

Autobiographical Memory, M. A. Conway, D. C. Rubin, H. Spinnler, and W. A. Wagenaar, eds. Dordrecht, Holland: Kluwer Academic Publishers. Pp. 13–29.

1993 Holy War or Wholly Unnecessary? Some Thoughts on the "Conflict" Between Laboratory Studies and Everyday Memory. In *Memory in Everyday Life*, G. M. Davies and R. H. Logie, eds. Amsterdam: North Holland. Pp. 532–536.

Banaji, Mahzarin R. and Robert Crowder 1989 The Bankruptcy of Everyday Memory. *American Psychologist* 44: 1185–1193.

Barclay, Craig R. 1993 Remembering Ourselves (with commentaries by S. Larsen, J. Robinson and rejoinder by C. Barclay). In *Memory in Everyday Life*, G. M. Davies and R. H. Logie, eds. Amsterdam: North Holland. Pp. 285–323.

1996 Autobiographical Remembering: Narrative Constraints on Objectified Selves. In *Remembering Our Past: Studies in Autobiographical Memory*, D. C. Rubin, ed. Cambridge: Cambridge University Press. Pp. 94–125.

Barsalou, Lawrence W. 1988 The Content and Organization of Autobiographical Memories. In *Remembering Reconsidered: Ecological and Traditional Approaches to the Study of Memory*, U. Neisser and E. Winograd, eds. Cambridge: Cambridge University Press. Pp. 193–243.

Bartlett, Frederic C. 1932 *Remembering: A Study in Experimental and Social Psychology*. Cambridge: Cambridge University Press.

Battaglia, Debbora 1992 The Body in the Gift: Memory and Forgetting in Sabarl Mortuary Exchange. *American Ethnologist* 19: 3–18.

Belli, Robert F. and Elizabeth F. Loftus 1996 The Pliability of Autobiographical Memory: Misinformation and the False Memory Problem. In *Remembering Our Past: Studies in Autobiographical Memory*, D. C. Rubin, ed. Cambridge: Cambridge University Press. Pp. 157–179.

Bourguignon, Erika 1996 Vienna and Memory: Anthropology and Experience. *Ethos* 24: 374–387.

Brewer, William F. 1986 What is Autobiographical Memory? In *Autobiographical Memory*, D. C. Rubin, ed. Cambridge: Cambridge University Press. Pp. 25–49.

1988 Memory for Randomly Sampled Autobiographical Events. In *Remembering Reconsidered: Ecological and Traditional Approaches to the Study of Memory*, U. Neisser and E. Winograd, eds. Cambridge: Cambridge University Press. Pp. 21–90.

1996 What is Recollective Memory? In *Remembering Our Past: Studies in Autobiographical Memory*, D. C. Rubin, ed. Cambridge: Cambridge University Press. Pp. 19–66.

Brewer, William F. and Glenn V. Nakamura 1984 The Nature and Functions of Schemas. In *Handbook of Social Cognition:* vol. I, R. S. Wyer, Jr., T. S. Srull, eds. Hillsdale, NJ: Lawrence Erlbaum, Pp. 119–160.

Brown, Roger and James Kulik 1977 Flashbulb Memories. *Cognition*. 1977: 73–99.

Bruce, Darryl 1989 Functional Explanations of Memory. In *Everyday Cognition in Adulthood and Late Life*, L. W. Poon, D. C. Rubin, and B. A. Wilson, eds. Cambridge: Cambridge University Press, Pp. 44–58.

Bruner, Jerome 1990 *Acts of Meaning*. Cambridge, MA: Harvard University Press.

Bruner, Jerome and Carol Fleisher Feldman 1996 Group Narrative as a Cultural Context of Autobiography. In *Remembering Our Past: Studies in*

Autobiographical Memory, D. C. Rubin, ed. Cambridge: Cambridge University Press. Pp. 291–317.

Cain, Carole 1991 Personal Stories: Identity Acquisition and Self-Understanding in Alcoholics Anonymous. *Ethos* 19: 210–253.

Christianson, Sven-Åke and Martin A. Safer 1996 Emotional Events and Emotions in Autobiographical Memories. In *Remembering Our Past: Studies in Autobiographical Memory*, D. C. Rubin, ed. Cambridge: Cambridge University Press. Pp. 218–243.

Cohen, Gillian 1989 *Memory in the Real World*. Hove, UK: Lawrence Erlbaum.

Cole, Michael 1991 Conclusion. In *Perspectives on Socially Shared Cognition*, L. B. Resnick, J. M. Levine, and S. D. Teasley, eds. Washington, DC: American Psychological Association. Pp. 398–417.

Cole, Michael and Yrjö Engeström 1993 A Cultural-Historical Approach to Distributed Cognition. In *Distributed Cognitions: Psychological and Educational Considerations*, G. Salomon, ed. Cambridge: Cambridge University Press. Pp. 1–46.

Connerton, Paul 1989 *How Societies Remember*. Cambridge: Cambridge University Press.

Conway, Martin A. 1993 Method and Meaning in Memory Research. In *Memory in Everyday Life*, G. M. Davies and R. H. Logie, eds. Amsterdam: North Holland. Pp. 499–524.

1996 Autobiographical Memory and Autobiographical Knowledge. In *Remembering Our Past: Studies in Autobiographical Memory*, D. C. Rubin, ed. Cambridge: Cambridge University Press. Pp. 67–93.

Conway, Martin A., David C. Rubin, Hans Spinnler, and Willem A. Wagenaar, eds. 1992 *Theoretical Perspectives on Autobiographical Memory*. Dordrecht, Holland: Kluwer Academic Publishers.

Crowder, Robert G. 1993 Commentary: Faith and Skepticism in Memory Research. In *Memory in Everyday Life*, G. M. Davies and R. H. Logie, eds. Amsterdam: North Holland. Pp. 525–531.

D'Andrade, Roy G. 1981 The Cultural Part of Cognition. *Cognitive Science* 5: 179–195.

1995 *The Development of Cognitive Anthropology*. Cambridge: Cambridge University Press.

Davies, Graham M. and Robert H. Logie, eds. 1993 *Memory in Everyday Life*. Amsterdam, Netherlands: North Holland.

Douglas, Mary 1986 *How Institutions Think*. Syracuse, NY: Syracuse University Press.

Ebbinghaus, Hermann 1964 *Memory: A Contribution to Experimental Psychology*. trans. H. A. Ruger and C. E. Bussenius. New York: Dover (originally published 1885 as *Über das Gedächtnis*, Leipzig: Duncker and Humblot).

Edwards, Derek and David Middleton 1988 Conversational Remembering and Family Relationships: How Children Learn to Remember. *Journal of Social and Personal Relationships* 5: 3–25.

Edwards, Derek, Jonathan Potter, and David Middleton 1992 Toward a Discursive Psychology of Remembering. *The Psychologist* 5: 441–446.

Fitzgerald, Joseph M. 1988 Vivid Memories and the Reminiscence Phenomenon: The Role of a Self Narrative. *Human Development* 31: 261–273.

1996 Intersecting Meanings of Reminiscence in Adult Development and Aging. In *Remembering Our Past: Studies in Autobiographical Memory*, D. C. Rubin, ed. Cambridge: Cambridge University Press. Pp. 360–383.

Fivush, Robyn, Catherine Haden, and Elaine Reese 1996 Remembering, Recounting, and Reminiscing: The Development of Autobiographical Memory in Social Context. In *Remembering Our Past: Studies in Autobiographical Memory*, D. C. Rubin, ed. Cambridge: Cambridge University Press. Pp. 341–359.

Gardner, Howard 1985 *The Mind's New Science: A History of the Cognitive Revolution*. New York: Basic Books.

Garro, Linda C. 1988 Explaining High Blood Pressure: Variation in Knowledge about Illness. *American Ethnologist* 15: 98–119.

1990 Continuity and Change: The Interpretation of Illness in an Anishinaabe (Ojibway) Community. *Culture, Medicine and Psychiatry* 14: 417–454.

1994 Narrative Representations of Chronic Illness Experience: Cultural Models of Illness, Mind and Body in Stories Concerning the Temporomandibular Joint (TMJ). *Social Science and Medicine* 38: 775–788.

Garro, Linda C. and Cheryl Mattingly 2000 Narrative as Construct and as Construction. In *Narrative and the Cultural Construction of Illness and Healing*, C. Mattingly and L. C. Garro, eds. Berkeley, CA: University of California Press. Pp. 1–49.

Gee, James Paul 1992 *The Social Mind: Language, Ideology, and Social Practice*. New York: Bergin and Garvey.

Goodenough, Ward H. 1957 Cultural Anthropology and Linguistics. In *Report of the Seventh Annual Round Table Meeting in Linguistics and Language Study*, P. Garvin, ed. *Monograph Series on Language and Linguistics*, No. 9. Washington, DC: Georgetown University. Pp. 167–173.

Halbwachs, Maurice 1925 *Les Cadres Sociaux de la Mémoire*, Paris: F. Alcan.

1980 *The Collective Memory*. trans. Francis J. Ditter, Jr. and Vida Y. Ditter. New York: Harper and Row.

Hirst, William and David Manier 1995 Opening Vistas for Cognitive Psychology. In *Sociocultural Psychology: Theory and Practice of Doing and Knowing*, L. M. W. Martin, K. Nelson, and E. Tobach, eds. Cambridge: Cambridge University Press. Pp. 89–124.

1996 Remembering as Communication: A Family Recounts Its Past. In *Remembering Our Past: Studies in Autobiographical Memory*, D. C. Rubin, ed. Cambridge: Cambridge University Press. Pp. 271–290.

Hutchins, Edwin 1995 *Cognition in the Wild*. Cambridge, MA: MIT Press.

Kotre, John 1995 *White Gloves: How We Create Ourselves Through Memory*. New York: The Free Press.

Landauer, Thomas K. 1989 Some Bad and Good Reasons for Studying Memory and Cognition in the Wild. In *Everyday Cognition in Adulthood and Late Life*, L. W. Poon, D. C. Rubin, and B. A. Wilson, eds. Cambridge: Cambridge University Press. Pp. 116–125.

Larsen, Steen F. 1988 Remembering Without Experiencing: Memory for Reported Events. In *Remembering Reconsidered: Ecological and Traditional Approaches to the Study of Memory*, U. Neisser and E. Winograd, eds. Cambridge: Cambridge University Press. Pp. 326–355.

Lave, Jean and Etienne Wenger 1991 *Situated Learning: Legitimate Peripheral Participation.* Cambridge: Cambridge University Press.

Linde, Charlotte 1987 Explanatory Systems in Oral Life Stories. In *Cultural Models in Language and Thought,* D. Holland and N. Quinn, eds. Cambridge: Cambridge University Press. Pp. 343–366.

1993 *Life Stories: The Creation of Coherence.* New York: Oxford University Press.

Linton, Marigold 1975 Memory for Real-World Events. In *Explorations in Cognition,* D. A. Norman, D. E. Rumelhart, and the LNR Research Group. San Francisco, CA: W. H. Freeman and Co. Pp. 376–404.

1986 Ways of Searching and the Contents of Memory. In *Autobiographical Memory,* D. C. Rubin, ed. Cambridge: Cambridge University Press. Pp. 50–67.

Loftus, Elizabeth F. 1993 The Reality of Repressed Memories. *American Psychologist* 48: 518–537.

Mankowski, Eric and Julian Rappaport 1995 Stories, Identity, and the Psychological Sense of Community. In *Knowledge and Memory: The Real Story,* R. S. Wyer, Jr., ed. *Advances in Social Cognition,* vol. VIII. Hillsdale, NJ: Lawrence Erlbaum. Pp. 211–226.

Mathews, Holly F., Donald R. Lannin, and James C. Mitchell 1994 Coming to Terms with Advanced Breast Cancer: Black Women's Narratives from Eastern North Carolina. *Social Science and Medicine* 38: 789–800.

Mattingly, Cheryl and Linda C. Garro 1994 Introduction. In *Narrative Representations of Illness and Healing.* L. C. Garro and C. Mattingly, guest eds. *Social Science and Medicine* 38: 771–774.

Middleton, David and Derek Edwards 1990a Introduction. In *Collective Remembering,* D. Middleton and D. Edwards, eds. London: Sage. Pp. 1–22.

1990b Conversational Remembering: A Social Psychological Approach. In *Collective Remembering,* D. Middleton and D. Edwards, eds. London: Sage. Pp. 23–45.

Miller, Peggy J. 1995 Personal Storytelling in Everyday Life: Social and Cultural Perspectives. In *Knowledge and Memory: The Real Story,* R. S. Wyer, Jr., ed. *Advances in Social Cognition,* vol. VIII. Hillsdale, NJ: Lawrence Erlbaum. Pp. 177–184.

Miller, Peggy J., Heidi Fung, and Judith Mintz 1996 Self-Construction Through Narrative Practices: A Chinese and American Comparison of Early Socialization. *Ethos* 24: 237–280.

Mullen, Mary K. 1994 Earliest Recollections of Childhood: A Demographic Analysis. *Cognition* 52: 55–79.

Neisser, Ulric 1978 Memory: What are the Important Questions? In *Practical Aspects of Memory,* M. M. Gruneberg, P. E. Morris, and R. N. Sykes, eds. London: Academic Press. Pp. 3–24.

1981 John Dean's Memory: A Case Study. *Cognition* 9: 1–22.

1988a Time Present and Time Past. In *Practical Aspects of Memory: Current Research and Issues,* vol. II: *Clinical and Educational Implications,* M. M. Gruneberg, P. E. Morris, and R. N. Sykes, eds. Chichester, England: John Wiley and Sons. Pp. 545–560.

1988b What is Ordinary Memory the Memory of? In *Remembering Reconsidered: Ecological and Traditional Approaches to the Study of Memory,*

U. Neisser and E. Winograd, eds. Cambridge: Cambridge University Press. Pp. 356–373.

Neisser, Ulric and Robyn Fivush, eds. 1994 *The Remembering Self: Construction and Accuracy in the Self-Narrative*. Cambridge: Cambridge University Press.

Nelson, Katherine 1989 Remembering: A Functional Developmental Perspective. In *Memory: Interdisciplinary Approaches*, P. R. Solomon, G. R. Goethals, C. M. Kelley, and B. R. Stephens, eds. New York: Springer-Verlag. Pp. 127–150.

    1993 The Psychological and Social Origins of Autobiographical Memory. *Psychological Science* 4: 7–14.

    1995 Stories in Memory: Developmental Issues. In *Knowledge and Memory: The Real Story*, R. S. Wyer, Jr., ed. *Advances in Social Cognition*, vol. VIII. Hillsdale, NJ: Lawrence Erlbaum, Pp. 185–191.

Peacock, James L. and Dorothy C. Holland 1993 The Narrated Self: Life Stories in Process. *Ethos* 21: 367–383.

Pillemer, David B. 1992 Remembering Personal Circumstances: A Functional Analysis. In *Affect and Accuracy in Recall: Studies of "Flashbulb" Memories*, E. Winograd and U. Neisser, eds. Cambridge: Cambridge University Press. Pp. 236–264.

Pillemer, David B., Martha L. Picariello, Anneliesa Beebe Law, and Jill S. Reichman 1996 Memories of College: The Importance of Specific Educational Episodes. In *Remembering Our Past: Studies in Autobiographical Memory*, D. C. Rubin, ed. Cambridge: Cambridge University Press. Pp. 318–337.

Poon, Leonard W., David C. Rubin, and Barbara A. Wilson, eds. 1989 *Everyday Cognition in Adulthood and Late Life*. Cambridge: Cambridge University Press.

Price, Laurie 1987 Ecuadorian Illness Stories: Cultural Knowledge in Natural Discourse. In *Cultural Models in Language and Thought*, D. Holland and N. Quinn, eds. Cambridge: Cambridge University Press. Pp. 313–342.

Quinn, Naomi and Dorothy Holland 1987 Culture and Cognition. In *Cultural Models in Language and Thought*, D. Holland and N. Quinn, eds. Cambridge: Cambridge University Press. Pp. 3–40.

Reiser, Brian J., John B. Black, and Peter Kalamarides 1986 Strategic Memory Search Processes. In *Autobiographical Memory*, D. C. Rubin, ed. Cambridge: Cambridge University Press. Pp. 100–121.

Resnick, Lauren B., John M. Levine, and Stephanie D. Teasley, eds. 1991 *Perspectives on Socially Shared Cognition*. Washington, DC: American Psychological Association.

Rice, G. Elizabeth 1980 On Cultural Schemata. *American Ethnologist* 7: 152–171.

Robinson, John A. 1986 Autobiographical Memory: A Historical Prologue. In *Autobiographical Memory*, D. C. Rubin, ed. Cambridge: Cambridge University Press. Pp. 19–24.

    1992 First Experience Memories: Contexts and Functions in Personal Histories. In *Theoretical Perspectives on Autobiographical Memory*, M. A. Conway, D. C. Rubin, H. Spinnler, and W. A. Wagenaar, eds. Dordrecht, Holland: Kluwer Academic Publishers. Pp. 223–239.

    1996 Perspective, Meaning, and Remembering. In *Remembering Our Past: Studies in Autobiographical Memory*, D. C. Rubin, ed. Cambridge: Cambridge University Press. Pp. 199–217.

Rosaldo, Renato 1976 The Story of Tukbaw: "They Listen as He Orates." In *The Biographical Process: Studies in the History and Psychology of Religion*, F. E. Reynolds and D. Capps, eds. The Hague: Mouton. Pp. 121–151.

Rubin, David C. 1986 Introduction. In *Autobiographical Memory*, D. C. Rubin, ed. Cambridge: Cambridge University Press. Pp. 3–16.

1996 Introduction. In *Remembering Our Past: Studies in Autobiographical Memory*, D. C. Rubin, ed., Cambridge: Cambridge University Press. Pp. 1–15.

Rubin, David C., ed. 1986 *Autobiographical Memory*. Cambridge: Cambridge University Press.

1996 *Remembering Our Past: Studies in Autobiographical Memory*. Cambridge: Cambridge University Press.

Rubin, David C. and Marc Kozin 1984 Vivid Memories. *Cognition* 16: 81–95.

Salomon, Gavriel, ed. 1993 *Distributed Cognitions: Psychological and Educational Considerations*. Cambridge: Cambridge University Press.

Schank, Roger C. 1990 *Tell Me a Story: A New Look at Real and Artificial Memory*. New York: Charles Scribner's Sons.

Schank, Roger C. and Robert P. Abelson 1995 Knowledge and Memory: The Real Story. In *Knowledge and Memory: The Real Story*, R. S. Wyer, Jr., ed. *Advances in Social Cognition*, vol. VIII. Hillsdale, NJ: Lawrence Erlbaum. Pp. 1–95.

Schwartz, Theodore 1978 Where is the Culture? Personality as the Distributive Locus of Culture. In *The Making of Psychological Anthropology*, G. D. Spindler, ed. Berkeley, CA: University of California Press. Pp. 419–441.

Shore, Bradd 1996 *Culture in Mind: Cognition, Culture, and the Problem of Meaning*. New York: Oxford University Press.

Shotter, John 1990 The Social Construction of Remembering and Forgetting. In *Collective Remembering*, D. Middleton and D. Edwards, eds. London: Sage. Pp. 120–138.

Singer, Jefferson A. and Peter Salovey 1993 *The Remembered Self: Emotion and Memory in Personality*. New York: The Free Press.

Steffensen, Margaret and Larry Colker 1982 Intercultural Misunderstandings about Health Care: Recall of Descriptions of Illness and Treatment. *Social Science and Medicine* 16: 1949–1954.

Strauss, Claudia 1992 Models and Motivations. In *Human Motives and Cultural Models*, R. G. D'Andrade and C. Strauss, eds. Cambridge: Cambridge University Press. Pp. 1–20.

Strauss, Claudia and Naomi Quinn 1994 A Cognitive/Cultural Anthropology. In *Assessing Cultural Anthropology*. R. Borofsky, ed. New York: McGraw-Hill. Pp. 284–300.

Teski, Marea C. 1995 The Remembering Consciousness of a Polish Exile Government. In *The Labyrinth of Memory: Ethnographic Journeys*, M. C. Teski and J. J. Climo, eds. Westport, CT: Bergin and Garvey. Pp. 49–58.

Teski, Marea C. and Jacob J. Climo, eds. 1995 *The Labyrinth of Memory: Ethnographic Journeys*. Westport, CT: Bergin and Garvey.

Tulving, Endel 1983 *Elements of Episodic Memory*. Oxford: Oxford University Press.

Wagenaar, Willem A. 1986 My Memory: A Study of Autobiographical Memory Over Six Years. *Cognitive Psychology* 18: 225–252.

Wegner, Daniel M. 1987 Transactive Memory: A Contemporary Analysis of the Group Mind. In *Theories of Group Behavior*, B. Mullen and G. Goethals, eds. New York: Springer-Verlag. Pp. 185–208.

Wikan, Unni 1989 Managing the Heart to Brighten Face and Soul: Emotions in Balinese Morality and Health Care. *American Ethnologist* 16: 294–312.

Winograd, Eugene 1988 Continuities Between Ecological and Laboratory Approaches to Memory. In *Remembering Reconsidered: Ecological and Traditional Approaches to the Study of Memory*, U. Neisser and E. Winograd, eds. Cambridge: Cambridge University Press. Pp. 11–20.

Winograd, Eugene and Ulric Neisser, eds. 1992 *Affect and Accuracy in Recall: Studies of "Flashbulb" Memories*. Cambridge: Cambridge University Press.

Part III

Continuity and change in cultural experience

6   The psychology of consensus in a Papua New Guinea Christian revival movement

Stephen C. Leavitt

During the first several months of 1984, the Bumbita Arapesh of the East Sepik Province of Papua New Guinea underwent a Christian "revival" unprecedented locally in its breadth and intensity. Expectations centered overtly on the Second Coming of Jesus which many thought would occur before the end of the year. More covertly, people hoped for such things as a reunion with the dead, the acquisition of wealth on the order of that of the Europeans, the transformation of black skin into white skin, and the eradication of all social conflict. Enthusiasm for the revival reached such a point that by the time I arrived in late August of that year, church services lasting for several hours occurred nightly in all Bumbita villages, and community school teachers complained that their pupils were not attending school for fear that when they returned home one day their parents would have abandoned them and gone to heaven. The revivalists directed their attention toward converting as many as possible, compelling people to confess their sins, trying to eradicate all adherence to traditional customs, and ferreting out hidden sorcery implements with the aid of the Holy Spirit. With these activities came rumors of miraculous events such as the return to life of the recently dead and the discovery of bags of rice and cartons of tinned fish in empty houses. But the single most significant act of the revival was the public revelation of men's cult secrets and artifacts to the women and uninitiated. In the people's minds, the revelation of the secrets severed all hopes of reviving the men's cult; for them, it was an act of sobering finality.

The 1984 Christian revival in Bumbita was a social movement of significant scope. In Bumbita village, less than 10 percent of the adults were Christian prior to 1984; at the height of the revival that number had climbed to nearly 75 percent. Church activities took up several hours of each day. Bible studies classes formed. Mass baptisms occurred regularly. Yet for all its dramatic early success, the revival of 1984 is probably most memorable for its just-as-rapid collapse. By the end of my field stay in 1986, nearly half of the Bumbita converts had already lapsed publicly, and more were soon to follow. In the end, the first-time-ever revelation of men's cult secrets seemed to have little durable effect on the movement as a whole.

The immediate aim of this chapter is to explain the rise and fall of the 1984 revival in terms of the aspirations of the participants as a part of a larger project to understand the personal significance of Bumbita religious conviction (see Leavitt 1995a, 1995b). Scholars working in Melanesia have had a continued interest in the dynamics of religious and social movements, and in Melanesia these movements are in fact well known for their often short lifespans. Whether they be concerned with development, religious revival, or the acquisition of cargo, the movements show a cycle of "over-enthusiastic adoption, trial, crisis and discontinuation" (Allen 1976: 281; see also May 1982). In the case of the 1984 revival in Bumbita, the crisis and discontinuation were likely affected by the fact that Jesus did not appear in November as had been planned by some. But when I asked people about their attitudes toward the movement, it was clear that their real concerns were more over the arguing and infighting that had broken out in the church. They were repelled by the bickering and dropped out as a result. In fact, in their view, the revival's success depended on the community's ability to foster an environment of near unanimous pursuit of its collective goals. It was consensus that would make the revival work, and without it, the revival would fail.

The inspirational potential of collective effort is well known to scholars of social movements, but what makes the Bumbita case unusual is the idea that consensus *itself* had the power to bring about the new age. The revivalist view was that ferreting out sorcery implements and revealing male cult secrets would build a new community where everyone shared their personal convictions and revealed their inner desires. The sheer power of the resulting consensus would then force the arrival of Jesus and propel the community into its new age. Local religious ideology had taken a desired social condition and made it a point of mystical doctrine.

The Melanesian view of the power of consensus is something that several scholars of Melanesian social movements have documented (e.g., Brunton 1989: 174, Ryan 1969: 116, Schwartz 1962: 350, Smith 1994: 60, Stent 1977). Brison (1991) and Smith (1994) in particular have outlined arguments linking social action to a central focus on the power of collective action. Smith argues that Kragur villagers "were struggling to bring about material plenty by harmonizing social relations" (1994: 105). In their view, the key to business success lay in replacing a traditional social system built on reciprocity with a new one built on the collective commercial spirit exemplified by Europeans. In Smith's words, "The contemporary concern with village-wide unity . . . must be understood in light of villagers' perceptions of white unity and cooperation and their own failings in that regard" (1994: 161). Brison, for her part, writes that among the Kwanga, neighbors of the Bumbita, "The idea that dramatic and general improvements in life

could result from short-term, but universal, cooperation and harmony was
. . . apparent in some form or another in virtually all of the programs to
promote social and economic change" (1991: 335). She argues that Kwanga
social initiatives have intense but short life cycles because an initial enthusiasm for potential cooperation inevitably leads some to feel coerced and to
register their objections. These in turn undermine the sense of collective
harmony and encourage people to abandon the project entirely (1991: 326).

I believe that it was this basic social dynamic that fueled and eventually
undermined the revival in Bumbita. This chapter therefore takes Smith's
and Brison's arguments as points of departure. I am interested in describing
just why it is, in the Bumbita view, that consensus must lie at the heart of
any vision of social transformation. To answer this question I define the
concept of consensus in local terms, outlining what was at stake in the drive
for unanimity in the revival. Then I show how achieving consensus was
essential to the new society envisioned by the movement. The key here is
recognizing that the ideological point about the power of consensus had its
roots in a traditional idea of collective potential coupled with a basic desire
for fundamental changes in the conditions of social interaction. Many
Bumbita say that their central moral failing is an inability to get along
together, and that this is caused by a social environment where one's actions
are coerced by others and where no one can be trusted because of hidden
motives. Their argument relies on a well-developed set of local understandings about the nature of self and society.

The Bumbita appeal to consensus as a new condition of social interaction
has implications for recent research on the psychology of social movements
more generally. In recent years, sociological studies of social movements
have shifted from a primary focus on resource mobilization – the pursuit of
political and material goals in the context of the political structure of
society at large – to an approach addressing "the construction of meaning,
consciousness raising, the manipulation of symbols, and collective iden-
tities" expressed in social action (Morris and Mueller 1992: ix). The editors
of one recent volume on social movements describe the trend as an attempt
to develop a "social psychology" that complements resource mobilization
approaches (Morris and Mueller 1992). It is a way to "bring culture back
in" to social movement research (Hart 1996: 87). The idea here is that
"social problems are not objective phenomena"; they are rather always perceived from within a culturally constructed world view (Klandermans 1992:
77). People's motivations have to be understood in terms of their prior views
of self and society. In building a vision for an improved world, social
reformers seek transformations in their most basic sense of their relation to
the community. As William Gamson (1992: 56) puts it, "Participation in
social movements frequently involves an enlargement of personal identity

for participants and offers fulfillment and realization of self." When people mobilize to create a transformed society, they are at the same time using the movement to refashion their sense of who they are. Because a transformed identity is often a goal in its own right, a movement's ability to tap into participants' basic self-definition can contribute significantly to its success (Melucci 1989).

These recent trends in the study of social movements reflect a growing awareness among sociologists of the central role of cultural understandings – and ethnopsychological understandings specifically – that have been for some time a central concern in psychological anthropology. While it is easy to talk in abstract terms about "transformations" in one's basic sense of "personal identity" through involvement in a social movement, it is much more difficult to explain exactly what that means in pragmatic terms. Psychological anthropologists have for some time been preoccupied with the ontological status of cultural concepts of "self" and "person" – to what extent do local cultural views define the range of experience available for the individual? To what extent can such views shape the trajectory of a social movement? I intend the case of the rise and fall of the Bumbita Christian revival as an illustration of how a perspective in psychological anthropology can shed light on these social processes.

From my viewpoint as a psychological anthropologist, one implication is that any study of the dynamics of social movements must contain a well-developed understanding of the problematics behind prior notions of self and community. Much recent work on the cultural construction of self has emphasized distinctive local constructions of self at the expense of a clear view of how these constructions create real problems for real individuals. In Melanesia, for example, researchers have sought to establish the "sociocentric" bases for self-understandings without asking much about what this means for individuals trying to live their lives on a day-to-day basis. The sociocentric self is, for many Bumbita, a severe burden. The revival's goals of achieving material wealth and transforming the conditions of society were grounded in fundamental dissatisfactions over how the self had been defined by their culture. In their particular situation the intoxicating sense of consensus that drove the revival in its early stages became an albatross when inevitable differences surfaced. The movement's distinctive trajectory emerged only because of the distinctive character of Bumbita self-understandings.

Specifically, the argument runs as follows: Bumbita self-schemas set up a tension between a desire for personal autonomy and an overwhelming sense that one is in fact defined by one's relations with others. While one may yearn to act on one's own, without regard for others, the reality is that for each action one must consider a myriad of factors relating to one's relatives and associates. Social conditions like these prevail in face-to-face societies everywhere. However, as the recent sociological research has pointed out, it is the overlay of specific local cultural understandings that gives each case its distinctive shape, and in Melanesia, notions of self and society emphasize the interconnected quality of human action to a striking degree. Consider some common examples: personal interactions are defined by exchange relations, so that even personal slights may be avenged by offering a gift to the offender; deaths are often explained in terms of human agents acting either through sorcery or outright murder; and religion takes its power explicitly from the spiritual efficacy of collective action. In a society so defined, day-to-day living can seem oppressive to individual actors. In a sense, one is continually being invoked by others into acting a certain way. Each individual faces a contradiction – one longs to be free of these social encumbrances while nonetheless maintaining a deep sense that one's social relations define who one is. The idea of consensus thus becomes immensely appealing because it neutralizes the contradiction – everyone, including oneself, is working toward the same goal while at the same time preserving a sense of personal autonomy. Thus, when the Bumbita revival sought to transform the society, there was an underlying promise that with consensus would come a release from the problems imposed by their definitions of who they are. When the prospects for consensus faltered, the movement lost its appeal.

The Bumbita Arapesh

During the time of fieldwork, the some 3000 Bumbita Arapesh occupied territory south of the Sepik highway between Maprik and Dreikikir in the East Sepik Province of Papua New Guinea. They live west of their nearest linguistic cousins, the Ilahita Arapesh (Tuzin 1976, 1980). Their language is Papuan (non-Austronesian), from the Torricelli phylum. Unlike the Ilahita, the Bumbita live in small, loosely defined villages of some 150–200 persons, with ritual moieties cutting across villages rather than serving to define village boundaries (see Tuzin 1976: 233–266). The Bumbita are horticulturists, cultivating yams, taro, and sago on lands owned by patrilineal sub-clans. These sub-clans are paired into larger clans that function as a unit only in ritual contexts. Garden cultivation is supplemented by modest individually owned coffee plantations that during the time of fieldwork generated between K100 and K200 for one family per year. The Bumbita and their neighbors are known for the ceremonial displays of large yams (over 6 feet in length) as an integral part of traditional religious activities. They also build men's cult houses (*haus tambaran*) for ceremonies of graded initiation for men, but the houses in Bumbita are neither as elaborate nor as large as those of their Ilahita and Abelam neighbors. Men use these houses on ceremonial occasions and otherwise reside in domestic houses with their wives and children.

Contact with Europeans is relatively recent, with only sporadic patrol visits before World War II. During the war, the area was occupied by Japanese troops for some months before they were ousted by the Allies in the closing months of the New Guinea campaign. People recalled vividly the initial Allied bombing runs and the subsequent supply drops from planes once the area had been taken from the Japanese. After the war there was relatively little contact until 1952 when the South Sea Evangelical Mission established a mission base in Brugam at the western edge of Bumbita territory. By 1958 the mission had completed an airstrip, established a literacy program for adults, and opened a community school for children; however, these affected mainly only those villages nearest the mission. Those further east, where I conducted my fieldwork, were still considered "backward" by those living nearer to the highway and mission.

In the 1960s and 1970s, enthusiasm for Christianity in the eastern Bumbita villages was sporadic at best. Several revivals and at least one cargo cult swept through the area, but the relative isolation of the eastern Bumbita villages meant that few people actually joined these movements. By 1984, the situation had changed. The mission had in the 1970s established an indigenous church (called the South Sea Evangelical Church or "SSEC") that used Melanesian pastors and missionaries to widen their outreach programs. In the early 1980s "teams" of proselytizers, mostly from the Solomon Islands, visited the area, introducing a more ecstatic vision of Christianity. As their techniques caught on, teams from areas neighboring the Bumbita began traveling as well, offering demonstration church services that featured exorcisms, speaking in tongues, and sleight-of-hand "discoveries" of sorcery implements. One service I attended made effective use of a precocious and charismatic 10-year-old girl who performed miracles and exhorted people to cast away their sins and join the movement. In the eastern Bumbita villages, these revival meetings generated considerable excitement, and once people felt a ground-swell of support growing, they converted in record numbers in the early months of 1984. Several men, in the process of confessing their "sins," spoke openly about secret men's cult activities. These confessions contributed to a sense that "everything had changed," and people began to hope that unanimous support for the movement would catapult the world into a new age.

The problem of self in Bumbita society

The early success and eventual failure of the 1984 revival depended ultimately on the personal commitments of individuals to the movement. An analysis of the dynamics of the movement must therefore address the revival's effects on the personal aspirations of individual people. In Bumbita, people built their hopes around the possible dissolution of tensions in traditional ways of relating self to society. The Melanesian concept of the self has received considerable attention in recent years. Most formulations begin with the observation that negotiating social relations in a face-to-face society has special problems. Each of one's actions has implications for many people, and many of these have a long-standing interest in one's affairs. The result is that people not only have to play their cards close to their chest, they also have to be very careful about guessing someone else's hand. Thus, for example, Melanesians are renowned for refusing to speculate about one another's motives (Fajans 1985: 383, B. Schieffelin 1990: 72–73). Edward Schieffelin notes that "imput[ing] feelings, motivations or intentions to a person which have not been made publicly clear . . . can have significant and troublesome social implications" (E. Schieffelin 1985: 174). But does this strategy simply reflect social prudence? According to several Melanesian ethnographers, there is more to it than that – deeply encoded cultural ideas about self and person frame individual experience in a particular way. Fajans notes that the reluctance among the Baining of New Britain even "to speculate about the personal motivations, actions, and feelings either of themselves or others" (1985: 367) suggests that they are "not predominantly individualistic" (1985: 383) in their view of themselves, preferring to see themselves as socially constructed persons defined as much through "particular contexts as through enduring 'human' qualities" (1983: 167). The refusal to speculate about intentions implies a cultural system stating that human action is better articulated in its social contexts, without regard for individuated intentions. M. Strathern has taken these and other examples and put forward some general conclusions about Melanesian concepts of person and self. She argues that Melanesian persons are conceived "dividually as [much as] they are individually," so that "persons are frequently constructed as the plural and composite site of the relationships that produced them" (1988: 13). Her point is that the ideological underpinnings of a distinctive way of thinking about self are so profound that it may not even be appropriate to conceptualize Melanesian action as produced by *in*dividuals. These authors articulate a Melanesian ethnopsychological pattern: individual selves are not to be conceptualized outside of the transactions and relationships they deploy.

However, as an analytical concept, the "sociocentric self" brings up a host of problems regarding the ontological status of concepts, and these problems plague ethnopsychological studies more generally. Does a fundamentally relational conceptual frame for human motivation make it impossible for individual actors to even think about the motives of others? In discussing the relation between speculations about motives and the sociocentric self, one needs to outline some relevant conceptual distinctions. First, it is possible that a refusal to speculate about motives is simply taking care to avoid boxing oneself into a difficult social situation. Such a refusal implies nothing about basic conceptual categories. On the other hand, a refusal could reflect the position that what another person thinks is fundamentally unknowable, so it is fundamentally inappropriate to speculate. It reflects a philosophical and moral position. Finally, a lack of speculation about motives could reflect the fact that, under the relevant cultural system, it makes no sense even to think in terms of individual motives – the cultural system defines motive in such a way as to make "individual" motivation meaningless (see, for example, Lutz's discussion [1988] of "emotions" as social categories on Ifaluk). In the case of the Bumbita concept of the self, the material presented below suggests that people were using Christianity as an opportunity to renegotiate the basic philosophical principles underlying individual action. It is not the case that social circumstances have become less intense, allowing more open speculation about motives; nor is it the case that the fundamental cultural categories are changing. Rather, the material presented below suggests that what is at stake here is a basic philosophical position about personal motives; individuals, because of their personal frustrations with existing values, are using the Christian framework to justify a more liberal approach to assessments of the motives of others.

The example discussed here below illustrates how ethnopsychological analysis can benefit from an inclusion of the pragmatic issues addressed by individuals in presenting their experience. An exclusive focus on how the self is defined by local understandings risks neglecting the very real problematics set up for individuals by their cultural surroundings. In the Bumbita case, while a sociocentric definition of self makes for a very effective and responsive approach to negotiating social problems, it is also easy to fall victim to others because their true motives are never made clear. Ethnographers in Melanesia have grappled with this issue from the earliest days of research in the area. Fortune's *Sorcerers of Dobu* (1932) highlighted the pervasive ambiance of mistrust in day-to-day interactions, and Benedict (1934) used that material to construct her well-known and controversial "paranoid culture configuration" for Dobu, attempting to apply a psychological construct to an entire culture. More recently, Schwartz has described the "sensitivity to the intentions and submerged meanings of others" as part of a broad cultural ethos that has, in his words, "paranoid" overtones (1973: 156–157). While the use of the term "paranoid" risks an inappropriate association of a culturally constructed world view with a clinical psychological condition, Schwartz uses this term not to denote pathology, but to characterize a general orientation to the world: "This view of being the center of malign or benign attention is natural to small-scale societies and . . . persists in large-scale societies" to a degree (1973: 169). While one is thinking about the implications of one's actions for others, one must also be wary of the hidden motives of others. While Schwartz points to problems shared by all small-scale societies, others have been more explicit about Melanesians having distinctive world views which become problematic. Writing about a small island off the north coast of Papua New Guinea, Smith, for example, describes this climate of mistrust as "the dark side" (1994: 61) of the personalistic world view and argues that Kragur villagers found such a world view "a strain" that became one basis for what Smith calls "the romance of community cooperation" (1994: 154).

In Bumbita culture these themes find expression in a preoccupation with secrets and the revelation of secrets – also a central theme of the revival. The complex attitude toward holding secrets can be illustrated through a brief look at the structure of Bumbita clan myths. These myths serve as charters for specific kin groups (clans), and they address the conditions for the formation of society as it is known today. They link together themes of personal autonomy and social regulation through the act of betrayal. I will outline in telescoped form the basic plots of three of these myths and then move on to their explication.

A. The Amoina Myth. This myth is the most important Bumbita myth. It is regarded as the charter myth for the society as a whole. In the myth an old man named Amoina had the ability to take off his skin and masquerade as a young and virile man. When no one was around he would take off his old skin and appear as a stranger at dances and festivals, always speaking in a foreign tongue. One day as his senior wife was scratching at his scabies, she discovered his youthful skin underneath. She told her co-wife that the young man who had been seducing all the women was in fact their own husband. At the next dance, they confronted him, and because he was ashamed, he left the area forever and founded the society of the Europeans. Amoina is now considered by the Bumbita to be God.

B. The Ambun Myth. This myth is the founding myth of the Ambun (Parrot) clan. The parrot Ambun came from red pandanus. He used to wash alone in a water hole that women used for bathing. One day, one of two sisters, disturbed by the murky water, decided to find out who was using their water hole. She discovered Ambun and he begged her to adopt him, and she became his mistress. He was later seduced by the younger sister and the older sister discovered them. Ambun was ashamed. One day, as they were out searching for food, the sisters asked Ambun to pick some red fruit for them (he could fly). The red fruit was a part of his own "body," so he was offended. He tricked them into looking away, rubbed the red fruit on himself transforming himself into a bird and then flew away forever. They begged him to return, but he would not. He is the founding ancestor of the Ambun clan.

C. The Tembaran Myth. Tembaran (hornbill) was originally not a bird but a man, but he had the ability to eat certain kinds of tree bark and nuts and regurgitate them as yams. His wife, angered by having to carry so many yams to the village, resolved to hide and discover his secret. She saw him regurgitating the yams and confronted him. He was ashamed. He smeared mud on his body to create a white patch and attached sword grass to his head for a comb. Transformed into a hornbill, he flew away. He is the founder of the Tembaran clan.

In each of these three myths, a significant social category (Bumbita society as a whole, the Ambun clan, and the Tembaran clan respectively) has its origins in the founder's sense of alienation in the face of betrayal – as the Bumbita put it: "They wronged him, so he left." The stories set out the pattern of an inaccessible ancestor who has been wronged, and this theme also dominates revival ideology. The idea is that ancestors are withholding prosperity because of some unknown slight or wrong. But even more significant is that in each case, the hero is ashamed because he is discovered doing an intimate bodily act (taking off skin, washing, regurgitating). While he is "ashamed" at being discovered, there is no intimation that he is actually doing anything wrong. It is rather that his personal, private act has been made public. In this conception, society itself is founded on the violation of a personal space, a personal sense of autonomy. In each case, the hero responds by leaving and (somewhat obscurely) creating social groups.

These myths are captivating because they reveal in a sympathetic way the flipside of the Bumbita sense of self. The conditions of social life that make everyone dependent upon everyone else, and that generate a preoccupation in the affairs of others, also rob one of one's sense of personal autonomy.

This theme appears as well in conceptions of one's relations with ancestral spirits. Stories of the spirits' engagement in human affairs often exhibit the idea that spirits deeply resent being invoked by their human counterparts to engage in some nefarious activity. For example, one older man, an admitted sorcerer who had become a deeply committed Christian convert, explained to me that for him Christianity meant getting into agreement with the wishes of his personal ancestral spirits – in short, with achieving a sense of consensus. He described a conversion experience in which he was actually confronted in the bush by the spirits of ancestors. They admonished him to reveal his sorcery activities, but they then went on to tell him that they were personally affronted for being themselves used for activities they did not agree with. He described it to me this way:

They said, "You went and stole our things [skulls, arm and finger bones, etc.] to use us, so that later you would make us not do the right thing, following you in this way that you have shown us, so that now we are going and killing women and men, that is not straight in our eyes. With God. We think that with these bad ways, you should leave them all behind." They told me that. "You can call out to us to kill pigs for you, and harvest yams, yes, we will follow you. But if you want to kill men, oh, that is not right. Doing these things and destroying your own flesh and blood." They thought that.

While he invokes the rather standard Christian theme of absolution through repentance and guilt over past evil acts (in this case sorcery), a theme undoubtedly genuinely felt but also likely suggested to him by his exposure to the mission, he devotes even more attention to the thought that his behavior had wronged the ancestors *themselves*, that he had selfishly manipulated *them*. They complain to him about being "used" against their will to carry out his magic. It is a peculiar construction, where spirits are being invoked to carry out deeds they themselves oppose. But from within the framework of Bumbita ideas about the relation of self to the community, this construction is not at all odd – in fact, it reflects a widespread feeling that one is continually being "invoked" to follow the wishes of others. What is most important is that this man has incorporated that perspective into his central conversion narrative. For him, becoming a Christian means aligning himself fully with the wishes of his ancestors, so that the problems created by invoking others against their will (or being invoked by them) becomes a nonissue. As Christians, he and the ancestors will find themselves "free."

Thus, in the Bumbita view of the articulation of self and society, the interconnectedness that is the bedrock of social life is accomplished only through a significant compromise in personal autonomy. All of the efforts to establish relations with ancestors, reflected in the cargo ideals of the Christian movement, have at their core an attempt to make up for or circumvent the basic conditions of social life. In the course of transforming society, the Bumbita revivalists were trying to renegotiate the basic parameters of their sense of self.

The character of consensus in the revival

The best way to convey the attempt to redefine the sense of self in the revival is to discuss the psychological significance of the commitment to consensus. The revivalists felt that they could not bring on the transformed society without first achieving complete consensus across the whole community. They took the missionaries' model of personal conversion and transformed it into a vehicle for the transformation of society as a whole. The aim of the movement was to create a local environment conducive to the arrival of Jesus, and to do this they had to first produce complete consensus. I shall discuss three features of this vision: the call for unity, the revelation of secrets, and the confession of sins. Taken together, these three features show how the call for collective harmony in the revival was really a call for a fundamental shift in the relation of self to society.

Perhaps the most important feature of the proposed Christian society was the maintenance or attainment of a state of *wan bel*, a Tok Pisin term translated roughly as "collective harmony" (see also Brison 1991). Achieving a state of collective harmony could, the Christians believed, do more than anything else to set the stage for the arrival of Jesus. *Wan bel* refers not only to a lack of open conflict and dispute but also to a united purpose of mind directed toward the apocalyptic goal. During the course of the revival movement, the term *wan bel* became a rallying cry for Christians. Whenever enticed into arguments, revivalists would call out to their adversaries with *Wan bel! Wan bel!* rather than continue the argument. It was their equivalent to turning the other cheek. In addition, *wan bel* replaced "good morning" or "good day" as the standard salutation when greeting someone or shaking hands. It was a theme stressed continually in church sermons. If the people were to get right with God, they had to be, more than anything else, united. Some people began to talk of *wan bel* as an important ingredient in miraculous events. In one sermon, a local pastor talked about *wan bel* in this way: "The revival is being *wan bel*. This is the core [*as*] of the revival. If there is unity [*wan bel*], then everything in the revival will happen [i.e., the new age will arrive]. If there is no unity, then the revival will stop like a cut tree which is stuck against the others as it tries to fall." He then went on to emphasize that Christians must seek to avoid all conflict in an attempt to remain pure. He pointed out that he personally had for three years avoided all contact with local magistrates because they dealt with disputes on a regular basis. Another man, in a revealing statement about the efficacy of miraculous "discoveries" of hidden sorcery implements, pointed out that discovery attempts by women filled with the Holy Spirit (*glas meri*) were only successful when the sorcerer himself had already been *wan bel*, had already agreed that they should be discovered. As he put it, "God will not allow her to see where the objects are hidden unless the owner is *wan bel*." These examples show how local views link the achievement of collective harmony to the efficacy of magical activities and to the success of the revival as a whole.

The emphasis on collective harmony clearly intends to redress what is viewed as a fundamental local failing. If asked to describe the primary difference between themselves and Europeans, the Bumbita inevitably point to the perception that they can never get along with one another (see also Smith 1994: 161). Europeans possess an almost miraculous ability to coordinate their actions, and they have demonstrated a capacity to put aside petty personal aspirations in favor of collective goals. The Bumbita themselves never seem to be able to accomplish that.

Besides the appeal to collective harmony and united action, the consensus called for by the revival hinged on the revelation of all cult secrets. Christian leaders offered at least three reasons why the revelation of the traditional men's cult secrets had been a necessary feature of the revival movement. The first was purely strategic. Once the men's cult secrets were revealed to women and the uninitiated, the traditionalists were, in their minds, effectively barred from any future attempts to start up cult activities. Second, they argued that many of the activities kept secret traditionally from women were morally wrong. It was simply wrong to hide in the bush and eat meat without sharing any with wives and children. In the new vision of society, it is wrong to practice deception. It is significant in this respect that most of the revelations of secrets occurred in testimonials in church, during which men, in the process of cleansing themselves just prior to conversion, revealed the "sins" they had committed in the men's cult. These men saw themselves as establishing a new basis for interaction, one that negated the secrets that had become the cornerstone of male power.

Third, and probably most important, the revealing of cult secrets symbolized the grand magnitude of the transformation that was claimed to be overtaking society. It was an essential ingredient to establishing the proper environment for the return of Christ. Christian leaders pointed out to me that, traditionally, any revelation of cult secrets was punished by death. Now the whole community had revealed the secrets without fear.[1] The revelation of the secrets provided palpable evidence that the premises of traditional society had been utterly transformed. Underlying the search for a transformed world was a feeling that once they had bared their secrets, the spiritual forces would, through the return of Christ, bare theirs. In this context, it is not insignificant that the European missionaries made it very clear that they opposed the oppression of women and children through the withholding of men's cult secrets. That position, when coupled with their emphasis on righting oneself with God as a prerequisite for entry into the Kingdom of God, fostered the belief that the cargo secrets would not be revealed until all the men's cult secrets were revealed.

When church leaders talked about the importance of revealing cult secrets, they likened it to the personal sense of relief one feels from confessing sins. Throughout the revival, Christians asserted that only by confessing sins could anyone really be "free." The senior pastor for the Bumbita area, Michael Uhiar, described it this way:

[When the revival teams] came and preached, asking who wanted to confess their sins, what they preached came out with power and touched one's stomach [*bel*] so that one would feel, "Oh, yes, I have such and such a sin." And your stomach would go around and around . . . and you wouldn't be afraid or feel ashamed, thinking, "Before I did this with that woman." You would not be ashamed anymore. You'd be free.

Much of the time in the long nightly service, people were in fact discussing their sins and basking in the "happiness" (*amamas*) that came with confession. The feeling was not so much one of unburdening oneself of gnawing crimes, for often the confessions involved relatively trivial things. Instead, the exhilaration came from knowing that one could talk publicly about things that had never been a part of open discourse. People had the sense that in the new order one would be "free" to talk about whatever it was they chose.

The feeling grew that the converse was the case as well, that if one tried to become a part of the revival but nevertheless withheld certain secrets, that this would cause irreparable psychological damage. Michael went on to describe the effects of a less-than-complete baring of one's soul before the church:

When [the visiting preachers] prayed and went on and on, some of us, those who weren't sorcerers and didn't have sorcery leavings or magic soil [*pen*] for [growing] yams and [catching] pigs, we felt inside ourselves like it was cool and we felt happiness rising within us. But those who had [hidden] these kinds of bad soils, for sorcery or for catching pigs, they got up and did all sorts of things, falling down, turning over and over, with spit appearing in their mouths. Because [God] was showing them these things, that these things of theirs were still there in their houses . . . When the spirit wanted to come and take us, if we were free, then we would just feel happiness like I said.

According to Michael, in order to be "free" to accept the Holy Spirit, people must confess their "sins." Otherwise, the powers of Christianity and the powers of Satan would clash and cause excessive ecstasy or even insanity. The underlying conviction here is that to become a complete Christian, one must change the very core of one's interaction with the world. Christians would no longer have any secrets from one another; they would be able to talk freely and openly about all that they did, and those who tried to retain some secrets would suffer psychological harm.

Through all of these examples, the idea of consensus emerges as something that has miraculous potential to heal body and soul. Any residue of the contention and dispute that characterized traditional Bumbita society now appears to be inimical to Christian action, to the point that individuals may react viscerally, even falling into seizures, if they do not wholeheartedly embrace the new vision. And residual disagreements also threaten the power of the movement as a whole. Thus, the ideas underlying the drive for consensus in the revival movement contained new visions for how one presents oneself to society, and this completely new way of living had an overwhelming appeal.

The mystification of collective action

One irony in the new vision of Bumbita social life is that with all of its attempts to transform the basis of social interaction through sustained consensus, the revival was drawing upon a well-established and thoroughly traditional view of the power of collective action. Traditional Bumbita religious life centered on a series of large-scale ceremonies conducted to shepherd men through a series of grades of initiation known collectively as the Tambaran. Tambaran ceremonies varied according to the ritual grade being celebrated, but all of the ceremonies generated religious power from the seemingly miraculous coordination of effort required to pull them off. Tuzin has written of the religious significance in neighboring Ilahita of the construction of the men's cult house itself, a grand cathedral-like structure that requires the cooperative efforts of all the members of the society. The tiers of bark paintings that adorn the front façade of the cult house depict generations of ancestors. Collectively, these paintings serve as potent reminders of the collective effort required to construct such a majestic structure (see Tuzin 1980: 116–167). In Bumbita, somewhat less ambitious cult houses were complemented by the erection of pairs of masts made from tree trunks, symbolizing cult flutes and wrapped with layers of coconuts donated by all the groups in the society. Ropes suspended from tree tops and attached to the masts to help hold them in place explicitly symbolized the array of clans participating in the building of the structure. The symbolism of the ropes mirrors the bark painting symbolism in Ilahita: each constituent group in the society had to work together to create a great religious edifice.

Tuzin argues that Tambaran ceremonies reflect a mystification of collective action that is the basis for Ilahita religious conviction in general. He writes:

The exaltation of the Tambaran is at once the celebration of personal and collective identity, reaching ultimately to a level of significance at which the metaphysics of self merge with, and are indistinguishable from, the highest values of the culture. This quality of sublime expressiveness is most evident in the symbolism of cult art, architecture and mythology; but it is equally present in the many areas of ritual action. When personal motivation is brought into such close accord with collective interests and ideological prescriptions, the necessary conditions are met for the formation of a rationalized ethic. (1980: 319–320)

A similar kind of mystification of collective action pervades Bumbita religious ideology. Not only are large structures and elaborate ceremonies evidence of the power of collective action, they also form the basis for men's attempts to preserve their power over women. In the traditional men's cult, many of the activities aimed at convincing women that men had miraculous powers were in fact the products of concerted cooperative action. Perhaps the most dramatic of these activities was the tradition of breaking off of coconut palms at the base of their trunks at the end of one of the Tambaran ceremonies. The women, who had been banished from the village for the duration of the ceremony, were told that at the ceremony's close, flying foxes had descended into the village and snapped the palm tree trunks like so many twigs. In reality, the men had used elaborate systems of ropes and pulleys to force the trees to sway back and forth to the point of breaking at their base.

Thus, in the minds of every Bumbita adult is a well-developed sense of the power of collective action in a religious context. One can actually see evidence of this world view operating in individual descriptions of the initial appeal of the revival movement and its persuasive effects. One young man whom I interviewed at length about his religious convictions described weighing his convictions about the return of Jesus by assessing the personal sense of excitement generated by the feeling that everyone was acting together in support of the movement. When I asked him about his wavering conviction about Christianity, the young man said:

> I will tell you that when the people come for the church and they say, "Sorry, you should challenge your sins, it is almost time now. Jesus will come." I think about it in my own thoughts. I weigh it. If my thinking starts to shake, if it really pulls at me, then it's true, this thing will happen. But if my thinking doesn't shake or whatever, then my thinking stays hard, saying, "He won't come," then he won't come. I think of it that way. In my thinking I think of it that way. It is really hard for us to believe and wait for him; it's hard. It's hard for us.

It is difficult to argue that this young man is actually saying that if you believe in something strongly enough it will happen, though that is what his words imply. What he actually means is that in his desire to become a part of the group (in this case becoming Christian), he weighs the extent to which he feels a sense of personal enthusiasm building to mirror the enthusiasm of others. If he feels that sense of shared conviction, he gains confidence that the miraculous event (in this case the return of Jesus) might very well happen. This way of looking at the power of consensus has its roots in the cultural construction of religious efficacy more generally. Whatever their attitudes about the revival itself, all Bumbita shared the conviction that miraculous things come from singleness of purpose and coordination of mind. The commitment to consensus in the revival was, in the end, an attempt to take a prior understanding of religious power through collective action and apply it to all of social life. The promise of such a new vision of one's personal place in the social arena had tremendous appeal.

The revival's collapse

In the end, though, the new vision of social harmony and consensus could not be sustained. People continued to die, and this meant that someone was still hiring sorcerers. There was inevitable bickering even at the core of the movement, and because of the way the movement had been constructed around the idea of consensus, the fractiousness had devastating effects on people's commitment to the movement. Most of the cases of falling away from the revival that I investigated were immediately precipitated by inter-personal conflicts rather than demoralization over Christ's failure to return. The issues behind the revival's disintegration can be approached by looking at what happened in specific instances. In what follows, I describe the devel-oping disillusionment of some key figures in the church in Bumbita village (the village in which I lived).

In early 1985, the church in Bumbita village had begun to show signs of weakening. Church services, which had occurred nightly some months before, were being convened more and more infrequently. While it is inevi-table that waning enthusiasm eventually will afflict any totalizing move-ment, the process of disillusionment is nevertheless instructive, for it reveals the extent to which the fall of the church was tied to disillusionment over the prospect of eliminating personal conflict. Take, for example, the case of Umatin.[2] Umatin was a man of thirty-five who with his wife had been a Christian and church leader for several years. He was one of the few Bumbita villagers who had developed an interest in Christianity some time before the revival of 1984. During the revival Umatin was perhaps the most consistently enthusiastic about the revival's potential. Nevertheless, in early 1985 Umatin quit being a Christian. His problem had not been with the failure of Jesus to arrive; rather, he left over an incident that showed him that the revival would not be able to transcend the problems of personal conflict that had always plagued Bumbita villagers. Umatin's break came over his problem with the interpretation of some things that had been said by other church leaders in a Bumbita church service. The local pastor, in a sermon, had reminded everyone that they should practice good behavior as an example to the non-Christians, and he accompanied his message with a passage from the Bible about marrying only one wife. Another leader then followed by saying that church leaders in particular should hold the stan-dard of moral behavior by not hitting their wives or fighting. Umatin, upon hearing these statements, inferred that they were referring obliquely to his own recent conflicts with his wife. After the service, both he and his wife argued with those who had spoken. Umatin charged that Christianity was worth nothing, and he stormed back to his house. He remained outside the church for some months but eventually returned.

Umatin's disillusionment had to do with the extent to which he saw behavior going on "as usual" inside the church. While his personal convic-tions to Christianity were not tied to the revival as such, the revival had prompted him to hope, along with many others, that Christianity could bring with it a new way of interacting freely. The oblique references in church to his marital difficulties convinced him that "nothing had changed," that the bickering would not end, as he had hoped. When he did return to the church some months later, he articulated themes of personal growth that had been a part of his Christianity before the revival arrived.

Another instructive case comes from the Bumbita village pastor, Mairen, who was my neighbor and good friend. Mairen discovered Christianity with the 1984 revival, and was one of the most vocal proponents of the movement in Bumbita village. He dutifully attended a mission course to become pastor, and he presided over many late-night ecstatic services in the village. In early March 1985, as we were walking alone between villages, he told me that he was thinking of taking up smoking (a reliable sign of lapsing from the church as no Christians smoked).[3] I asked him why, and he said that there were "too many roads" to follow, that some people say that one has to pray to the angels, that others emphasize the ecstatic qualities of the revival, and others want people to listen to those affected by the Holy Spirit. Everyone was saying something different; there was no consensus. As I asked him more intently about his impending decision, he brought up the bickering that had recently afflicted the church in our village. A couple of weeks earlier, a major dispute had erupted when a Christian man well known for his unstable and volatile behavior overheard some others talking badly about the church. He allegedly attacked them verbally, accusing them of undermining the revival by continuing to think of the customs. This incident would have been of little consequence, but he then took it a step further by pulling a spear out of his house and allegedly throwing it at his "father," the senior man of the village. To Mairen, the incident showed a disturbing lack of commitment to the movement (even though it was the Christian man who had resorted to unacceptable behavior). Mairen's complaint about there being "too many roads" was an articulation of a nagging feeling that his church was unable to achieve the kind of consensus that the revival required. The church seemed to be provoking conflict instead of eliminating it.

It was conflict in his own personal life, though, that provoked Mairen into a final break with the church. A few weeks after our earlier conversation, I noticed him conspicuously smoking tobacco and chewing betel nut in front of his house. I asked him why he was doing this, and he replied that he wanted to leave the village to find work at the plantations. He went on to say that his wife's family had complained about him, saying that he did no work and that he beat his wife. He and she had had a bitter argument about whether she was properly taking care of their daughter; she had called him a "fake" Christian, referring to his proclivity for extramarital affairs, and he had beaten her in response. After their argument, he said, she began smoking and chewing betel and he, upon seeing her, decided to do the same.

Mairen had articulated his disillusionment as stemming from a lack of consensus over how the Christian movement should succeed, but now he was leaving the church in the wake of personal conflicts that had little to do with Christianity as such. Earlier he had told me that one appeal of Christianity for him had been the hope that with everything out in the open, there would be no reason for disputes or conflict. The persistence of these conflicts undermined his confidence in the power of Christianity as a whole.

In both these cases, the secretive and potentially two-faced behavior that in the Bumbita view plagued traditional society reappeared, and the individuals involved expressed their frustrations by pointedly retiring from the movement. Instead of freeing them from the strains of social action, the revival was beginning to exacerbate them. These two incidents and several others occurred within a period of a few weeks. After Mairen's lapse, the church quickly fell into disarray. During that time, many of the Bumbita Christians left the church for good, saying that the church was no good if it was fighting all of the time. In many cases interpersonal conflict was a catalyst: people understood that if they were not able to live in harmony with one another, they had no hope of ushering in the new age. The vision of consensus that had energized so many people and had become the cornerstone of the movement, was, in the end, unattainable, and the revival failed as a result.

Conclusion: self-construction through religious aspirations

I have not intended this analysis as an assessment of the overall appeal of the revival movement. Much of it had to do with relations with ancestors, with feelings of betrayal, with perceptions of inferiority in the face of colonization. But the important role consensus played in people's efforts to transform their society had a significant impact on the initial appeal of the movement and its eventual demise. I have argued that the movement took the conceptual shape it did by drawing on pre-existing problematics in people's sense of self, specifically a tension between the desire for personal autonomy and the recognition that all behavior has social repercussions. When Bumbita communities seized upon the Christian revival as an opportunity to transform society, people saw as well a possible new basis for social interaction, one that would free them from the usual pressures built into a sociocentric sense of self. This point is significant because others have argued that the same general patterns of self-conception appear in other Melanesian societies. Similar problems with the demands of consensus may help explain why the pattern of enthusiastic support followed by pronounced disillusionment has characterized many different types of Melanesian social movements, both religious and secular.

Nor does the analysis imply that the Bumbita case is unique. The feeling of commitment to a sense of unity and a common goal is central to social and religious movements everywhere. And movements everywhere must also cope with the problems of routinization and the inevitable fissures and factions that develop as the movement tries to establish a new basis for organizing social life (Wallace 1956). But in the Bumbita case (and other Melanesian cases as well), the movement's demise was particularly dramatic and precipitous. It is tempting under such circumstances to argue that either (a) the movement's ideals were not sufficiently compelling to sustain strong membership or (b) people's naivety about their cargoistic expectations led them to be overly credulous about such things as Jesus' return. The analysis here suggests that it was neither of these things. The issues involved were deeply compelling, and the revival's persistence did not hinge on Jesus' return. Rather, because local cultural constructions made the prospect of consensus so highly appealing that it became an integral objective to the movement, the inevitable failure to sustain consensus resulted in a collapse of the movement as a whole.

The trajectory of the brief revival movement in Bumbita underscores the importance of attending to both local cultural constructions and personal psychological needs in explaining the appeal of religious movements generally. While sociologists of religion are thinking more about how local cultural codes affect social movements, there is a perception that such studies "are often focused too narrowly on codes and their structures. Recent studies of movement structure suggest the importance of the culture-making processes by which codes are crafted in particular practical contexts" (Hart 1996: 89). Psychological anthropology, with its long history of relating local cultural constructs to the practical psychological needs of adherents, can make significant contributions to a sociology of religion that is framed in this way.

The analysis also underscores another point recognized by anthropologists studying the aspirations of adherents to religious and social movements – namely, that while these movements reflect genuine dissatisfactions with the post-colonial conditions of life, they take their characteristic shape from pre-existing culturally constructed conceptions of self and society (see especially Clark 1992, Lattas 1992, 1993). This research supports the recent recognition of the importance of cultural understandings in the study of the sociology of social movements.

Finally, the argument calls for an approach to psychological anthropology that looks at the experiential implications of culturally constructed notions of self. The Bumbita ideas about self and society lead to individual dissatisfactions which reveal themselves in the yearning for fundamental transformation in the revival. These dissatisfactions have a very real experiential basis, and they fuel the widespread self-deprecating comparisons to Europeans and their supposed superior capacity for coordinated action based on consensus. So, while the conditions of postcolonial life offer many reasons for social action, the movements themselves take the shape they do from individual efforts to grapple with problems posed by local constructions of social life.

NOTES

1 This was, of course, not true. The revelation of the secrets appeared frequently as one of the possible causes for an untimely death. The sorcerers or the traditionalists supposedly retaliated against the public recognition of their secrets. Nevertheless, the significance of a widespread recognition of things that had before been kept scrupulously secret cannot be overestimated.

2 This name is a pseudonym, as are all other Bumbita person names.

3 Among the Bumbita, as with other groups in the area, solidarity in the revival was demonstrated by the unanimous renunciation of tobacco and betel nut. Everyone who smoked and chewed betel was not Christian and, with a few exceptions, everyone who abstained was Christian. Smoking and chewing betel were thus effective external markers of the individual's current affiliation.

REFERENCES

Allen, Bryant J. 1976 *Information Flow and Innovation Diffusion in the East Sepik District, Papua New Guinea*. Ph.D. Dissertation, Australian National University, Canberra.

Benedict, Ruth 1934 *Patterns of Culture*. Boston, MA: Houghton Mifflin.

Brison, Karen 1991 Community and Prosperity: Social Movements among the Kwanga of Papua New Guinea. *The Contemporary Pacific* 3: 325–355.

Brunton, Ron 1989 *The Abandoned Narcotic: Kava and Cultural Instability in Melanesia*. Cambridge: Cambridge University Press.

Clark, Jeffrey 1992 Madness and Colonization: the Embodiment of Power in Pangia. *Oceania* 63: 15–26.

Fajans, Jane 1983 Shame, Social Action, and the Person among the Baining. *Ethos* 11: 166–180.

    1985 The Person in Social Context: The Social Character of Baining "Psychology." In *Person, Self, and Experience*, G. M. White and J. Kirkpatrick, eds. Berkeley, CA: University of California Press. Pp. 367–397.

Fortune, Reo 1932 *Sorcerers of Dobu: The Social Anthropology of the Dobu Islanders of the Western Pacific*. New York: Dutton.

Gamson, William A. 1992 The Social Psychology of Collective Action. In *Frontiers in Social Movement Theory*, A. D. Morris and C. M. Mueller, eds. New Haven, CT: Yale University Press. Pp. 53–76.

Hart, Stephen 1996 The Cultural Dimension of Social Movements: A Theoretical Reassessment and Literature Review. *Sociology of Religion* 57: 87–100.

Klandermans, Bert 1992 The Social Construction of Protest and Multiorganizational Fields. In *Frontiers in Social Movement Theory*, A. D. Morris and C. M. Mueller, eds. New Haven, CT: Yale University Press. Pp. 77–103.

Lattas, Andrew 1992 Skin, Personhood and Redemption: The Double Self in West New Britain Cargo Cults. *Oceania* 63: 27–54.

   1993 Sorcery and Colonialism: Illness, Dreams, and Death as Political Languages in West New Britain. *Man* 28: 51–77.

Leavitt, Stephen C. 1995a Seeking Gifts from the Dead: Long-Term Mourning in a Bumbita Arapesh Cargo Narrative. *Ethos* 23: 453–473.

   1995b Political Domination and the Absent Oppressor: Images of Europeans in Bumbita Arapesh Narratives. *Ethnology* 34: 177–189.

Lutz, Catherine 1988 *Unnatural Emotions: Everyday Sentiments on a Micronesian Atoll and Their Challenge to Western Theory*. Chicago, IL: University of Chicago Press.

May, Ronald J. 1982 Micronationalism: What, When, and Why. In *Micronationalist Movements in Papua New Guinea*, R. J. May, ed. Canberra: Department of Political and Social Change, RSPS, Australian National University. Pp. 421–448.

Melucci, Alberto 1989 *Nomads of the Present: Social Movements and Individual Needs in Contemporary Society*. Philadelphia, PA: Temple University Press.

Morris, Aldon D. and Carol McClurg Mueller, eds. 1992 *Frontiers in Social Movement Theory*. New Haven, CT: Yale University Press.

Ryan, Dawn 1969 Christianity, Cargo Cults, and Politics Among the Toaripi of Papua. *Oceania* 40: 99–118.

Schieffelin, Bambi B. 1990 *The Give and Take of Everyday Life*. Cambridge: Cambridge University Press.

Schieffelin, Edward L. 1985 Anger, Grief, and Shame: Toward a Kaluli Ethnopsychology. In *Person, Self, and Experience*, G. M. White and J. Kirkpatrick, eds. Berkeley, CA: University of California Press. Pp. 168–182.

Schwartz, Theodore 1962 The Paliau Movement in the Admiralty Islands, 1946–54. *Anthropological Papers of the American Museum of Natural History* 49(2).

   1973 Cult and Context: The Paranoid Ethos in Melanesia. *Ethos* 1: 153–174.

Smith, Michael French 1994 *Hard Times on Kairiru Island*. Honolulu, HI: University of Hawaii Press.

Stent, William R. 1977 An Interpretation of a Cargo Cult. *Oceania* 47: 187–219.

Strathern, Marilyn 1988 *The Gender of the Gift*. Berkeley, CA: University of California Press.

Tuzin, Donald F. 1976 *The Ilahita Arapesh*. Berkeley, CA: University of California Press.

   1980 *The Voice of the Tambaran*. Berkeley, CA: University of California Press.

Wallace, Anthony F. C. 1956 Revitalization Movements. *American Anthropologist* 58: 264–281.

7 God and self: the shaping and sharing of
     experience in a cooperative, religious
     community

Susan Love Brown

In sleep, I walked beside a wide, calm river. The road parallel to my footpath and
the river was broad and well-traveled. In the distance, I could hear an approaching
procession with bells, flutes and small cymbals. As I turned to look behind me, the
procession drew nearer and I could see the joyful, innocent faces of the participants. At the very end of this group of probably 100 was Yogananda. My heart
stopped for a moment, and I thought, "I *must* get to him." However, no sooner had
the need been registered than he was surrounded by an impenetrable crowd. I felt
desperate and sick. Suddenly though, the crowd began to shift and, to my surprise
and consternation, master was forcibly parting the crush to come and stand in
front of me. I thought I would burst as I fell to the ground and touched his feet.
"Divine teacher," I pleaded, "I want to be with you." He calmly replied, "You
already are." Frantic that he didn't understand and I would lose this opportunity to
join him, I repeated my request with tears – "But I want to be with you!" He bent
down, raised my chin so I was looking into his eyes and said after a pause, "Child,
you already *are*." He then turned, walked back through the crowd, and I was left
there without joining the procession as it moved away, puzzled by his words yet no
longer frantic, peaceful but uncomprehending. I awoke immediately and wasn't
tired but amazingly refreshed and ready to act on the still puzzling message of the
dream. It was 4: 20 a.m. I'd gone to bed at 4. Typically, I wouldn't have entered a
dream state of sleep for some time. Whatever else may have been a mystery, I knew
I'd encountered Yogananda.[1]

These words describe the dream of a 36-year-old woman who had
recently joined Ananda Village. She was one of many people at Ananda
who could be called "baby boomers" and who had been embroiled in the
turmoil of the 1960s in the United States, spending her college years in the
countercultural atmosphere of northern California (Berkeley, Haight-
Ashbury), eventually crashing and seeking psychiatric help. Finally realizing that "the purest and best desire I'd ever had was for a complete union
with God," she returned to the church of her parents, attending a seminary
with the intention of becoming a theologian. "I lasted two quarters and
made no friends among the theologians – men who knew much *about* God
but were, in many ways, afraid to *know* God."

She read the works of the British writer C. S. Lewis and referred to him as "my first guru." When, after ending an abusive marriage, she finally severed her ties with her church, she realized her approach to Christianity was altering:

I believed He was the only truth, not words in a book, but the vibrant indwelling spirit. I needed nor desired no other authority for my beliefs. And, my, how rapidly they changed. I realized the necessity of reincarnation – God allows us as much time as we need, rather than the do-or-die three score and ten the Bible supposedly allots.

She gradually began to read the works of Eastern religions, eventually chancing upon *Ananda Magazine*. Soon after that, she fell asleep at 4 a.m. reading *Autobiography of a Yogi* (Yogananda 1985) and had the experience described at the beginning of this chapter.

The case of this woman, whom I call Laura, is instructive, because it contains so many of the elements that characterize attempts by many young people to reconcile self and culture after the societal disruptions known as "the sixties" in the United States. The new religious movements and new religious communities that arose in the United States in the seventies served the revitalization function that Wallace described as resulting from culture stress and change (1956). These communities and religions were the means of "getting saved from the sixties" that Tipton refers to (1982). Perhaps the most important point about these religions and communities is that they served a therapeutic function, helping to reconcile what have always been potentially contradictory elements in American culture and in the psyches of its people: the need for self-reliance and the quest for community, rationality and emotion, and self-interest and altruism.[2]

The problem of how people reconcile the contradictory elements of any culture is a theoretical problem arising from the nature of culture itself with its overlapping social and individual aspects and inherent variations that arise due to individual differences and changes in the environment, both of which can potentially clash with existing cultural understandings. Contemplation of the problem of the individual and social manifestations of culture absorbed the attentions of Edward Sapir (1994) and A. Irving Hallowell (1967: 75–110). Sapir noted: "In the psychological sense, culture is not the thing that is given us. The culture of a group as a whole is not a true reality. What is given – what we do start with – is the individual and his behavior" (1994: 139). Hallowell stated that "the individual's self-image and his interpretation of his own experience cannot be divorced from the concept of self that is characteristic of his society" (1967: 75–76). Since then, anthropologists have evaluated the relative importance of individual and society in the production, maintenance, and change of culture with varying degrees of success (for a summary see Strauss and Quinn 1997: 13–47). Theodore Schwartz, in offering a distributive model of culture based on *internalization* ("the continuous process in which individuals form, modify and store derivatives or representations of events" [1978: 423]), mounted a solution that acknowledged both internal and external reality and provided "an approach to describing and studying the distribution of culture among the members of a society . . . [that] provides a useful basis for articulating culture with social structure and personality" (1978: 424).

Schema theory, as it has developed over the last ten years (see D'Andrade and Strauss 1992, Holland and Quinn 1987, and Strauss and Quinn 1997), has provided a more detailed look at how individuals process culture in a range of cross-cultural circumstances, while at the same time recognizing culture as a social and not just an individual phenomenon. Strauss and Quinn, in particular, have theoretically sustained the view that culture, while subject to change, has an undeniable "durability" in both individuals and across generations – a so-called "centripetal" movement that tends to reinforce cultural meanings (1997: 89–98;111–115).

The Ananda example demonstrates both centripetal and centrifugal forces at work in culture (or, in older terms, continuity and change) through the examination of community members who mostly come from a single generation, living in an environment different from their parents, but whose problem stems from their acceptance of shared American cultural meanings with the older generation. Although the individual is the locus of culture, the ways in which individuals channel their experiences often depend on cultural predispositions and even human nature. In the United States (and in other societies as well) religious ideology emerges as a frequent medium for the negotiation of meaning in the face of radical or stressful social change, and Ananda members have chosen this general path, stamping on it their own specific approach to it.

The particular religious ideology that Laura found at Ananda – the Self-Realization of Paramahansa Yogananda, as taught by his direct disciple Sri Kriyananda – integrated these oppositions through the use of yoga, which provided the experience demanded by these young people as the only valid approach to knowledge and truth, and which promised direct contact with God. As one Ananda man put it, "Essentially, it all boils down to religion as experience of God rather than belief."

In this chapter I explore the way in which Ananda members emphasize experience as the means of mediating the inner conflict of self and culture that arose from their particular circumstances. In the course of doing so, I hope to shed light on the appeal of Eastern religious practices to those Americans known as baby boomers. The Ananda example also demonstrates motivations to seek out new resources for the mediation of conflict and sheds new light on the power of syncretism. All of these illustrate the

Thesis

ways in which internal and external realities interact in the production, maintenance, and change of culture.

Psychology, drugs, and experience

The emphasis on experience rather than belief among so many Americans of the baby boom generation arose from at least two major factors: (1) the rise of a psychological consciousness and (2) the use of hallucinogenic drugs. Together, these factors created a shift in American consciousness. But the roots of this shift and the ideas that would characterize it lie in the fifties – in a quest to find new meaning in life in a society characterized by affluence, success, and conformity.[3]

Following World War II, the United States had experienced an unprecedented growth that led to its rise as both a key military power in the world, as well as an industrial giant. Americans themselves experienced an unprecedented affluence that increased the middle class from 13 percent to 46 percent of the total population (Strickland and Ambrose 1985). Yet, in spite of this economic and political success, Americans confronted major problems that constituted what Maslow referred to as "the neurosis of success" (1959: vii). Maslow saw the United States as being in "an interregnum between old value systems that have not worked and new ones not yet born, an empty period which could be borne more patiently were it not for the great and unique dangers that beset mankind. We are faced with the real possibility of annihilation, and with the certainty of 'small' wars, of racial hostilities, and of widespread exploitation . . . " (1959: vii–viii).

The remedy for this state of affairs, according to Maslow and those who joined him in the Research Society for Creative Altruism, was a "usable system of values, values that we can believe in and devote ourselves to because they are true rather than because we are *exhorted* to 'believe and have faith'" (Maslow 1959: viii, emphasis in original).

Psychologists, more than any other group of professionals, would supply the rhetoric of the sixties and lead the way to the therapeutic point of view. Maslow's own work in self-actualization would be taken up by the young people of the sixties and used as a model for self-design (Alexander 1992: 36–38, 41–43). Ananda members interviewed by Nordquist during his field-work there in 1975 and 1976 indicated that their prime reasons for coming to the community were psychological (1978: 86).

The emergent psychological movement, later to be called the Human Potential Movement, proposed that the self could be retrofitted and refined. But why the turn toward the psychological?

Between 1956 and 1976 the American view of self shifted from a socio-centric view to one focused on self-fulfillment, and the self detached from social roles. This shift is documented in a longitudinal study done by Veroff, Douvan, and Kulka (1981). They attribute this "psychological revolution" to a change in child-rearing methods following World War II:

Impelled by this goal [raising perfect children] and the advice of child-raising experts, women sought to mold children's attitudes and motives to a degree previously unheard of. Where in earlier times parents sought obedience/compliance from children and left their internal psychological world alone, they now aimed at creating the attitudes and motives that would lead the child to behave properly on the basis of her/his own desires. They invested the child with "potential" and took the goal of socialization to be the realization of that unique potential. The child was invested with unique value, and to a real degree, the world . . . was to be judged by the criterion of realizing or releasing that value. (Veroff, Douvan, and Kulka 1981: 14–15)

But the shift to a psychological view of self in which fulfillment became a key goal led to a less socially integrated individual with its equivalent loss of "power to provide people with meaning, identity elements, satisfaction" (Veroff, Douvan, and Kulka 1981: 17). This "distancing" of people from the social structure also "represents a potential psychological loss" evidenced by the "increased sensitivity to interpersonal relations" (Veroff, Douvan, and Kulka 1981: 17, 20). Thus arises the irony of seemingly individualistic selves in constant search of companionship.

The coming of age of baby boomers with a different perspective from that of the parental generation accounts for the shift in the view of self and the subsequent "generation gap" so remarked upon by observers. However, it was this view of self coupled with an awareness of the possibilities of expanded consciousness that led to the emphasis on experience. This approach was facilitated by the use of LSD and other hallucinogens.

The connection between drug use and an affinity for Eastern religions has not been lost on those doing research on new religions and communities in the United States. For example, Zablocki reports that 96.4 percent of those who joined communes based on Eastern religious ideology had used drugs before joining the commune but only 16.1 percent did so after joining such a community (1980: 118). Nordquist found that many Ananda members were former drug users (1978: 91–92), and members told me the same during my work there.[4]

Robbins has also noted the affinity of drug users for Eastern religions that promise an extension of the experience of an expanded consciousness. "The ability of Oriental mysticism to serve as the means whereby persons terminate drug usage derives, in part, from the elements of similarity between mystical experiences and drug experiences which permit 'pure,' i.e., non-chemical, mysticism to serve as a *substitute gratification* for psychedelic trips" (1969: 310, emphasis in original).

Those people who first came to Ananda and helped to establish it as a community in the late sixties were refugees from this drug culture, and many of them reported having experiences that led them in a spiritual direction. But this was not, in itself, enough to keep people at Ananda. Many people drifted into and out of the community in its early years. Those who stayed and built the community into what it is today found something more.

Ananda village and self-realization

The members of Ananda Village are followers of Self-Realization, the religion founded by Paramahansa Yogananda (often called Swami Yogananda), their guru. Yogananda came to the United States from India in 1920 to attend the International Congress of Religious Liberals and ended up staying. After four years of lecturing and touring the country, Yogananda founded the Self-Realization Fellowship (SRF) in 1925 in southern California, dubbing it "the Church of All Religions," a notification that Yogananda had "respect for all religions as constituting various paths to God. Such temples, dedicated to the one God that all religions worship, should be built everywhere . . . East and West should destroy forever narrow divisions in the houses of God" (1982: 14). Headquarters were located in Los Angeles, and the church became a home to the monks and nuns who joined its monastic order and conducted the services for lay members.

Swami Kriyananda, who tells his story in *The Path* (1979a), was a direct disciple of Yogananda. Swami Kriyananda later left SRF and founded his own community to honor Yogananda's call for world brotherhood communities. Ananda Village began as a meditation retreat in 1967 on land owned by Kriyananda and others and expanded into a community in 1969 when additional lands were purchased by Swami Kriyananda, the spiritual leader and founder of the community (for a full explanation see Nordquist 1978: 28–33). Finding its stable form only later, the community nevertheless was founded upon the teachings of Paramahansa Yogananda.

In the seventies, when many young people became interested in Eastern religions, some people doubted the applicability of these teachings to Western lives. But anthropologists know that syncretic religions form because people find similarities of structure and meaning that are easily incorporated into their pre-existing systems of belief and practice. This does not occur only because people are confronted with new religions by force through the process of acculturation, but also because people confront problems that can only be remedied by the espousal of new ideas and approaches that are compatible with their own culture. Such was the case with Self-Realization and Ananda community members (Brown 1992).

The declared purpose of Ananda is a religious one – members seek to show how one might live a simple life devoted to God in a community in which one's home, one's work, and one's church are all in the same place – and to do this through the practice of kriya yoga (a type of meditation). To become a member, one must accept Yogananda as one's sole guru, be initiated into the practice of kriya yoga, and be willing to follow the rules of the community. Because the sense of community and inclusion is so strong for those visiting the community to participate in its educational programs, the Ananda membership process is designed to discourage those whose attraction is not based on the ultimate religious purpose.[5]

The community was designed to be cooperative rather than communal in its structure, and this was a conscious decision on the part of Kriyananda, the community's founder and spiritual director. "The simplest management is simply to give people the incentive to manage themselves. When they must look out for their own needs, they will bestir themselves well enough to produce." He believed that a "communistic" society had a tendency to "force people to overwork," and Kriyananda thought that an individual decision-making process would allow people to decide for themselves how much time to devote to work and to worship or leisure activities.

The difference between the economic system here proposed and a normal system of free enterprise is that here the member remains, as in any cooperative, a part owner of the community. Whether in higher wages, discounts, stock dividends, or special benefits, he receives his share of the community's prosperity. It is up to him, by the contribution of his labor, to increase that prosperity or to keep it lower. (Kriyananda 1979b: 32–33)

This approach has been a successful one. Although Kriyananda financed much of the expense of the community in the early years through his lectures and teaching, the community today is self-sufficient, owning a number of profitable businesses (a market, a restaurant, a boutique, a bookstore, a publishing company, and so on), which gave it a gross income of around $3 million in 1985. Each business has its own manager, its own income, and its own checkbook. Twelve percent of the income of each business goes into a general fund to pay for overheads, mortgages, and support for various projects (for specific details see Brown 1987: 87–94).[6]

Ananda offers a wide range of educational programs at its outreach facility, The Expanding Light, and its ministers often travel to conduct services and programs at locations where there are no Ananda churches or colonies.[7] It is from this kind of outreach that potential members come. Potential members must have a familiarity with the community and "be in attunement" with it. This is usually accomplished by taking a course or two at The Expanding Light or by living at an Ananda center. One prerequisite was to take the correspondence course, *14 Steps to Perfect Joy*; another at the time of my fieldwork was that all Ananda members had to be members of the Self-Realization Fellowship, Yogananda's church. Individuals then formally applied to become potential members, which included interviews and acceptance by the Membership Committee.

Once accepted, potential members make a substantial investment in the membership process. They enter a three-month course at $500 per month (including room and board) and live at the Meditation Retreat. They receive instruction during this time in the different kinds of yoga, keep journals, and deepen their meditation skills under the guidance of Ananda ministers and teachers. They attend daily meditations and engage in work projects at the Meditation Retreat. They learn the history of the community, the financing of the community, and how to solve problems constructively. Finally, in the third month, they are integrated into the community itself through classes and by serving apprenticeships within the community. They also receive guidance in finding jobs and housing within the community.

All potential members have to be self-supporting within the community. Living on welfare is discouraged. They are allowed to take their time becoming full members, because there is a $1500 nonrefundable, one-time membership fee ($2500 for couples) for those wanting to be full members, and a smaller fee for those who prefer to be supporting members. (In 1986 full members could live on the land, but supporting members, while participating in all community activities had to live off the land.) For this reason, people who become Ananda members are generally people with a work history and some savings or marketable skills.

Although all of the land is owned by the Ananda community or the Ananda church (depending on its location), members are allowed to build houses on the land with the understanding that they will be reimbursed for the cost (but not allowed to make a profit) should they leave the community or be transferred at a later time. Both single houses belonging to individuals or families and group houses with multiple individual units sharing a common kitchen can be found in the community. There is a planning department that guides members in this process and assures conformity to state and local planning guidelines and a housing committee that handles the "buying" and "selling" of housing. The great investment in time and money made by potential members makes membership a serious proposition.

Members either find employment in an existing Ananda business or in an outside business, and Ananda members are also encouraged to start their own businesses. In 1986 Ananda generally paid its members between $550 and $990 per month, depending on the business and how well it was doing, and the community made some effort to see that a couple with a child had a

combined income of at least $1200 per month. While these figures seemed
low even at the time, one must remember that Ananda members had fewer
expenses and considered themselves to be living lives of selfless service
within a supportive community.

The financial director told me that Ananda members at the time of my
fieldwork paid monthly residence fees ($185 for a single; $355 for a couple;
$225 for a couple with preschool children; $400 for a couple with school-
age children; $220 for a single parent). These fees helped in part to support
the Ananda school and to defray community expenses involved with living
on the land. Full members also voluntarily gave a portion of their monthly
incomes to the community. Members were not required to give their personal savings or property to the community upon joining, nor were they
required to sever relationships with family and friends outside of the community, so that many people had alternate sources of income. Members at
that time were required to follow two rules: no drugs (including no alcohol)
and no dogs. Other behavior, such as vegetarianism, was customary.

After a full year of Ananda membership, persons are eligible to join the
Friends of God, a renunciant order whose members agree to devote their
lives to God. After five years of membership, a member might be asked to
join the Fellowship of Inner Communion, the official church of Ananda.
Members are voted into the group by current members. Long-time membership in the community is greatly valued and respected, and it is the
primary source of prestige enjoyed by members at Ananda.

Ananda members as I found them in 1986 had a mean age of 37.7 years,
were mostly married, had children from current or previous marriages, and
had been members on average for almost seven years (Brown 1987: 120).
These mostly middle-class, Caucasian, college educated people came from
a predominantly Protestant Christian background, and were more liberal
than their parents, although they had not been politically active before
coming to Ananda, and most of them came to the community for spiritual
reasons (Brown 1987: 122–136).

Self-Realization provided all of the elements by which young American
adherents could resolve their psychological problems in the cause of their
spiritual pursuits. Self-Realization, like its psychological counterpart, self-
actualization, allowed its practitioners to concentrate on "doing" in an
effort to enhance "being."

Young people in the United States had three main problems to solve in
their retreat from the anomie of their coming-of-age decade: (1) reconciling
the isolated self that they had adopted with the community they yearned
for; (2) reconciling their cultural proclivity toward science and rationality
with the presence of emotion and intuition; (3) reconciling self-interest
stemming from American individualism with the altruism stemming from

their mostly Judeo-Christian backgrounds. Yoga helped them to accomplish all three.

Reconciling self and community

The parental generation had the problem of reconciling the experience of a sociocentric self with the cultural ideal of individualism, and it solved this problem partially by projecting lone heroes into its collective representations (Brown 1993). The baby boomer generation, experiencing the isolated self focused on self-fulfillment, had the opposite problem: how to reestablish ties to the human community – how to put an end to the problem of unattachment.

In order to reconcile self with community, Ananda members draw upon the Hindu idea of the greater Self that is God and to which all selves struggle to return. The essence of this idea is captured metaphorically in a chant sung frequently at Ananda, whose refrain is: "I am the bubble, make me the sea."[8]

Yoga means "union" in Sanskrit, and the particular kind of yoga emphasized at Ananda is kriya yoga, a form of raja yoga that emphasizes the practice of meditation. Through meditation, one listens to God and achieves unity with God once again. Ananda members are first taught two other forms of meditation, the Hong Sau method and the Om technique. When they have mastered these and the written lessons of Yogananda and Kriyananda, they are spiritually prepared to be initiated into kriya. Its secrecy accomplishes the creation and possession of property but also functions to "reinforce the belief in its claims" (Luhrmann 1989: 136–137). It functions to make its possessors both different from the world at large, from which they have fled, and part of a community in league with others at the same time.

In his book, *Philosophy of Meditation*, Haridas Chaudhuri explains the nature of meditation:

Meditation in its full fruition is the total self's existential understanding of the total reality. It aims at perfect realization of the self in its active relationship to the Supreme Being. To achieve that end, the ego has to be transcended. Also to be transcended are the fixed ideas and stereotyped molds imposed by sociocultural conditions. As an essential condition of ego transcendence, the practice of meditation has to assume the form of total self-opening to the light of Being. All preconceived notions of the mind and tumultuous desires of the psyche have to be hushed into silence so that the voice of truth can be heard in the stillness of the soul . . . It is when the mind stops chattering and perfect silence settles within, that the indwelling light of truth shines out and an individual clearly perceives his destiny in the total scheme of life . . . (1965: 3)

Meditation is the heart of experience at Ananda Village. Ananda members indicated to me that they meditated at least twice a day and three times was ideal. Every space occupied by Ananda members included an altar or a meditation room with the appropriate items to encourage a good meditation: pictures of Yogananda and his line of gurus, of Kriyananda, and of other spiritual leaders, flowers, incense, candles, and other religious items. I found altars in work places (even construction sites), as well as in homes and meeting rooms. For some members, the practice of meditation actually led them to the Ananda community. One Ananda member, a woman in her fifties, said:

I tried everything else in the effort to make life meaningful: LSD, encounter groups, therapists, music, sports, travel, lovers. The yogic way of life here does it for me. As soon as I started meditating (before I came here) life began to improve. The more I learned about this path, the more sense it made to me. I finally decided to commit myself to formal discipleship and later took kriya. Life kept on improving, and finally I wanted more than anything else to live in a community of devotees. It was a joyful decision. There is a great bond of love that connects everyone at Ananda, and I find it amazing that people can live like this.

A 32-year-old Ananda man said that he realized that "communion with God is the only answer to finding meaning and joy in life." He had "a sudden inward realization that I needed to find out how to meditate." He began "daily meditation and study of Yogananda's teachings . . . After starting the SRF lessons of Yogananda's teachings in order to find out how to meditate, I asked for an outward sign from God if this was the path I should take and was granted that sign."

A 39-year-old female, describing the change in her outlook that led to her joining Ananda, said:

I now see the purpose to life is to know God and return to God. Before, I couldn't find a purpose that made sense – the material world was never enough for me – everything always seemed so tentative. Happiness was fleeting . . . The change took place over several years beginning when I started to turn within – begin meditation practices and affirmations – and then coming to Ananda as a guest and realized Yogananda as my guru and began to accept his guidance . . . I decided to move to Ananda and dedicate my life to serving God . . . Here one can always put God first – practice the presence of God in a supportive and loving environment. Everyone else is attempting to do the same – live their life for God. So the distractions that can pull one away are lessened.

Although meditation is a solitary activity in which the individual communicates with God, this activity becomes transformed into a community activity on many occasions at Ananda. At those times, the power of the individual meditation is enhanced by the energy of the group. Thus,

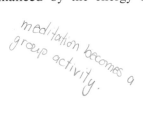
meditation group activity becomes a

members have the best of both worlds – a practice that is individual and collective at the same time, satisfying both the need for individual striving and the need for collective participation. Every business meeting, party, house warming, or church service incorporated meditation.

Through the proper use of kriya yoga, Ananda members told me, a person can successfully overcome bad karma without having to go through the usual long process of many lifetimes. In other words, kriya constitutes a spiritual short-cut through the world of illusion back to the Self from which all selves come. But, equally important, through yoga members re-established the lost connections fostered by the cultural shift to an isolated self, doing so through repetitive experience rather than mere belief.

Meditation reconstitutes, again and again, the mystical experiences that brought many Ananda members to the community. For example, one young man described this experience as the "loss of ego as usually experienced merging with all . . . leaving body consciousness and returning with a feeling of ever new joy." Another spoke of "a vision of creation . . . with the saint . . . beyond creation. Each time, both the world and myself ceased to exist. I was pure experience – no body, no mind, no emotions, no thoughts, just aliveness."

One man recounted this experience: "Once, on LSD, I experienced great lightness and joy and was thinking of how enjoyable it was, when the strong thought entered my mind, 'It's not the drug.' It was the last time I did drugs."

Meditation and the other practices of yoga provide individuals with a steady program of both effort and experience that is psychologically more satisfying than drugs, because it integrates them back into the social fold without mitigating the experience of self:

I lost consciousness and tumbled down a long tunnel with light at the end during which seemingly answers to all questions past, present, and future were understood. Later, when I was conscious, looking up at a very bright star or planet which divided and became the eyes of God, he spoke to me saying why do you continue this, I have shown you the way, I have given you Yoga.

Reconciling rationality and emotion

One of the main problems faced by young people during and after the sixties was the disillusionment with the efficacy of science and of rationality in general. Members of the baby boom generation – a highly idealistic generation with high expectations of the world – came of age seeing the evil in the world: racism, inequality, poverty, hypocrisy, and war. Rationality and science had aided and abetted these evils rather than mitigating or eliminating them.

As scholars probed history to discover the way in which science was really carried out and to rediscover the contributions of previously invisible participants such as African-Americans and women, many young people abandoned their faith in science and progress. They were left, then, with the desire to abandon rationality altogether but with nothing to put in its place other than mysticism and nature. But these highly educated, middle-class young people, who, for the most part, shared many of their parents' values, could not totally erase their cultural preference for the scientifically valid, even while giving vent to emotion or intuition as more fundamental forms of experience. As one member said, "My only problems with these beliefs was that I felt they were very much on the surface of people's lives and, thus, were somewhat hypocritical."

A 35-year-old man who had majored in philosophy reported that his life changed after:

finding western philosophy and the rational mind couldn't give me the truth. I learned this in college . . . After I saw the rational mind wasn't the answer, I thought maybe God was. I realized that my ego was in the way of experiencing God but didn't know how to get rid of it. I prayed that if there was a God that he show me how to get rid of ego so I could find Him. He gave me a very profound experience . . . I felt God was real and with me in everyday life. I talked to Him and thanked Him for his love.

That man "wanted to experience God and felt that Ananda was the best place to do it." A 37-year-old Ananda member, describing his change in outlook, noted:

I was materialistic and scientific. I'm still scientific, but see the universe descending down from spirit; intentional from absolute intelligence/consciousness . . . The fruit was ripe, I guess. I began to wonder if there were higher realities beyond my human self, my immediate world, and this world's "reality."

Part of this member's change in outlook came from a mystical experience that he says is "too sacred to write about" but which he described as "an experience of perfect bliss," which had come about during the course of his regular meditations. He subsequently had successive experiences involving "a vision of creation" and another "beyond creation." He stated: "Each time, both the world and myself ceased to exist. I was pure experience – no body, no mind, no emotions, no thoughts, just *aliveness*" (speaker's emphasis). That these experiences led him to reformulate his views about the nature of the universe are evidenced in this written account, that illustrates how he reconciles the belief in science with his new emphasis on experience:

I have a special interest in dogma vs. truth. Even Ananda cannot escape a certain amount of dogma. Let's define dogma. A dogmatic belief can be true (regarding some fact) but, in Ananda's definition, it is untrue in the sense that a person is believing blindly, without direct personal knowledge (experience). So, how can I rightly believe in all our dogmas, that is, about our gurus, miracle working, metaphysical states, etc.? Well, several reasons. For one thing, every spiritual truth, both in broad scope and in details, that has been possible for me to prove as true or false has been proven to me to be true. This has even included not only directions for achieving true happiness but some of the weird stuff as well. Once, in a very dramatic fashion, Swami [Kriyananda] told me of a slight passing thought that I'd had about six months earlier and never mentioned. I nearly fell off my chair! On Swami's last birthday, a brilliant rainbow appeared in the sunny, clear blue sky. One person told me he was just sitting there, waiting for it to appear, and that a rainbow had appeared in a blue, cloudless sky on each of Swami's birthdays (during the celebration) for the past four years. As he told me this while I was watching it, I said, "Wow, I have just stepped into the Twilight Zone!" You know, that "peak experience" comes from *someplace*. It's not just some random collision of mental electrons. There is a *ghost* in the machine. All major religions teach the same ideals and values, if you look beneath the apparent separating dogmas. There are universal principles which are one with this universe. They indicate where the universe emerged from.

Yogananda's teachings were particularly resonant with the consciousness of young Americans searching for something more than the familiar, both because of his openness to people from all religious denominations but also in his concentration on meditation and first-hand knowledge of God. Yogananda taught that religion need not be dogmatic and that God need not be accepted on faith:

Science and religion should go hand in hand. All the results of scientific investigation are definite and are connected by reason, whereas religion is often dogmatic. When Jesus urged his disciples to have faith, he didn't mean blind belief. It breaks my heart when I see blind dogmatism, for it is one reason why the majority of people have no real interest in God . . . Those who want to seek Him earnestly should learn how to do so scientifically. (1982: 48)

In taking up the practice of yoga, Ananda members are able to reconcile the scientific bent of American culture with the need to trust feeling and intuition. "Yoga is definite and scientific. Yoga means union of soul and God, through step-by-step methods with specific and known results. It raises the practice of religion above the differences of dogma" (Yogananda 1982: 48).

The experience of God that Ananda members achieve through the practice of kriya yoga serves as a means of empirical verification of His existence. Through meditation one knows God for oneself, not having to rely upon second-hand information. And when one has shed the cloak of illusion that comes from clinging to the dogmas of everyday life, one can rely upon one's intuition. Science and intuition, or rationality and feeling, are no longer at odds with one another.

Reconciling self-interest and altruism

Americans have always had a problem reconciling their ideal of rational self-interest with the necessity of charity toward others, both of which constitute major components in their belief system. Self-interest is the outgrowth of the core principle of individualism or self-reliance. Charity toward others is the outgrowth of the Judeo-Christian religious teachings that are the moral foundation of American life. Yet, in the pursuit of one, it is easy to lose sight of the other.

At Ananda the primary way in which these contradictions are reconciled is through karma yoga, union with God through action and selfless service. This selfless service consists primarily of one's everyday work. When Gardner visited Ananda in 1973, he noted the industriousness of its members and referred to it as a bastion of free enterprise (1978). Ananda members are encouraged to start their own businesses, as well as staffing community businesses and seeking work in the outside world. Whatever they do, they are expected to do in a spirit of cooperation rather than competition. They are also expected to be cheerful and to put their best foot forward in whatever they do. Service to others is held in very high regard within the community.

In many ways, Ananda members have invested the old Protestant work ethic with a new vitality born out of their understanding of yoga. But actual work constitutes experience in everyday life that is in accord with their spiritual goals. In one of his writings, *How to Use Money for Your Own Highest Good* (1981), Kriyananda gives Ananda members the following advice:

Whatever you do, therefore, put your full energy into it. If you have to earn money, don't work at it with half your mind, while, with the other half, regretting what you are doing . . . It isn't really important what you do, so long as you see everything that you do as an opportunity for service, for applying energy creatively, for working for the welfare of all. Remember, God is in money, too. God is in business. God is in the banks just as much as He is in the mountains and in the clouds. And though it is, I grant you, more difficult to see Him in the marketplace, nonetheless, He is there. If you look deeply enough, you *must* find Him, wherever you are. (1981: 32–33)

Yet, Ananda members live simply. They see their work as putting out positive energy in a spirit of nonattachment. They are encouraged to work only in those places in which they can retain a positive spiritual attitude, and full members are expected to return part of their income to the community in the form of voluntary tithes.

A 33-year-old male, reflecting on his life at Ananda, said, "It's the only way to live. If one must live in the world, then he must find an outlet to direct his energy (giving) to something greater than himself or his family if he hopes to find any happiness whatsoever." Other members wrote:

My work, like all parts of my life, is part of my spiritual search. I meditate to find God but also feel we have to bring God into all parts of my life. Working for God is just as important as meditating. It doesn't matter really what you do – work, play, meditate – as long as you do it for God. (35-year-old, man)

It's part of the spiritual path. We in the store work consciously as devotees all day, doing our best to serve our customers and to channel God's love and joy as best as we can. Work is not separate. (39-year-old, woman)

Everyone at Ananda is trying to improve his or her own behavior rather than someone or some group outside of self. Giving is the key. (If one lacks love, one can get it by giving it away. If joy, likewise.) All sorrow comes from thinking of the self with a small "s." (41-year-old, woman)

My work is a great opportunity and challenge to continuously attempt to be a healing channel and see all my patients as God's light as well as coworkers and doctors in the usual dynamics of an intensive care ward. (39-year-old, woman)

I view my work as service and work for God in Joy. I love working with other devotees. (33-year-old, woman)

Ananda members are called upon to make personal sacrifices, mostly in the form of being willing to move to another colony or changing jobs if asked to do so. Many of them told me that they merely accepted this as part of their commitment to the community itself. Yet, I was also told on many occasions that the well-being of the individual was held to be very important at Ananda, and more than one member expressed the view that they saw themselves as a community of eccentrics and individualists – a view not substantiated by my own research within the community. And, although Ananda members describe their community as cooperative, there was a decided lack of anomie that indicated to me a much more communal spirit than was generally acknowledged. The longer members reside in the community, the more in harmony they are expected to be and the more likely they are to become ministers, and this seems to involve more of a willingness to think in communal terms.

Conclusion

In a society like that of the United States in which change is cultivated as an end in itself, contradictions involving self, culture, and environment will readily arise, widening the gap between the real and the ideal at an accelerated rate. When change is the result of serious social problems, as was the case in the years preceding the sixties, then the gulf widens even more. Analyzing the creative way in which Ananda members and those in other successful intentional communities have drawn upon new resources and experiences to make sense of the world and to provide safe havens for themselves, provides valuable data about the interaction of centripetal and centrifugal forces within culture. It also requires us to broaden the applicability of theories of self, revitalization movements and their functions, the nature of syncretism, and the way in which cultural models provide enough flexibility within systems to allow for and encourage necessary change while maintaining continuity.

The relationship between American individualism and self is problematic and often subject to evaluation according to a monolithic view of the Western self (see Spiro 1993). That the American self is changeable has been demonstrated by Veroff, Douvan, and Kulka (1981), but any disparity between the view of self and external environmental conditions or the view of self and cultural ideology can cause dissonance. The isolated self that emerged out of the detritus of the sixties might have been more compatible with the cultural ideology of individualism than the parental generation's sociocentric self, but it left people longing for community as a remedy for that isolation.

The need for a deeper understanding of the relationship between individualism and self in the United States requires new theory, such as that of Mageo's "reconfiguring self" (1995), which can be applied to American discourse. Mageo's approach represents "a path between cultural relativism and essentialism" in which "sociocentric or egocentric representations of self" constitute part of a larger picture of cultural premises and the resistance to them within the process of socialization. The struggle of Ananda members to reconcile ideas and experiences of self with their cultural requirements for individualism indicates both a fundamental psychological need (connection with others, community) that had been neglected and a more relative need (self-reliance) indicated by their cultural ideology. Mageo's positing of different discourses that "encompass stray experiences of self within a descriptive system" provides a means by which the array of American selves emerging in specific circumstances might be explained.

Precisely because of the constant and often traumatic changes in the United States, religious experience remains an important factor in helping people adjust and provides a venue in which conflicting cultural symbols can be mediated. American culture often emphasizes practical action based on scientific knowledge or practical market solutions to such an extreme that it drives its own citizens in pursuit of religious experience as a palliative, as De Tocqueville noted in the early nineteenth century when he wrote that "certain momentary outbreaks occur when their souls seem suddenly to burst the bonds of matter by which they are restrained and to soar impetuously towards heaven" (1945: 142).

important

Thus, revitalization movements – which include the formation of new religions and intentional communities in state societies – are distinctly therapeutic. They are the means through which psychological security is restored and people are protected against the ravages of change. New religion formation and intense periods of community building become important measures of the disturbance of well-being in complex societies. Zablocki mentions four distinct periods of communitarianism in the United States before the fifth period that took place in the 1970s (1980: 31–40).

Most of these communities do not last very long, but the ones that do, which tend to be overwhelmingly religious in their focus, presumably meet some permanent or long-term need that the mainstream society was not meeting. Ananda Village, at almost thirty years old, constitutes a successful intentional community if longevity is the measure (see Gardner 1978, Kantor 1972, and Kramer 1955 for various criteria for judging intentional communities). In spite of its high scores on measures of community viability (see Brown 1987: 144–158), the true insight into Ananda's long-term appeal is better verified by responses to the Value Orientation Interviews I conducted there (see Brown 1987: 101–115).

The results of these interviews indicated that the dominant orientations of Ananda members deviated substantially from those of American society generally in that they tended to relate to each other collaterally rather than individualistically, they tended to see themselves in harmony with nature rather than in mastery over nature, and their time orientation placed the emphasis on the present over the future, because of their belief in the principle of karma by which the present influences the past and the future (Brown 1987: 114; cf. Kluckhohn and Strodtbeck 1973).[9] Thus, this research instrument demonstrated that substantial differences from mainstream American society were real enough to motivate people to find solace elsewhere.

I used to think that the commitment mechanisms that so many social scientists concentrated on in trying to explain the longevity of some intentional communities were the key elements. But insights provided by the Value Orientation Interview have led me to focus more on the deep need of baby boomers to reconcile the dissonance in their lives. In other words, the forces that led people to found and flee to intentional communities in the first place are the same forces that determine the longevity of these communities and the commitment of people to them.

Wallace notes that revitalization movements seek "a more satisfying way of life" for their members (1956: 264), and, as I have demonstrated above, the Ananda community has certainly done that. Over the years since Ananda's inception, American society has in many ways moved closer to the beliefs and experiences of Ananda members. But the continuing pursuit of community indicates that this problem has not been solved for many Americans. The longevity of religions and communities left standing after periods of intense revitalization might be used as measures of the perceived deficiencies that a society has had to redress.

Finally, the formation of new religions and communities that combine Eastern and Western cultural elements signals the necessity of broadening our concept of syncretism to include cultural blends that are voluntarily and consciously made. Generally, religious syncretism is presented as the result of acculturation – the clash of two or more different cultures and the imposition of cultural values by a dominant culture upon the subordinate, resulting in new forms in which elements of the dominant culture often mask those of the subordinate culture, which continue to flourish. The revitalization movements most often studied are the consequence of change caused by such clashes – the Ghost Dance and Handsome Lake in native North America (Kehoe 1989 and Wallace 1969, respectively), Voudou in Haiti (Bourguignon 1976), cargo cults in Melanesia (Schwartz 1976), and Mau Mau in Kenya (Edgerton 1989).

However, in the case of Ananda village people actively sought out foreign elements to help them come to terms with their own ways of life. These Eastern elements have been a part of the culture for some time (Diem and Lewis 1992, Ellwood 1992), as have other elements of the New Age religion that emerged after the sixties. But these elements lay dormant until the right combination of events led to their conscious appropriation and proliferation. Ananda still offers an easier resolution of conflict and shelter from a cruel world for some than the larger society will ever be able to do, and it does so by bringing in fresh but compatible solutions from the East that emphasize experience rather than mere belief.

Acknowledgments

My fieldwork at Ananda Village was conducted in the summer of 1986. I returned to the village briefly in 1987 to observe Spiritual Renewal Week. I then attended regular meditations with Ananda affiliates in San Diego from 1986–87. I also attended church services during the 1987–88 year when members from the Ananda community attempted to establish a church in San Diego. I wish to thank Vivian Rohrl, Roy D'Andrade, and Ted Schwartz for their assistance along the way in dealing with this material. Vivian Rohrl supervised the original research at Ananda Village and gave me many suggestions about the presentation of this material from the beginning. Roy D'Andrade's course in national character helped me to establish the context within which much of the Ananda and baby boomer material could be understood. Ted Schwartz gave me the first opportunity to present this material publicly. I also wish to thank the members of the Ananda community and Sri Kriyananda (James Donald Walters) for their assistance during the time of my fieldwork there and in San Diego.

NOTES

1 This quotation and all the other quotations from Ananda members (unless otherwise stated) are taken directly from their written comments on a comprehensive survey that I administered in the community during the summer of 1986 (see Brown 1987 for survey and results).
2 On the subject of intentional communities as therapeutic vehicles, see Zielke (1972).
3 For the problem of conformity in the United States and its coexistence with an ideology of individualism see Kluckhohn and Strodtbeck (1973). However, I believe that what social scientists glossed as conformity was really the manifestation of the sociocentric view of self posited by Veroff, Douvan, and Kulka (1981). In other words, although Americans possessed an ideology of self-reliance (individualism), their environment required a different kind of behavior and self-orientation. The scholarly expectation of an American individualistic self masked the sociocentrism of American self-image at this time. For a summary of the baby boom generation during the 1960s see Brown (1999).
4 It is important to note that Ananda members prided themselves on the fact that their community had only two formal rules: no drugs and no dogs. This fits with Zablocki's findings that few people joining Eastern religious communities use drugs after joining.
5 The community directors told me this during an interview in 1986. The membership process described here is based on data collected at that time. However, Ananda is always undergoing change, so it is possible that elements of the process have been refined or changed since then. Dollar amounts subsequently referred to were accurate at the time of my fieldwork and have almost certainly changed since then.
6 The Ananda community and the Ananda church are separate legal entities. The community, its members, and businesses pay taxes. The church has the same status as other churches in the United States.
7 Ananda Village refers to the original community located at Nevada City, California. This community has had a number of names over the years, including Ananda World Brotherhood Village and Ananda Cooperative Village. Most people refer to it simply as Ananda. Ananda has operated a number of centers, mostly in California, Oregon, and Washington, but it has two additional full-fledged communities, which members refer to as colonies, in Assisi, Italy, and in Mountain View, California.
8 This chant can be found in Yogananda's *Cosmic Chants* (1974).
9 In 1987 from a full membership of 160 persons (85 men and 75 women) in residence at the time, I chose a random sample of 10 men and 2 alternates and 10 women and 2 alternates. Of these, I received interviews with 8 women and 7 men. In administering the Value Orientation Interviews, I ran into a problem

with the activity orientation for which Kluckhohn and Strodtbeck provided only two alternatives, Being and Doing, although they acknowledged a third alternative, Being-in-Becoming, without providing questions (Kluckhohn and Strodtbeck 1973: 77). The dominant orientation among Americans was Doing. Because of the emphasis on both Being (meditation) and Doing (karma yoga), Ananda members' responses split right down the middle – producing a statistically nonsignificant result. That this would happen was clear to me during the interviews as interviewees struggled to answer questions that clearly dichotomized their views and did not allow for their orientation. From ethnographic data collected, I would predict a Being-in-Becoming orientation for Ananda members.

REFERENCES

Alexander, Kay 1992 Roots of the New Age. In *Perspectives on the New Age*, James R. Lewis and J. Gordon Melton, eds. Albany, NY: SUNY Press. Pp. 30–47.
Bourguignon, Erika 1976 *Possession*. Prospect Heights, IL: Waveland Press.
Brown, Susan Love 1987 *Ananda Revisited: Values and Change in a Cooperative Religious Community*. Masters Thesis. San Diego, CA: San Diego State University.
   1992 Baby Boomers, American Character, and the New Age: A Synthesis. In *Perspectives on the New Age*, James R. Lewis and J. Gordon Melton, eds. Albany, NY: SUNY Press. Pp. 87–96.
   1993 Individualism and the Transformation of Self in the US. Paper presented at the 92nd Annual Meeting of the American Anthropological Association, Washington, DC.
   1999 Baby Boomers. In *The Sixties in America*, vol. 1, Carl Singleton, ed. Pasadena, CA: Salem Press. Pp. 55–57.
Chaudhuri, Haridas 1965 *Philosophy of Meditation*. New York: Philosophical Library.
D'Andrade, Roy and Claudia Strauss, eds. 1992 *Human Motives and Cultural Models*. Cambridge: Cambridge University Press.
De Tocqueville, Alexis 1945 *Democracy in America*, vol. II. Henry Reeve translation as revised by Francis Bowen. New York: Vintage (originally published 1835).
Diem, Andrea Grace and James R. Lewis 1992 Imagining India: The Influence of Hinduism on the New Age Movement. In *Perspectives on the New Age*, James R. Lewis and J. Gordon Melton, eds. Albany, NY: SUNY Press. Pp. 48–58.
Edgerton, Robert B. 1989 *Mau Mau: An African Crucible*. New York: Ballantine Books.
Ellwood, Robert 1992 How New Is the New Age? In *Perspectives on the New Age*, James R. Lewis and J. Gordon Melton, eds. Albany, NY: SUNY Press. Pp. 59–67.
Gardner, Hugh 1978 *The Children of Prosperity*. New York: St. Martins Press.
Hallowell, A. Irving 1967 *Culture and Experience*. New York: Schocken Books (originally published 1955).
Holland, Dorothy and Naomi Quinn, eds. 1987 *Cultural Models in Language and Thought*. Cambridge: Cambridge University Press.

Kantor, Rosabeth Moss 1972 *Commitment and Community*. Cambridge, MA: Harvard University Press.

Kehoe, Alice 1989 *The Ghost Dance*. New York: Holt, Rinehart and Winston.

Kluckhohn, Florence Rockwood and Fred L. Strodtbeck 1973 *Variations in Value Orientations*. Westport, CT: Greenwood Press.

Kramer, Wendell Barlow 1955 *Criteria for the International Community: A Study of the Factors Affecting Success and Failure in the Planned, Purposefull, Cooperative Community*. Ph.D. Dissertation. New York: New York University.

Kriyananda, Sri 1979a *The Path: Autobiography of a Western Yogi*. Nevada City, CA: Ananda Publications.

    1979b *Cooperative Communities: How to Start Them and Why*. Nevada City, CA: Ananda Publications.

    1981 *How to Use Money for Your Own Highest Good*. Nevada City, CA: Ananda Publications.

Luhrmann, Tanya M. 1989 The Magic of Secrecy. *Ethos* 17(2): 131–165.

Mageo, Jeanette Marie 1995 The Reconfiguring Self. *American Anthopologist* 97(2): 282–292.

Maslow, Abraham H. 1959 Preface. In *New Knowledge in Human Values*, Abraham H. Maslow, ed. New York: Harper and Row. Pp. vii–x.

Nordquist, Ted A. 1978 *Ananda Cooperative Village: A Study in the Beliefs, Values, and Attitudes of a New Age Religious Community*. Uppsala, Sweden: Religionhistorika institutionen.

Robbins, Thomas 1969 Eastern Mysticism and the Resocialization of Drug Users: The Meher Baba Cult. *Journal for the Scientific Study of Religion* 8(2): 308–317.

Sapir, Edward 1994 *The Psychology of Culture: A Course of Lectures*, reconstructed and ed. Judith T. Irvine. Berlin and New York: Mouton de Gruyter.

Schwartz, Theodore 1976 The Cargo Cult: A Melanesian Type-Response to Change. In *Response to Change: Society, Culture, and Personality*, George A. De Vos, ed. New York: D. Van Nostrand. Pp. 157–206.

    1978 Where Is the Culture? Personality as the Distributive Locus of Culture. In *The Making of Psychological Anthropology*, George D. Spindler, ed. Berkeley and Los Angeles, CA: University of California Press. Pp. 419–444.

Spiro, Melford E. 1993 Is the Western Conception of the Self "Peculiar" Within the Context of the World Cultures? *Ethos* 21(2): 107–153.

Strauss, Claudia and Naomi Quinn 1997 *A Cognitive Theory of Cultural Meaning*. Cambridge: Cambridge University Press.

Strickland, Charles E. and Andrew M. Ambrose 1985 The Baby Boom, Prosperity, and the Changing Worlds of Children, 1945–63. In *American Childhood: A Research Guide and Historical Handbook*, Joseph M. Hawes and N. Ray Hinter, eds. Westport, CT: Greenwood Press. Pp. 533–585.

Tipton, Steven M. 1982 *Getting Saved From the Sixties: Moral Meaning in Conversion and Cultural Change*. Berkeley and Los Angeles, CA: University of California Press.

Veroff, Joseph, Elizabeth Douvan, and Richard A. Kulka 1981 *The Inner American: A Self-Portrait from 1957 to 1976*. New York: Basic Books.

Wallace, Anthony F. C. 1956 Revitalization Movements: Some Theoretical

Considerations for Their Comparative Study. *American Anthropologist* 58(2): 264–281.

1969 *The Death and Rebirth of the Seneca*. New York: Alfred A. Knopf.

Yogananda, Paramahansa 1974 *Cosmic Chants*. Los Angeles, CA: Self-Realization Fellowship.

1982 *Man's Eternal Quest*. Los Angeles, CA: Self-Realization Fellowship.

1985 *Autobiography of a Yogi*. Los Angeles, CA: Self-Realization Fellowship.

Zablocki, Benjamin 1980 *Alienation and Charisma: A Study of Contemporary American Communes*. New York: The Free Press.

Zielke, Alfred R. 1972 *The Use of an Intentional Community as an Educative and Therapeutic Vehicle: A Case Study*. Ph.D. Dissertation. New York: New York University.

Part IV

A reinvigorated comparative perspective

8 Cross-cultural studies in language and thought: is there a metalanguage?

Eve Danziger

For any discipline that seeks to understand human nature, a necessary goal is the defining of boundaries between those aspects of humanity that are culturally universal, and those that are elaborated only in particular cultural contexts. This is so whether the researcher is more interested in celebrating diversity by describing the particular, or in emphasizing unity by identifying the universal. As scholarly pursuits, both are at the outset, and, of necessity, comparative activities.[1]

Within anthropology, however, the explicitly comparative enterprise is largely out of fashion. A justified anthropological wariness has grown up about the possibility of any genuinely culturally sensitive comparative research. The commitment to thinking in terms of systems rather than units makes anthropology reluctant to compare individual fragments of what may be very different conceptual complexes. And, at the methodological level the use of standardized tasks for exploration becomes suspect. What is the nature of the activity that each such task represents in different cultures, and therefore what sort of knowledge is being tapped in each case? Yet if tasks are not standardized – not at *any* level the same – surely comparison cannot even begin.

It is critical that psychological anthropology, in particular, once again take up the comparative challenge. Cross-culturally comparative questions are now being addressed in the new discipline of cognitive science, and anthropology has a crucial role to play. The tenets which to anthropologists seem mere background assumptions – that things might be different elsewhere, that what appear intuitively to be basic and natural categories of analysis ought to be questioned on cultural grounds – constitute rare and precious insights in the workaday world of the psychologist and the linguist. Anthropology offers a necessary caution to cognitive science against ethnocentric intuition. It is important that anthropologists turn once again to the elaboration of perspectives and techniques that will allow us to determine when comparison is justifiable – if only in order to be able to say when it is not. At the same time, the careful search for comparative data in domains that are frankly acknowledged to be circumscribed by the interests of a particular research community is an antidote to the existential malaise currently afflicting anthropology. Although one response to the realization that there is no such thing as decontextualized knowing is to cease to desire to know, another is to seek an identifiable context for one's own intellectual program, and to accept the contextualized nature of one's discoveries without rejecting them because they are contextualized.

As an illustration, I outline below the recent history of cross-cultural investigation into the domain of spatial expression and cognition. This domain has recently become a focus of interest for scholars in psychology, linguistics, and now anthropology (Levinson 1996, Miller and Johnson-Laird 1976, Talmy 1983). Questions as to the universality of organization of this domain – both in language and in thinking – have been of great concern. The relationship of linguistic variation to possible variation in habitual thought has once again been taken up. But a close look at the nature of the domain, in light of cross-cultural and cross-linguistic evidence, reveals that it has itself not been sufficiently problematized. The domain as proposed simply does not exist universally across languages and cultures. Far from serving merely to structure perceptions within a necessary domain of space, it can be argued, linguistic (and therefore cultural) expression serves actually to *create* the domain as a relevant one in the minds of speakers. If recognized and carefully handled, however, this fact need not render comparison impossible in all cases.

The question is investigated with respect in particular to observations from speakers of Mopan Maya. Mopan is a Yucatecan language, spoken by about 5000 people in southern Belize and in the Peten region of Guatemala. Belizean Mopan are shifting cultivators of maize, beans, and rice. They live in a small and intimately known region within which access to spatial resources (such as those necessary for hunting, residence, animal husbandry, and agriculture) is negotiated through prayer and offerings directed to the supernatural owners (Mopan *u yumil*) of the landscape (Danziger 1998, Thompson 1930). [2]

Spatial expression and spatial cognition

When cognitive scientists enquire as to the universality of linguistic expression in space they are usually talking about the translational equivalents of relations encoded in English expressions such as *in front of*, *to the right of*, *behind*, and so on (cf. Jackendoff 1987). That is, interest has centered on terms that specify the relationship of one object to another within a matrix of surrounding space, and on the nature of the reference points that are invoked to state this relationship. Initial formulations (Clark 1973, Olson and Bialystok 1983) proposed that the universal reference points for this domain in language and in conceptualization were, as observable in the English expressions, those of the physical body. Recent work in cognitive and linguistic anthropology has shown that this is not the case – at least not for the ways that spatial relations are expressed in language. John B. Haviland (1979, 1993, 1998), working with speakers of Guugu Yimithirr in Northern Australia, reports that these speakers do not make their own bodies the reference points for locutions about spatial locations or regions. Instead, the cardinal directions provide such reference points – even when distances are very small. According to Haviland (1979: 75) these people

routinely use such words [i.e., cardinal point terms] to give immediate and local directions. Instead of saying "There on your right" or "right behind you" they employ a term like *gungga=gunggaarr* "a bit Northwards".

Again, Brown and Levinson (1993) show how Tzeltal Maya regularly use expressions translated as *uphill* and *downhill* rather than equivalents of *left* and *right* to locate objects in space. Does this kind of variation in the ways that people talk in fact mean something for the way that these people conceptualize spatial relationships? If, as is increasingly the case in modern theoretical linguistics (Jackendoff 1983, Langacker 1986), linguistic cognition is understood to be linked to other kinds of cognition, issues of classic linguistic relativity will have to be seriously considered once again. We find ourselves again asking the old anthropological question: what does it mean for thinking, if languages vary?

The writings of Benjamin Lee Whorf (esp., 1956a) are traditionally associated with the twentieth-century formulation of this intriguing question. Whorf suggested that the different linguistic structures of individual languages might influence speakers' everyday habits of thinking and acting at levels well outside our awareness. Given the perceived difficulties of designing appropriate psychological measures, especially in the behaviorist environment of mid-century psychology, work on the Sapir–Whorf hypothesis proceeded for some time in a largely suggestive vein (see, for example, Bright and Bright 1969, Lee 1959, Trager 1959). More recently, however, new studies of Whorfian issues using the experimental methods of cognitive psychology began to appear (Bloom 1981, Heider 1972, Kay and Kempton 1984, Lucy 1992b, Lucy and Shweder 1979; Lucy 1992a provides a fuller review and discussion of some of the critical past research on Whorfian issues). The field of language and thought studies is now seeing something of a revival, with cognitive psychology (Hunt and Agnoli 1991) and linguistic anthropology (Hill and Mannheim 1992, Lucy 1997) both finding new interest in the issues.

As an instance of the new kind of linguistically oriented cognitive anthropology which is now taking up these classic questions of linguistic relativity, Levinson (1998) undertakes an explicitly comparative experimental investigation of the differences in non-linguistic spatial problem-solving between individuals whose language calls for habitual use of *north/south* translation equivalents (Guugu Yimithirr), and those whose language calls for *right/left* translation equivalents (Dutch). Levinson's experiment exploits the fact that spatial relations that have been encoded using systems that are based on the physiological body (left/right) are reversed when the individual rotates. That is, when you turn around 180 degrees, the region you now call *left* is precisely that which a moment ago you called *right*. This is not the case for the region you call *north*.

In the experiment, consultants were asked to contemplate a simple schematic map (Figure 8.1 shows the version of this task for which Mopan results are reported below). Participants were told that this was a diagram of an incomplete route, and they were asked to decide upon the kind of path that would complete the route. The contour of the (imaginary) path that would complete the route was quite distinctive and highly constrained – it had to avoid pools of water, thickets of brush etc., that were depicted on the map. Having indicated that he or she was ready, the consultant was then led into another room, at 180 degrees rotation from the first. He or she was asked to choose, from among three route-completions displayed on cards there, the one that represented the completion for the route that he or she had just seen. One of the three route-completion cards, called the Relative solution, showed a path that would only fit the original map correctly if the consultant had maintained a physiological encoding of it as he or she rotated (that is, if he or she had mentally carried the original map along, and now imagined it as it would appear if laid out in front of him or her – therefore rotated 180 degrees from its actual position). A second route-completion card, called the Absolute solution, showed a path that would only fit the original map if the consultant had maintained a non-physiological encoding of it as he or she rotated – that is, if he or she imagined the original, still in place in the first room, unrotated. The third route-completion card, the Distractor or non-solution, showed a path that would never fit the original map under any rotation. Over five trials, Levinson found that every one of fifteen Dutch-speaking subjects preferred to select the Relative route-completion card. By contrast, of twelve Guugu Yimithirr-speaking subjects, eight preferred to select the Absolute route-completion card in a majority of trials.

More recent collaborative work in the same vein (Pederson *et al.* 1998) expands the range of languages examined, using a slightly different experimental technique.[3] Here, predictions were made for the choices of consultants who were first-language speakers of Arandic (a Central Australian language using *north/south* translation equivalents to express spatial

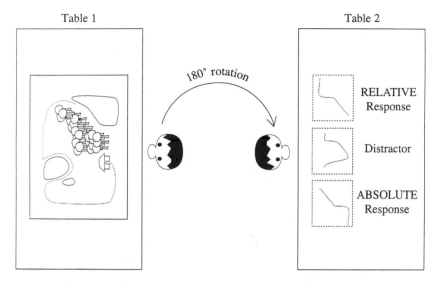

Figure 8.1 The Route-Completion task (Copyright of the Max Planck Institute for Psycholinguistics and reprinted with permission.)

relations), of Tzeltal (a Mayan language using *uphill/downhill* translation equivalents to express spatial relations), of Longgu (an Austronesian language using *seaward/inland* translation equivalents to express spatial relations), of Dutch, and of Japanese (languages using *left/right* translation equivalents to express spatial relations). Consultants were shown a row of three toy animals (three of cow, sheep, pig, and horse), lined up nose to tail and with all three noses pointing either left or right across the consultant's line of vision. Consultants were asked, in their own language, to contemplate this arrangement carefully. When the consultant was ready, the arrangement of animals was destroyed. After a 30 second interval, the consultant was led to a second experimental area, at 180 degrees rotation from the first. Here, he or she was supplied with toy animals identical to those just observed, and was asked, again in his or her own language, to "make it again, just as it was." The consultant was expected to line the animals up in an arrangement that would preserve either the left/right orientation of the original with respect to his or her body (the Relative solution, actually reversing the environmental direction that the animals were facing in the original display) or in one that would preserve the north/south orientation of the animals in the original (the Absolute solution, reversing the original left/right relations).

It had been hypothesized that individuals who spoke a language that expressed spatial relations with reference to the body (Dutch, Japanese) would also choose to solve this non-linguistic problem in such a way as to preserve the orientation of the arrangement to their own bodies – even under rotation (the Relative solution). It had been further hypothesized that individuals speaking a language in which spatial relations were encoded nonphysiologically, would not do so: instead these individuals would solve the problem in such a way as to preserve the environmental orientation of the arrangement under rotation (the Absolute solution). Results showed solid support of this hypothesis. In all five samples, the number of individuals employing the solution predicted as favored for their language community, relative to the number employing the one predicted as disfavored for the language community, was a proportion of at least four to one (see Levinson and Nagy n.d.).

These experimental data seem to support the hypothesis of linguistic relativity in the domain of spatial cognition. A certain variability in the processing of spatial information has been demonstrated that departs from initial European-based claims about the primacy of the physiological body as point of reference. But the problem of the formulation of the comparative question has not yet been addressed. How can it be possible to compare ways of thinking across speech communities, if one of the primary hypotheses of the research is the possibility that conceptual categories might be fundamentally different? Can we be sure, in short, that the domain of spatial relations itself is a valid comparative framework within which to set experimental tasks across cultures?

The work in spatial reference and spatial cognition, like most existing empirical studies dealing with issues of universalism and relativism in language and thought can be characterized as "domain-based" (Lucy 1997). Such studies have started by defining a semantic domain of investigation (like "color," "kinship," "botany" or "space"), and have proceeded to discover how different languages deal with it. This procedure is opposed, for example, to studies like those of Whorf which look first for observable typological differences in language structure and then seek ways to identify correlations in behavior. Previous domain-based studies have been criticized (Dougherty 1978, Hunn 1985, Lucy 1992a: 146–156, Needham 1971, Randall and Hunn 1984, Schneider 1984) – and research in some domains actually abandoned – for lack of attention to the niceties of comparative desiderata. The difficulties stem from the fact that a full reading of the Sapir–Whorf hypothesis must envisage the possibility that any preconceived semantic domain might not be a valid unit in some existing alternative cultural world view. But since the domain is the methodological starting point of the investigation, true differences in global conceptualization are unlikely to appear. Because it defines the framing question which is asked of every participant, the original domain will necessarily emerge as universal – any discoveries of cultural and linguistic divergence from the original will consist only in differences of *organization* of the same conceptual territory. Radical differences will be invisible except to the extent that certain peoples may appear less proficient than the original group at organizing this same territory. No people will emerge as *more* proficient, since any unexpected complexity in cultural understandings of the elements of the original domain are excluded from consideration by the rules of the game – freshness is not color; function is not taxonomy; solidarity is not kinship.

The recent spate of work in spatial cognition is in danger of falling victim to these same errors. However, by taking full account of the acknowledged problems of this sort of approach, I aim to show here how a domain-based comparison, if cautiously handled, may actually suggest radically relativist conclusions. I will first report the discovery that not all groups of people make the expected linguistic distinctions within the domain of lateral spatial relations as it has been defined to date. I insist however that this observation be taken as evidence of the failure of the proposed domain, rather than a failure of the group in question. I do this from anthropological but also from comparative methodological first principles. A first finding therefore is that the domain of spatial relations as initially conceived by European researchers (myself included) cannot be considered a universal arena of linguistic reference. I then apply that discovery to the question of cognition. To the extent that my experimental investigations do not support a natural nonlinguistic understanding of this same domain of lateral spatial relations on the part of Mopan Maya speakers, they also suggest that, rather than language and culture being factors only in the *organization* of a pre-existing conceptual domain of spatial relations, this conceptual domain is culturally contingent – it is in fact nonobligatorily *created* through cultural and linguistic experience.

The domain of spatial relations

In order to elicit expressions of spatial relationship in what was hoped would constitute a comparable activity context, a standard interactive task, presented as a game, was used across all of the speech communities represented in the Animals-in-a-Row experiment (Pederson *et al.* 1998). In the task, two members of the same speech community sit beside one another, but are separated by a screen so that neither participant can see objects or pictures that the other may be manipulating. Both participants are given an identical set of twelve photographs, each photo only slightly different from the others. One participant is now identified as the "director" and he or she is asked to characterize, using language alone (i.e., without the aid of gesture), one picture of the twelve. The "matching" participant is asked to try to identify the particular photo by asking questions of his or her partner. This continues through the entire series of twelve photos.[4]

Interactive games of this type have been used in well over a dozen different cultural contexts (Pederson and Roelofs 1995), consulting at least three pairs of native speakers in each community. In all cases, participants engage with the activity, and endeavor to find the right match for the photo being described. The comparative project exploits this fact, using the standardization of game materials, and the acceptance of the imposed motivations of the game, to constitute an artificial but comparable situation in each speech community. It becomes possible deliberately to create contrast sets of very similar pictures, each of which ideally differs from its fellows only in terms of a single spatial-relational property. Whether or not this is actually achieved, the juxtaposition of the particular contrasts embedded in such sets becomes a *de facto* metalanguage for the domain envisaged by the comparative enterprise.[5]

The particular game that is crucial in the context of the experiments described is one in which six different photographs show the same toy man and the same toy tree side by side (see Figure 8.2). The man and the tree are arranged laterally across each photo: from the viewer's perspective they are always beside one another. In the different photos, the man is shown in different postures with respect to the tree: turned sideways, facing it, or with his back to it, for example. In three of the photos the man appears to the left of the tree from the viewer's perspective, and in three he appears to the right, again from the viewer's perspective. In order to distinguish linguistically among the six photos, speakers must articulate and conjoin a variety of contrasts. Of particular interest has been the contrast that distinguishes between the three photos in which the man stands on the left-hand side of the photo (numbers 3, 4 and 7), and the three in which he stands on the right (numbers 5,6 and 8).

As we have seen, this contrast can be expressed in different functionally equivalent ways in language. In the interactive game context, speakers of different languages indeed choose different means to do so. The three pairs of Dutch speakers consulted all used translation equivalents of *left* and *right*.[6] Two pairs of Arandic speakers used translation equivalents of *north*, *south*, *east*, and *west*, and the third pair referred to the shadow cast by the tree in order to distinguish between the two series of photos. Two pairs of Tzeltal speakers used translation equivalents of *uphill* and *downhill*, and a third used translation equivalents of *sunrise* and *sunset*. But, in three pairs of speakers of Mopan Maya, this contrast was never made at all.

The Mopan speakers who were consulted characterized each photo in

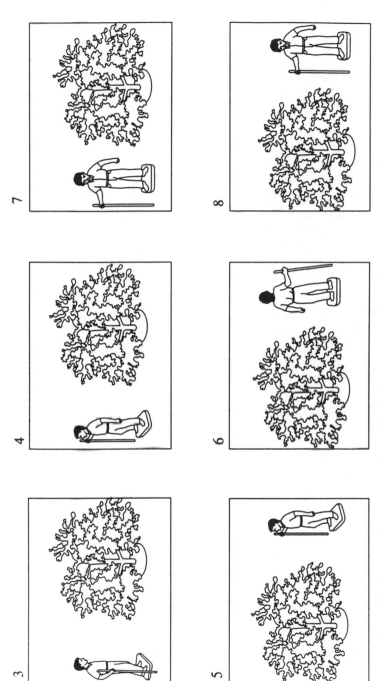

Figure 8.2 Various arrangements of man "beside" tree for the Man and Tree Game (Copyright of the Max Planck Institute for Psycholinguistics and reprinted with permission.)

terms of the relations that the parts of the man have to the tree. One Mopan description of photo number 4 for example, was of the following form:

Ka'-a-käx-t-e'	a	nene'	tz'ub'	a	la-Ø',
You-should-find-him	the	little	child	who	is-here

a	t-u-pach	ke'en-Ø	a	top'-o.
who	at-his-back	is-located	the	bush.

Environmental co-ordinates (e.g., *sunrise, north*) are never used by Mopan speakers playing this game to locate the man and the tree with respect to one another. In only one instance is a translation equivalent of the English words *right* or *left* used by a Mopan speaker to locate either the man or the tree. In a description of photo number 8 (see example below), one speaker states that the tree is to the right of the man. In this photo, the man faces us as viewers of the photograph. The tree is at his right hand – and he is on the right-hand side of the photograph. There is no sense in which, for this picture, 'the tree is at the right of the man' can be taken to refer to anything but the man's own parts:

D:	Käx-t-e'	a	tz'ub'	a	w-a'an-Ø	yok'ol	tunich.
	You-should-find-him	the	child	who	is-standing	on	a stone

	... B'a'al-a'	yan-Ø	top'	t-u-tzeel-i.
	... Like this	exists	bush	at-his-side.

M:	Ich	lef	waj	ich	rait?
	At	left	or	at	right?

D:	Ich	rait	ke'en-Ø	a	top'-o.
	At	right	is-located	the	bush.

	A-käx-t-aj-Ø waj?
	Did-you-find-it?

M:	In-käx-t-aj-Ø.
	I-found-it.

The fact that Mopan speakers do not make a global contrast between these two sets of photos means that apparent underdifferentiation of certain photos occurs in Mopan. In two photos (number 3 and number 5), for example, the man faces the tree; in photo number 3 the man stands on the left side of the photo. In photo number 5 he stands on the right. Mopan speakers, who otherwise appear well motivated and engaged in the task, systematically do not produce language which will distinguish these two photos from one another. The example below is the full description of photo number 5 given by one Mopan player. Her partner did not question the description, and confidently matched it with photo number 3. Note that, in light of the description that was offered, this is not an incorrect match. Both photo number 5 and photo number 3 fit a description in which the bush is located [at his chest]. What is noteworthy here is that neither Mopan player found it necessary to distinguish these two photos any further from one another.

Ka'-a-käx-t-e'	a	nene'	tz'ub'
Let-you-find-him	the	little	child

a	t-u-ta'an	ke'en-Ø	top'-o.
who	at-his-chest	is-located	bush.

Also outside the interactive game context, in spontaneous discourse, Mopan usage can be observed to show similar characteristics. Cardinal direction terms are rare to nonexistent, and specific orientational information is rarely important in Mopan life. For example, although the form of the cross is important in Mopan ritual procedure (censing with *pom* incense should envelope the four corners and then the center of the object being purified), the four corners are not separately named, and one can proceed through the ritual in any orientational order as long as the final point is the center.

Mopan expressions denoting the coming out and the going in of the sun (Mopan *jok'eeb' k'in* and *okeeb' k'in* respectively) which might be taken to translate *east* and *west* are in fact at best ambiguous as between spatial and temporal meanings. On one occasion, for example, my intended question as to whether one should start an important ritual in the East (*jok'eeb' k'in*) met with a negative answer. My interlocutor then continued to speak, informing me that one should start at 11o'clock at night and not at dawn (*jok'eeb' k'in*) for such an important event. On another occasion, a question which I had phrased more specifically in spatial terms (*tub'a walak u jok'ol a k'in?* [Where does the sun come out?]) received the accurate but non-directional answer "*Tu yit ka'an*" [At the horizon]. Meanwhile, no indigenous translation equivalents of *north* and *south* appear to exist at all: Said one acquaintance in English, expressing the sentiment that such terms may once have existed but have now been forgotten, "Maybe my grandfather in his grave knows!" Terms borrowed from Spanish and English for *north* and *south* are rare in natural speech and not all Mopan informants even recognize these terms.

Translation equivalents of *right hand* and *left hand* do exist in Mopan, and they occur sometimes in elicitation. The indigenous term *seeb'* [speedy, quick] designates the right hand or side of a human or an animal. A term borrowed from Spanish, *suldeero* [deaf] designates the left hand or side of humans and animals. No indigenous Mopan term for the left hand survives. (In colonial Yucatec the term *tz'iik* [angry, malevolent] was used [Barrera Vásquez 1980: 884].) Recently, the terms *rait* and *lef* have been borrowed into Mopan from English and are used in the same spatial contexts as *seeb'* and *suldeero* respectively. All of these expressions, however, indicate only actual human or animal parts, and not regions of abstract space (Danziger 1996b; see also Levinson and Brown 1994). In the sense that Dutch, Japanese, Guugu Yimithirr and Arandic use them, Mopan Maya uses neither translation equivalents of *left/right* nor translation equivalents of *north/south* to indicate horizontal relations in space.

In order to understand these Mopan linguistic facts, we are led seriously to examine a distinction made in perceptual psychology between ways of encoding spatial relationships that are considered "Orientation-Bound" and those that are considered "Orientation-Free" (Cohen and Kubovy 1993, Just and Carpenter 1985, Takano 1989). Consider an English expression such as *the truck stood at the nose of the plane*; unless either the truck or the plane moves independently of the other, the sentence remains true. The Gestalt configuration of truck-and-plane, the speaker, or even the entire cosmos (north etc.), can rotate without consequences for the truth of the sentence. This defines the use of an Orientation-Free encoding of the relationship between truck and plane. Such encoding in language is characteristically phrased in terms of a part of the first object (*nose*), and it depends upon a construal of strict dyadic contiguity between the two objects related (if the truck is a long distance from the plane, or if a large object stands between the two of them, the sentence loses its felicity). But because it remains true under all external rotation, its applicability in a given situation can be quickly assessed without resort to time-consuming mental rotation (cf. Just and Carpenter 1985). By contrast, so-called Orientation-Bound frames of reference (such as those invoked by English *left*, but also by English *north*) commit the user to some form of fixed orientation, and, as a consequence, to various calculations as to the relationship of the particular point of reference invoked (users of *north* must know where north lies at any given moment; users of *left* must know how the relevant physiological body is positioned).[7]

Just as for speakers of many of the world's languages, for Mopan speakers it is quite usual to specify the relation between two objects in space by stating the proximity of one to some part of the other: locutions making use of the translation equivalents of *head, nose, foot, tooth*, and so on, are common. What is unusual about Mopan in the context of other languages investigated is that it is *not* common to use linguistic expressions of any other kind to encode horizontal spatial relations on the dimension lateral to the speaker's body. Linguistic expressions used in Mopan Maya to specify the kinds of relationships instantiated in the Man and Tree game – even those involving words specifying *right hand, left hand, front, back*, etc. function in the manner of English *nose*.

Experimental results from Mopan Maya

We are now in a position to remark that the alternative solutions in both the Route-Completion and the Animals-in-a-Row experiments instantiate actual alternatives only in Orientation-Bound space: in an Orientation-Free characterization the two solutions are equivalent. (That this is so can be seen clearly by noting that the Relative and Absolute solution cards in the Route-Completion game are identical if either one of them is rotated 180 degrees.) But the data from Mopan Maya indicate that, certainly in language, what is known as Orientation-Bound encoding of the relevant kind of spatial relationships does not occur. What is the case then for Mopan spatial conceptualization?

Given its linguistic profile, could Mopan Maya constitute a natural laboratory in which we could observe the conceptualization of spatial relations untrammeled by the obfuscatory effects of language? Since the Mopan language does not supply a ready-made formula into which individuals might transpose the experimental problems, might we expect the performance of Mopan Maya speakers on our experimental tasks to show us the workings of natural cognition with respect to Orientation-Bound spatial relations in the lateral dimension – unaided, but also unimpeded by facile or superficial facts of linguistic encoding? In August of 1993 I asked a number of Mopan consultants to solve both the Animals-in-a-Row and the Route-Completion puzzles for me.

Animals-in-a-Row

As described above, in this experiment, consultants are asked to consider an arrangement of three toy animals, aligned before the consultant as if traveling across his or her line of vision. The consultant is asked to consider the arrangement carefully, and when she or he has seen enough, the original arrangement is destroyed and the consultant is asked to "make it again" after a 30 second waiting period, and on a surface rotated 180 degrees from the original one.

The first Mopan consultant whom I asked to perform this task arranged the line of animals on the second table in such a way that they faced, not laterally across her line of vision, but roughly toward herself. The second, to my relief, preserved the lateral orientation of the line of animals, but over five trials this person persisted in reconstructing the line of animals in a single orientation. That is, although the original line of animals varied in its orientation on the first table (right-facing or left-facing across the consultant's body), the orientational solution arrived at on the second table took no account of this variation.[8] My third consultant combined both this "monodirectional" strategy with the indifference to lateral orientation displayed by the first consultant. When the next consultant also chose a monodirectional solution, it was quite clear that something was badly wrong.

I now altered the experimental protocol, and started asking explicitly that consultants pay attention to the orientation of the animals. In the absence of any direct way of expressing this in Mopan I asked consultants, in the initial instruction, to pay attention to the identity of the animals (horse, pig, cow) and also to notice *tub'a tun-cha'an* [where they are looking]. From the point of view of response codability things improved. Of the seventeen consultants who solved the Animals-in-a-Row puzzle under these new conditions [where they are looking], nine showed a preference for an Absolute solution over five trials, and three for a Relative solution.

Fearing that the instructions, and particularly the word *tub'a* [where] were too environmentally oriented, I enlisted twelve more consultants to solve the problem when asked to pay attention to [how] (Mopan *b'ikij*) the animals were looking. Of the twelve, nine showed a preference for an Absolute solution and none for a Relative one.

Route-Completion

The Route-Completion experiment investigates a consultant's preference for a rotated path-completion when they themselves have been rotated 180 degrees (recall Figure 8.1). We have seen that Guugu Yimithirr speakers ([north/south] speakers) often prefer a completion that preserves the orientation of the original, while Dutch speakers ([left/right] speakers) overwhelmingly prefer the rotated completion.

Mopan consultants were asked to consider a diagram like the one shown on the left in Figure 8.1, spread before them on a table top. Consultants were told that certain areas were shaded to represent bush, certain others water, and that the dark line represented a path. Consultants were asked to think of the house shown as their house, and to see themselves as having walked the path shown until they reached its end. On the understanding that woods and water were dangerous, consultants were asked in Mopan "How could there be a new path so that you could get home quickly?"

B'ikij	ka-yan-ak-Ø	a	tumul	b'ej,
How	let-it-exist	a	new	path,

ka-usk'-ak-ech	ti jomol?
let-you-reach_home	soon?

Having seen as much as they wished of the original map, consultants were led over to a different table at 180 degrees rotation from the first. After a 30 second interval, consultants were asked to choose the right path for getting home from among three cards showing possible candidates. One card (Absolute solution) showed a path that would complete the maze in its original orientation. One (Relative solution) showed a path that would complete it if rotated 180 degrees. And one (Distractor, non-solution) showed a path that would not complete the maze under any circumstances.

In coding, an individual's choices over five trials were compared. Consultants who chose the Distractor solution more than once over five trials were eliminated from further analysis. Those remaining who chose either the Relative or the Absolute solution at least three times over five trials were coded for their preference.

It was once again extremely difficult to code the preferences of the eight Mopan consultants who assisted me in solving the Route-Completion puzzle under the conditions outlined above. Of eight consultants, only four showed a codable (3/5) preference.[9] In hope of achieving a more codable result, this experimental protocol also was modified. Sixteen consultants were asked to perform the same Route-Completion task, except that these consultants were asked to draw the new path that they had imagined onto the original (plastic) map with a marker. They were invited to contemplate the resulting configuration for as long as they wished, after which it was covered with a cloth and an interval of 30 seconds allowed to pass. As before, consultants were then led over to a different table at 180 degrees rotation from the first, and were asked to choose the right path for getting home from among three cards showing the three possible candidates as outlined above. Consultants were now being asked to remember and match, not the shape and orientation of an imaginary line, but that of an actual one which they themselves had drawn. Under these conditions, consultants showed more consistency in their preferences across trials. Of sixteen consultants, fourteen were codable: nine preferred the Relative solution, and five preferred the Absolute.

Mopan experimental results

Clearly, no monolithic Mopan preference toward Absolute or Relative nonlinguistic strategies is identifiable. The overall trend is toward preferring the Relative solution in the modified Route-Completion task, and toward preferring the Absolute solution in the modified Animals-in-a-Row task. There seems to be a great deal of influence of the particular task conditions and instructions on the solution that an individual chooses.

Most striking of all, however, is the difficulty of implementing, with Mopan consultants the experiments as they were originally described, and as they were administered by other researchers without comparable problems among speakers of other languages around the world (Baayen and Danziger 1994). The main result from Mopan is not that under different conditions of instructions and experimental material, responses varied across tasks. It is the fact that without further clues – whether explicit in the instruction to pay attention to where/how the animals are looking, or implicit in the addition of a bodily gesture (drawing in the path) – the issues of spatial relations which the researchers had assumed were incorporated in obvious fashion into the task, did not appear obvious at all to Mopan speakers.

In understanding this difficulty as a significant Mopan result, it is also important to recall, not just that Mopan people showed difficulty with the tasks as initially implemented, but that it *was* ultimately possible to construct versions of the tasks which Mopan did find comprehensible. The mere fact of the experimental context and the mere appearance of the experimental materials were not the sources of the difficulty. Rather, in both Route-Completion and Animals-in-a-Row, it was the assumption implicit in the experimental materials themselves – that a difference in lateral Orientation-Bound relations alone would appear to all humanity as an obvious one – that constituted the difficulty.

A fortuitous stretch of unintentionally recorded videotape captured the experience of one Mopan woman in her 50s (ES), as she interacted with the materials of the Route-Completion task for a few moments while I was unexpectedly called out of the room. In order to understand her reactions it is important to know that before finalizing the modified version of the Route-Completion puzzle as described above, I experimented with a version in which a first stage of training was conducted with the task materials laid out together in a single orientation. Before being introduced to the fact that they themselves were to be rotated 180 degrees, consultants piloting this version of the task were shown that, in this constant orientation, only the Relative solution card, but not the Absolute or Distractor cards, could be lifted to fit neatly onto the map. ES was one of four consultants with whom I piloted this version of the task (it was partly because of her puzzled reaction that I moved on to the modified version described more fully above). In the moments immediately before I left ES alone in the experimental room, we had just completed several explanatory exchanges during which I had been showing her that only the Relative solution card, but not the Distractor or the Absolute solution card would fit the map. Under this condition of no rotation, she had already twice succeeded – although with some hesitation and diffidence – in picking the Relative solution card as the correct answer from among the three provided. I had not yet introduced the complication of the 180 degree rotation of the consultant to ES. In a way that clearly illuminates her sense of the proceedings, the video camera records how she contemplated and manipulated the three plastic solution cards during my brief absence.

After I left the room, ES moved to the side of the small table on which we had been working, and she began to handle the three solution cards, comparing them under various spatial rotations. The camera records how she first reached for the Relative solution card, and laid it down in front of herself – upside down. It now would have looked from her perspective just like the Absolute solution card which she was also contemplating (recall that only moments ago she had been told that only one of these was the correct solution). She then rotated the Relative solution card clockwise through 90 degrees, so that it was perpendicular to the other two cards on the table, and she held it alongside them to compare again. Now she pulled the Absolute solution card toward herself (without rotating it) and she compared it more closely to the Relative solution card, giving a short helpless chuckle. Finally, she rotated the Absolute solution card a full 180 degrees, pausing for a moment at the 90 degree point in her rotation (at that point the Absolute solution card would have looked from her perspective maximally different from the Relative solution card which she also continued to contemplate). As she was finishing the full rotation of the Absolute solution card, I returned to the room. ES said to me:

> Ma' jedeek in-b'etiki.
> Not possible I-do-it.

She used at this point a Mopan form of words which does not refer in particular to the individual abilities of the speaker, but (by default) rather to the affordances of the physical world. I replied encouragingly. Turning slightly to me, she now rotated the Absolute solution card another 90 degrees clockwise. This last rotation yielded the Absolute solution card looking identical to the Relative solution card as it appeared at that moment on the table. My sense is that this last rotation was for my benefit; it offered from just outside the channel of explicit spoken interaction the evidence of her difficulty. She now spoke again:

> Ma' patal-en-i.
> Not I-am-capable.

This time, perhaps out of courtesy to me, she used a predicate form which emphasized her own inability rather than the insufficiency of my materials. Once again, I replied encouragingly and she allowed me to guide her through the standardized procedures of further training and of coded trials. During coded trials involving 180 degree rotation of her own body, ES favored the Relative solution over the Absolute one. But although she evidently understood my instructions sufficiently to realize that I was asking her to take account of orientatioɪ ι in selecting her solution, she had in fact already told me (in a way that I did not fully appreciate until later) that this did not appear to her to be a particularly easy or a particularly sensible request.

As the fortuitous videotaped excerpt shows, and as the quantitative data confirm, the problem of orientation posed in the two experiments does not appear to have made much sense to Mopan speakers. Far from providing a view of any a-linguistic and natural approach to the problem, the Mopan reaction to the experiment is evidence that the problem itself is a culturally relative one – even when posed in the non-linguistic realm. The Mopan results constitute initial evidence that, even nonlinguistically, the domain of lateral Orientation-Bound spatial relations is a cultural construct.

To the extent that languages do not encode Orientation-Bound relations in the lateral dimension, it seems that individuals may also have little sense that they are relevant even in nonlinguistic tasks which, to members of other speech communities, appear to embody aspects of these relations in an intuitively obvious way. If this is true, the particular facts of linguistic encoding not only *structure* conceptualization within the domain of spatial relations – a domain once thought to be invulnerable to cultural influences – they may actually *create* the domain as a functional entity.

Conclusion

Within the proposed domain of spatial relations we can draw the conclusion from the data outlined here that – certainly in language and arguably in conceptualization – Orientation-Free encoding of spatial relations stands as a candidate universal. We now know, however, that – again, certainly in language and arguably in conceptualization – Orientation-Bound encoding of spatial relations in the dimension lateral to the human body is not. Where such encoding does appear in language and in thinking, its structure varies across cultures – yielding differences between what have been called Relative and Absolute patterns of linguistic and cognitive encoding.

The Mopan pattern is rare across speech communities sampled (Pederson *et al.* 1998) and it is not observable to the same degree in all Mopan individuals (Danziger 1999). Nevertheless, its appearance as described here is enough to disconfirm the intuitive assumption that sensitivity to orientation across the lateral dimension of the human body is a *necessary* component in human apprehension of the tasks presented. To that extent, the notion of an obvious and natural domain of lateral spatial relations, appropriately represented for cross-cultural research in the form of these sorts of materials, must come under heavy scrutiny.

To draw a more general conclusion, it seems that certain intuitively natural domains of cognition may in fact be cultural constructs facilitated by language. They are not necessary components of human cognition, and can be expected to vary in their organization across cultures and languages. Indeed, they need not even appear in all cultural cases. The domain of lateral spatial relations as instantiated in the contrasts embedded in the Man and Tree game appears to be one such case. Mopan linguistic patterns, and Mopan responses to the experimental tasks designed to investigate this domain, indicate that comparison of Mopan with other cultures with respect to this postulated domain is not justifiable. Mopan speakers do not readily make linguistic distinctions in Orientation-Bound space in the lateral dimension. While it may be initially illuminating to note that all human groups are not alike – nor even functionally equivalent – in their treatment of these materials, further comparison of Mopan speakers with speakers of languages in which such distinctions are obligatory or even habitual is an error of metalanguage. Comparison among communities that can be shown to make Orientation-Bound distinctions in lateral space, however, but which make use of different ways of doing so (as in the case of the five-community experimental study described above), remains defensible.

Finally, it is significant that the cultural relativity of the domain of Orientation-Bound spatial relations appears at first glance to be highly counterintuitive. His many demonizers and mythologizers to the contrary, Whorf's main pessimism in outlining his linguistic relativity principle (Whorf 1956b) was not over any belief that he had discovered that humans were unable to think in any manner not dictated by their language. On the contrary, it was over the fact that he believed he had uncovered in language a mechanism which ensured that most speakers would believe they didn't need to. He warned that culturally variable and language-borne habits of thought could make their way into intuitive conceptualization so early and so easily that they were likely to take on the character of an unexamined second nature. Whorf's primary warning was to science, and not to the layman, lest culturally and linguistically constructed domains should appear so natural as to pass unexamined in scientific investigation. This is a lesson which anthropology is uniquely placed among the cognitive sciences to understand and convey. Collaborating with other students of human nature in such a way as to do so constitutes a context for anthropological inquiry in which anxieties about claims to knowledge can actually become a truly scientific contribution.

Acknowledgments

In this paper, the data from Mopan Maya and the argument as to its significance are my own. But all of the other work reported here has been

massively collaborative, both in its origins and in its continuing development. Where possible, individual contributions have been mentioned in
footnotes. But the work of intellectual creativity is as much in unrecorded
argument as in the final product. I would therefore like to acknowledge a
general debt to all of the members of the Cognitive Anthropology Research
Group from 1991 to 1997. I would also like to thank the Department of
Archaeology in Belmopan, Belize, and to extend my gratitude to my
Mopan consultants, especially those who obliged me by grappling with the
different standardized games and puzzles described. This research was
funded by the Cognitive Anthropology Research Group of the Max Planck
Institute for Psycholinguistics. Figures 8.1 and 8.2 are copyright of the Max
Planck Institute for Psycholinguistics and are reprinted with permission.

NOTES

1 As has been very often remarked, exactly what any cultural researcher finds
   reportable is always a matter of implicit comparison both with the researcher's
   own cultural experience, and with existing-previous reports in the particular
   intellectual tradition to which he or she belongs (cf. Munroe and Munroe, this
   volume).
2 Throughout this chapter, all non-English words and expressions are italicized.
   English words and expressions cited purely as language examples are also italicized. Glosses for non-English expressions appear in square brackets.
   Quotations within text citations appear in single quotes. Double quotes are
   reserved for actual quotes in English or other languages, and for the first presentation of technical or specialized terms in the text. Mopan orthography follows
   the conventions outlined in England and Elliott (1990). Lengthier Mopan
   examples appear with their English glosses in dedicated example paragraphs. In
   these paragraphs, I have provided neither exact morpheme by morpheme
   glosses nor free translation into English. Instead I have preferred to translate
   closely into English, retaining Mopan syntax and word formations where possible. In the English translations, a hyphen indicates that the conjoined items are
   represented by separate parts of a single word in Mopan. An underscore indicates that the conjoined items are inseparable parts of the same lexical unit in
   Mopan. For more detail on the Mopan language the reader is referred to
   Danziger 1994, 1996a, and Ulrich *et al.* 1986.
3 The specific design of this experiment was piloted by Stephen Levinson, and
   finalized by Stephen Levinson and Bernadette Schmitt, under brainstorming
   conditions in which various members of the Cognitive Anthropology Research
   Group participated in early 1993. Linguistic analysis and experimental imple-
   mentation in the various locations was carried out by Penelope Brown and
   Stephen Levinson (Tzeltal), Deborah Hill (Longgu), Kyoko Inoue (Japanese),
   and David Wilkins (Arandic). Misja Schroeder Peters implemented the Dutch
   version of the experiment.
4 This interactive game technique was pioneered in cognitive anthropology by

Lourdes de León (1991), on the model of work by Clark and Wilkes-Gibbs (1986). The particular series of photos eliciting contrasts on the horizontal plane was designed by Eve Danziger and Eric Pederson, and the analysis in terms of functional equivalence was developed by David Wilkins.

5 In many domain-based comparative studies, the physical apparatus and the controlled procedures through which the domain is presented to speakers of different languages become the implicit third term with respect to which the comparison is actually effected. The interactive games described here are designed to elicit particular contrasts that have struck the researchers as interesting or valid; they are therefore ill-equipped either to uncover unexpected contrasts within the domain as proposed, or to provide expansions to the researchers' own understandings of the scope of the domain. Researchers cannot rely exclusively on these games as ethnographic tools.

6 Note that the interactive game context allows us to make the crucial distinction between resources potentially available in language and those actually used in a given context. Dutch, after all, has a word corresponding to English *north*. It simply is not used in this, the designated comparative context.

7 Although habitual users of Orientation-Bound frames of reference become very skilled at this, it is worth pointing out that children in general master left/right and north/south systems only long after truly part-based systems of spatial expression (De León 1994: 880, Johnston and Slobin 1979, Piaget 1928). The properties of Orientation-Free frames of reference (dyadic, non-transitive, stable under rotation), are very much those which characterize Piagetian early-acquired "topological" space (Piaget and Inhelder 1963; see also Levelt 1984).

8 Other researchers elsewhere in the world have also reported this kind of choice.

9 Of these, three chose the Relative solution and one the Absolute.

REFERENCES

Baayen, Harald and Eve Danziger (eds.) 1994 Cognitive Anthropology Research Group. *Annual Report 1993.* Max Planck Institute for Psycholinguistics. Nijmegen, Netherlands. Pp. 63–98.

Barrera Vásquez, Alfredo 1980 *Diccionario Maya Cordemex.* Merida, Yucatan: Ediciones Cordemex.

Bloom, Alfred 1981 *The Linguistic Shaping of Thought.* Hillsdale, NJ: Erlbaum.

Bright, Jane and William Bright 1969 Semantic Structure in Northwestern California and the Sapir–Whorf Hypothesis. In *Cognitive Anthropology*, S. Tyler, ed. New York: Holt, Rinehart and Winston. Pp. 66–78.

Brown, Penelope and Stephen C. Levinson 1993 'Uphill' and 'Downhill' in Tzeltal. *Journal of Linguistic Anthropology* 3: 46–74.

Clark, Herbert 1973 Space, Time, Semantics, and the Child. In *Cognitive Development and the Acquisition of Language*, T. E. Moore, ed. New York: Academic Press. Pp. 27–64.

Clark, Herbert and Deanna Wilkes-Gibbs 1986 Referring as a Collaborative Process. *Cognition* 21: 1–39.

Cohen, Dale and Michael Kubovy 1993 Mental Rotation, Mental Representation and Flat Slopes. *Cognitive Psychology* 25: 351–382.

Danziger, Eve 1994 Out of Sight, Out of Mind: Person, Perception and Function in Mopan Maya Spatial Deixis. *Linguistics: An Interdisciplinary Journal of the Language Sciences* 32: 885–907.

1996a Split Intransitivity and Active-Inactive Patterning in Mopan Maya. *International Journal of American Linguistics* 62: 379–414.

1996b Parts and their Counter-parts: Social and Spatial Relationships in Mopan Maya. *The Journal of the Royal Anthropological Institute N.S.* (incorporating *Man*) 1: 1–16.

1998 Getting Here from There: The Acquisition of Point of View in Mopan Maya. *Ethos* 26: 48–72.

1999 Language, Space and Sociolect: Cognitive Correlates of Gendered Speech in Mopan Maya. In *Language Diversity and Cognitive Representations*, Catherine Fuchs and Stéphane Robert, eds. Amsterdam: Benjamins. Pp. 85–106.

Dougherty, Janet 1978 Salience and Relativity in Classification. *American Ethnologist* 5: 66–81.

England, Nora C. and Stephen R. Elliott 1990 *Lecturas Sobre la Linguistica Maya.* Guatemala: Centro de Investigaciones Regionales de Mesoamerica.

Haviland, John. B. 1979 Guugu Yimithirr. In *Handbook of Australian Languages,* vol. I, R. M. W. Dixon and Barry Blake, eds. Canberra: Australian National University Press. Pp. 27–182.

1993 Anchoring, Iconicity and Orientation in Guugu Yimithirr Pointing Gestures. *Journal of Linguistic Anthropology* 3: 3–45.

1998 Guugu Yimithirr Cardinal Directions. *Ethos* 26: 25–47.

Heider, Eleanor Rosch 1972 Universals in Color Naming and Memory. *Journal of Experimental Psychology* 93: 10– 20.

Hill, Jane and Bruce Mannheim 1992 Language and World-View. *Annual Review of Anthropology* 21: 381–406.

Hunn, Eugene 1985 The Utilitarian Factor in Folk Biological Classification. In *Directions in Cognitive Anthropology*, J. Dougherty, ed. Urbana, IL: University of Illinois Press. Pp. 117–141.

Hunt, Earl and Franca Agnoli 1991 The Whorfian Hypothesis: A Cognitive Psychology Perspective. *Psychological Review* 98: 377–389.

Jackendoff, Ray 1983 *Semantics and Cognition.* Cambridge, MA: MIT Press.

1987 On Beyond Zebra: The Relation of Linguistic and Visual Information. *Cognition* 26: 89–114.

Johnston, Judith R. and Dan Slobin 1979 The Development of Locative Expressions in English, Italian, Serbo-Croatian and Turkish. *Journal of Child Language* 6: 529–545.

Just, Michael A. and Patricia Carpenter 1985 Cognitive Coordinate Systems: Accounts of Mental Rotation and Individual Differences in Spatial Ability. *Psychological Review* 92: 37–172.

Kay, Paul and Willet Kempton 1984 What is the Sapir–Whorf Hypothesis? *American Anthropologist* 86: 65–89.

Langacker, Ronald W. 1986 *Foundations of Cognitive Grammar:* vol. 1, *Theoretical Prerequisites.* Stanford, CA: Stanford University Press.

Lee, Dorothy D. 1959 Linguistic Reflection of Wintu Thought. In *Freedom and Culture – Essays.* Englewood Cliffs, NJ: Prentice Hall. Pp. 21–30.

de León, Lourdes 1991 Space Games in Tzotzil: Creating a Context for Spatial Reference. Working Paper No. 4, Cognitive Anthropology Research Group, Max Planck Institute for Psycholinguistics. Nijmegen, Netherlands.

1994 Exploration in the Acquisition of Geocentric Location by Tzotzil Children. *Linguistics* 32(4/5): 857–884.

Levelt, Willem J. M. 1984 Some Perceptual Limitations on Talking About Space. In *Limits in Perception*, A. van Doorn, W. de Grind, and J. Koenderink, eds. Utrecht: VNU Science Press. Pp. 323–358.

Levinson, Stephen C. 1996 Relativity in Spatial Conception and Description. In *Rethinking Linguistic Relativity*, John Gumperz and Stephen C. Levinson, eds. Cambridge: Cambridge University Press. Pp. 177–202.

1998 Studying Spatial Conceptualization Across Cultures: Anthropology and Cognitive Science. *Ethos* 26: 7–24.

Levinson, Stephen C. and Penelope Brown 1994 Immanuel Kant among the Tenejapans: Anthropology as Empirical Philosophy. *Ethos* 22: 3–41.

Levinson, Stephen C. And Lazlo K. Nagy n.d. Look at Your Southern Leg: A Statistical Approach to Cross-Cultural Field Studies of Language and Spatial Orientation.

Lucy, John A. 1992a. *Language Diversity and Thought*. Cambridge Studies in the Social and Cultural Foundations of Language. Cambridge: Cambridge University Press.

1992b *Grammatical Categories and Cognition*. Cambridge Studies in the Social and Cultural Foundations of Language. Cambridge: Cambridge University Press.

1997 Linguistic Relativity. *Annual Review of Anthropology* 26: 291–312.

Lucy, John A. and Richard Shweder 1979 Whorf and his Critics: Linguistic and Nonlinguistic Influences on Color Memory. *American Anthropologist* 81: 581–615.

Miller, George A. and Philip N. Johnson-Laird 1976 *Language and Perception*. Cambridge, MA: Harvard University Press.

Needham, Rodney 1971 Remarks on the Analysis of Kinship and Marriage. In *Rethinking Kinship and Marriage*, R. Needham, ed. London: Tavistock Publications. Pp. 1–34.

Olson, David and Ellen Bialystok 1983 *Spatial Cognition*. Hillsdale, NJ: Erlbaum.

Pederson, Eric, Eve Danziger, Stephen C. Levinson, Sotaro Kita, Gunter Senft, and David Wilkins 1998 Semantic Typology and Spatial Conceptualization. *Language* 74: 557–589.

Pederson, Eric and Ardi Roelofs (eds.) 1995 Space. *Annual Report 1994*. Max Planck Institute for Psycholinguistics. Nijmegen, Netherlands. Pp. 65–88.

Piaget, Jean 1928 *Judgment and Reasoning in the Child*. M. Warden, trans. New York: Harcourt, Brace and Company.

Piaget, Jean, and Bärbel Inhelder 1963 *The Child's Conception of Space*. F. Langdon and J. Lunzer, trans. London: Routledge and Kegan Paul.

Randall, Robert, and E. Hunn 1984 Do Life-Forms Evolve or Do Uses for Life? Some Doubts about Brown's Universals Hypotheses. *American Ethnologist* 11: 329–349.

Schneider, David 1984 *A Critique of the Study of Kinship*. Ann Arbor, MI: University of Michigan Press.

Takano, Yohtaro 1989 Perception of Rotated Forms: A Theory of Information Types. *Cognitive Psychology* 21: 1–59.

Talmy, Len 1983 How Language Structures Space. In *Spatial Orientation: Theory, Research, and Application*. H. Pick and L. Acredolo, eds. New York: Plenum. Pp. 225–320.

Thompson, J. Eric 1930 *Ethnology of the Mayas of Southern and Central British Honduras*. Chicago, IL: Field Museum of Natural History, Anthropological Series 17(2).

Trager, George L. 1959 The Systematization of the Whorf Hypothesis. *Anthropological Linguistics* 1: 31–35.

Ulrich, Matthew, Rosemary Ulrich and Charles Peck 1986 *Mopan Mayan Verbs*. Guatemala: Summer Institute of Linguistics.

Whorf, Benjamin L. 1956a The Relation of Habitual Thought and Behavior to Language. In *Language, Thought, and Reality: Selected Writings of Benjamin Lee Whorf*. John B. Carroll, ed. Cambridge, MA: MIT Press. Pp. 134–159 (originally published 1939).

1956b Science and Linguistics. In *Language, Thought, and Reality: Selected Writings of Benjamin Lee Whorf*. John B. Carroll, ed. Cambridge, MA: MIT Press. Pp. 207–219 (originally published 1940).

9   Comparative approaches to psychological anthropology

Robert L. Munroe and Ruth H. Munroe

The arguments for and against comparison in psychological anthropology are well rehearsed, and individuals on one side of the issue are rarely converted to the other. Our main purpose here is thus not so much to try to persuade others as to alert them to various endeavors within the comparative sphere. When Sperber (1994: 6) refers to "the work of comparison, which is always planned but rarely undertaken," he overlooks a thriving industry of research. Most of this chapter will be devoted to sketching a selection of recent results that have emerged from such inquiry. The presentation of findings will be accompanied by a thread of commentary on theory and method.

A second purpose is to suggest that comparativists and particularists have embarked on a division of labor which tends to obscure their engagement in a common enterprise. We will turn to this point in the latter part of the chapter.

Range of variation

Cross-cultural comparisons are often implicit, with the anthropologist's own culture serving as the unstated but assumed baseline against which the "other" is assessed. Weisner and his colleagues (Weisner, Bausano, and Kornfein 1983) have reversed the typical direction of this comparative strategy while carrying out explicit measurement in their study of nonconventional families in US society. In this study, families with non-normative values and life experiences, such as those living in collective urban houses or in unusual religious or ideological communities, differed from conventional families in their natural-organic beliefs (e.g., dislike of plastic items, dislike of material possessions), and in their commitment to a warm, emotionally expressive family, and a relaxed, low-conflict family life. In child rearing practices, they breast-fed rather than bottle-fed, weaned late from the breast, fed infants on demand, co-slept with the baby, and used carrying devices that promoted close and direct body contact. These parents believed that they were very innovative, and had put dramatic and unusual changes into practice. When compared with similar data from a world sample of societies, however, it was evident that, overall, "the parents in pronatural, nonconventional families [had] moved only a relatively small distance from their conventional counterparts" (Weisner, Bausano, and Kornfein 1983: 293). The research allows us to conclude that among the changes inspired by social movements of the 1960s, this one, when taken in cross-cultural perspective, was minor – even though it was effected by some of those most committed to radical modifications.

One of the two major advantages to systematic comparative investigation, according to John Whiting (1994), is that it provides an increased range of variation, which is precisely what the interpretation of Weisner and his colleagues has relied upon. Numerous instances of this type of research can be cited, but we will refer to only one other, which also dealt with infant care. Hewlett (1991) carried out several hundred hours of systematic observations among the Aka Pygmies of the Western Congo Basin. Fathers around the world are involved in direct care of infants no more than about 2–3 percent of their time (compared with the 20–25 percent of the time of mothers). The level for fathers tends to be somewhat higher among hunter-gatherers, but, for the Aka, Hewlett found something unique: fathers spending 47 percent of their day holding or within arm's reach of their infants, and, in the Aka's forest-camp setting, staying within view of the baby a remarkable 88 percent of the time. One might say, "Why remarkable? It could happen anywhere." The evidence of course indicates that it *has* happened – but without the Aka case before us, we would have no empirical basis for arguing its likelihood; and without the rest of the comparative data, no basis for understanding its high rarity.

Generality

The other advantage to comparison noted by Whiting (1994) is the question of generality, i.e., whether a finding is bound to a single culture or relates to human behavior in general. Whiting's own research on father absence and male sex identity is relevant here. Father absence in one sense marks the scalar opposite of the Aka Pygmy case – it is, as one psychologist has termed it, paternal *deprivation* (Biller 1976). A meta-analysis of Western research on father absence affirms that, consistently, boys without fathers display inappropriate sex-typing behavior, i.e., behavior which is either exaggeratedly male or not male enough (Stevenson and Black 1988). Whiting's cross-cultural investigations of this connection have focused on putative institutionalized responses to early father absence and to other, similar experiences (Burton and Whiting 1994, Munroe, Munroe, and Whiting 1994). This research, however, has not directly measured behavioral responses to father absence at the cross-cultural level. Such a project

Table 9.1 *Correlations between father presence/absence in the home and children's attention to males in their immediate social environments*[a]

| | Sex | |
Culture	Boys	Girls
Black Carib	-0.40^{b}	0.16
Logoli	-0.43^{b}	0.03
Newars	-0.46^{b}	-0.18
Samoans	-0.05	-0.02
Total sample	-0.36^{c}	0.00

Notes:
[a] $n = 24$ boys and 24 girls each culture except Black Carib where $n = 23$ for boys and 22 for girls, and Newars where $n = 23$ for girls. Total sample size = 188.
[b] $p < 0.05$; [c] $p < 0.001$
Source: Munroe and Munroe in Hewlett, 1992, p. 221. Copyright 1992 by Walter de Gruyter, Inc. Adapted with permission of the publisher.

was initiated by the present authors in four societies chosen for their cultural and geographic diversity, namely, in Samoa, Belize, Kenya, and Nepal (Munroe and Munroe 1992). The approach was to compare father-absent and father-present children, ages three to nine, with respect to their selective attention to others. Our interest was whether in natural settings the father-absent children, and especially the boys, would pay more attention or less attention to the males in their social environments. The sample totaled 188 children, approximately 47 from each society. On the basis of systematic, standardized observations designed to record a child's direction of eye gaze, scores were constructed indexing each child's relative attentiveness to males, taking into account the degree to which males were represented (*vis-à-vis* females) in the environment of the child. For example, a child who directed 70 percent of its attentional gazes at males when the males constituted, say, only 50 percent of that child's social environment would receive a high score.

The findings, shown in Table 9.1, are clear-cut for boys. In three of the societies and for all boys taken together, absence of the father was associated with higher scores on the attention-to-males variable. (Negative signs indicate an association with father absence, positive signs with father presence.) The exception, American Samoa, was marked by frequent shifting of household membership and a highly fluid visiting pattern. These social conditions may have contributed to the lack of findings for this one case.[1]

Given our interpretation, girls' attentional behavior to males should not differ by household presence of fathers. And the relationships for girls did not differ, in no case reaching anything approaching statistical significance. Concerning attentional behavior, young females did not differentially respond to the presence or absence of the father.

In these societies father absence was of varying frequency – ranging all the way from the unusual to the modal – and it occurred due to variable sociocultural factors, such as migrant wage labor and fragile consensual unions. Nonetheless, despite these conditions that differed from one community to the next, the father's presence or absence in the home was related cross-culturally to boys' attentional behavior. For the father-absent boys, we are assuming that heightened attention to males is compensatory and that it serves to allow boys to form a model for male behavior. Such a relationship between father absence and attention to males indicates to us the importance of fathers in the development of appropriate sex-typed behavior. This generalization then holds not only in the West, where the hypothesis was developed, but in diverse cultural settings.

Universals

Now, to take up another of the contributions of comparisons: Geertz (1965: 100) has argued that universals are of no help in constructing an understanding of human behavior because their contentless character prevents us from linking them to the interesting and crucial variations that constitute "the essentials of the human situation." On the contrary, universals are important in aiding our understanding, and the primary way in which this is being done today is precisely through comparative study of their variability. This is not a contradiction in terms. Universals are obviously set apart from other sociocultural phenomena by the pervasive central tendencies and patterns of regularity and similarity that they display cross-culturally, and these regularities point us toward robust biopsychological points of reference that are critical and necessary for the framing of generalizations about humankind. But within any class of phenomena, universals included, we will inevitably find variation, whether in magnitude, intensity, or frequency; and it is in this variation, i.e., it is in these "variform universals" (Lonner 1980), that we will find a rich source of statements about the nature of human nature.

Let us look briefly at a few of the relevant studies. In the domain of kinship, marriage, and the family, the universal incest taboo is no longer seen as a monolithic, unvarying entity. From the work of Fox (1962), Wolf (1970), and Talmon (1964), we have learned about cultural variation in the intensity and direction of the taboo, and from the recent contributions of Schlegel (1994) and Spain (1994), we have begun to make distinctions between *avoidance* – the avoidance of sexual relations with close kin, which occurs not only in human societies but in many sexually reproducing animal species; and *taboo* – the beliefs surrounding incest, which are highly variable culturally. Additionally, comparative research has documented the conditions under which, in matrilineal societies, father–daughter or brother–sister incest is more strongly interdicted (Schlegel 1994).

There exist systematic and limited sets of kin-term types in all human societies. Among types of sibling terms, according to the analysis of Nerlove and Romney (1967), principles of "cognitive economy" were able to account for 98 percent of the cases in a sample of almost 250 societies. And D'Andrade (1971) has shown that differential predictions about kinship terminologies can be made to a high degree of precision from features of social organization, correct predictions exceeding 99 percent in some cases.

Another cultural domain with psychological relevance is that of language. First, a case in point on the value of a comparative approach. One of the most powerful generalizations discovered about language is that all known writing systems encode spoken language: "Writing is speech put in visible form . . ." (Coe 1992: 13).[2] This may seem a truism, but for a century after the discovery of the Mayan ruins, almost none of the written records (except for calendars) could be read; the leading scholars held that Mayan writing conveyed ideas directly, independently of the spoken language, and was thus impenetrable to us today. Benjamin Whorf's (1956) early attempts to establish that the writing system phonetically recorded Mayan language were rebuffed. And resistance continued to be considerable even after a Soviet linguist (Knorosov 1952), following along the lines of Whorf's general argument, made a strong case that Mayan writing was based on the same principles as scripts in other parts of the world. J. Eric S. Thompson, the dominant Mayanist of his generation, maintained until his death in 1975 that translation was unattainable.

The reluctance was not due to simple wrongheadedness. We can see in Figure 9.1 how the written language was inconsistently phoneticized – the spellings for *balam*, "jaguar," were rendered in at least five different ways, only one of which was fully phonetic-syllabic, and one of which was purely logographic. Nevertheless, as Coe (1992) points out, a sound and earlier application of the comparative method could have saved generations of Mayanists from the fatal assumption of Mayan "uniqueness."

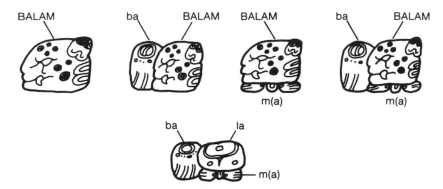

Figure 9.1 Alternative spellings for *balam* "jaguar." According to his whim, the scribe could write this purely logographically; logographically with phonetic complements; or purely syllabically. (From *Breaking the Maya Code* [1992: 264], by Michael D. Coe, New York: Thames and Hudson. Copyright 1992 by Michael D. Coe. Reprinted with the permission of the publisher.)

The universals in language, from sound to syntax, are numerous, and they have been aptly summarized by Greenberg (1966) and by other researchers since (Brown and Witkowski 1980, Talmy 1987). Rather than attempting either a listing or an explication of a group of them, we want to take a single universal, illustrate the accompanying fact of variability, and demonstrate how investigating it can be productive.

As Greenberg (1966) noted, all languages possess syllables composed of a consonant followed by a vowel – that is, simple CV syllables, as in the English words *to* (CV) and the two-syllable *tuba* (CV-CV). Every language also generates more complex syllabic forms (English, despite the examples just given, has a large proportion of syllables with clusters of consonants, as in the word *strict* [CCCVCC]); but the simple CV is easily the most common type of syllable in the world's languages. And, as well, this "canonical syllable," as it has been termed (Oller and Eilers 1992), is produced by infants at an early age, usually 5 to 10 months.

The universality of CV is probably due to its status as a prototypical or "ideal" syllable: According to Studdert-Kennedy (1976: 270), "the consonant is transient, low in energy, and spectrally diffuse; the vowel is relatively stable, high in energy, and spectrally compact. Together they form the syllable, each fulfilling within it some necessary function." When CV sequences are employed, advantages accrue to both hearer and speaker. The hearer benefits from perceptual distinctness, and the speaker, in conveying messages with these minimal syllabic units rather than more complex ones, achieves economy of articulation. Thus, the likely effect of

CV usage is efficient communication (in the sense of optimal signal processing).

Although CV is ubiquitous, in some cases it dominates the syllabic corpus of a language and in others it makes up only a minority of the syllables. Taking a standard world sample of societies, viz., a sample selected for cultural and geographic variability, well described ethnographically, and frequently used in comparative studies, we compiled a list of up to 200 words for all the sample languages, which numbered 53 languages in total (Munroe, Munroe, and Winters 1996). Each word from a list was analyzed in order to determine the percentage of CV syllables, this information permitting the calculation of a mean CV score for each society.

For the entire sample, the mean CV percentage was 55, indicating that the stated ubiquity and language-specific commonness of CV was manifested in these representative languages. The variation in CV from language to language was also reflected in the scores, which ranged from a high of 85 to a low of 16.

Table 9.2 gives the grouped CV scores (mean percentage of consonant-vowel syllables) for indigenously spoken languages in this sample, the scores being separated into those for warm/moderate *versus* cold-climate areas. The results indicate a striking association between temperature and CV score, with all cold-climate cases clustered between the middle and the bottom of the distribution. The highest 24 scores, in fact, belong without exception to societies in the warm- to moderate-temperature areas. These 24 scores run from the top, the Mexican Tarahumara at 85, down to the Greeks at 58; whereas the cold-climate cases do not exceed a high score of 57, for the Fox, and descend to a low score of 16 for the Scots. The difference between the overall means of 59 for the warm/moderate cases and 42 for the cold-climate societies is, as Table 9.2 indicates, highly significant.

We have interpreted the finding according to the following assumptions: that (a) people in warm to moderate climates, as inhabitants of "outdoor" cultures, would on average engage in more distal communication than people in cold climates; and (b) such distal communication would create a need for optimal transmittal of messages, that is, high CV usage (Munroe, Munroe, and Winters 1996: 60).

This interpretation offers an account of the climate/syllable-type association in terms of oral communicability and its constraints.[3] What we would emphasize, however, is not the specific hypothesis at issue but the family of explanations to which it belongs, namely, one that involves the adaptiveness of sociocultural phenomena. Early theoretical statements about the promise of neo-Darwinian principles, made by Campbell (1965) for the behavioral sciences in general and by LeVine (1973) for psychological anthropology, have been followed with a good deal of empirical research,

Table 9.2. *Climate and CV^a scores*

Grouped CV Scores	Climate	
	Warm/Moderate	Cold
80 and above	Aymara Hausa Lozi Tarahumara Tonga Trobriands	
70–79	Cuna Dogon Lau Fiji Yanoama	
60–69	Andamans Aranda Ashanti Cagaba Caraja Ganda Kpelle Mescalero Pemon Santal Teda Toradja	
50–59	Caingang Greeks Ifugao Lebanon Masai San (Bushmen) Toba	Fox Lapps Serbs
40–49	Iban Mundurucu Pashtun Rwala Truk	Copper Eskimo Iroquois Korea Ojibwa Ona Yakut
30–39	Garo Fang Tiv Tzeltal	Blackfoot Klamath Tlingit
29 and below	Khasi Vietnamese	Highland Scots
Mean CV Scores:^{a}	59	42 $t(51) = 3.43$ $n = 53$ $p < 0.005$ (1-tailed test)

Note:
^{a} Although the sample societies are arranged according to class
  intervals, the statistical analysis was carried out with actual scores.
Source: Munroe, Munroe, and Winters, 1996, 30: 72–73.
Copyright 1996 by Sage Publications. Reprinted with permission.

much of it in the aforementioned areas of kinship, marriage, and the family (cf. Buss 1994, Chagnon and Irons 1979, Daly and Wilson 1988, Draper and Harpending 1982). Closely related optimality arguments have been made for such diverse phenomena as trial-and-error learning, the evolution of science, and the development of personality (cf. Shweder 1979). What we are suggesting here is that the components of language may be worth investigating along the same lines. Certainly the numerous universals found in this domain, together with the regularities of language acquisition among children in diverse cultures (Slobin 1982), give us reason to hope that elements of phonetics/phonemics, morphology, and syntax eventually will be seen to display adaptive qualities of the sort discovered elsewhere in nature and culture.

By way of concluding this presentation of the advantages and a few examples of comparative approaches, we note that several *types* of comparison have been discussed in some detail – the case study, with its implicit comparison, as in the work on Aka Pygmy fathers; the within-cultures study, as in the investigation of father absence and attention to males; and the worldwide study, as in the investigation of climate and the CV syllable. And the range of comparative strategies goes even beyond this to include within-region (Johnson 1991) and historical comparisons (Burton and White 1991).

Needed: recognition of a common enterprise

Let us turn to our second purpose. As we said at the outset, the comparativist and the ethnographer who works within a single society are divided in their labor, but not necessarily in their aims. We would argue that we need both – the comparative *and* the minutely contextualized study. By way of illustration of the point, we discuss briefly a topic, emotion, that has received a great deal of attention in the recent history of psychological anthropology.

Symbolic meaning, the central interest of interpretivists, might seem beyond the reach of comparative study. Meaning depends upon nuanced contextual usages and, often, special rhetorical devices, as, for example, antiphrasis and paralipsis in English. For subject matter as complex as emotion, the singularities of each unique culture may not appear to lend themselves to analysis of meaning beyond any one system. Yet recent work by Romney, Moore, and their students (Moore *et al.* 1999, Romney, Moore, and Rusch 1997) has demonstrated that the semantic structure of emotion terms can be reliably measured and compared for languages and cultures as diverse as (American) English, Chinese, and Japanese. Based on judged similarity tasks, the technique allows precise assessment of the degree to which said semantic structures are universally shared, culture-specific, or unique to individuals. Perhaps surprisingly, results indicate that American, Chinese, and Japanese individuals share to a large extent the same internal representations of the semantic structure of emotion terms. Correspondingly, their culture-specific and uniquely individual representations account for much less of their emotion-relevant semantic structures. Thus, the research has allowed a change in focus from the question of "universal *or* culture-specific" to "how much of each," and it has shown that some aspects of symbolic meaning, the key concern of current cultural anthropology, can be approached successfully via the comparative method.

Further support for the idea of generality concerning emotional life comes from the long-term program of Ekman and associates, who found that both the facial expression and the recognition of "basic" emotions (*happiness, sadness, anger, fear, surprise,* and *disgust*) were highly comparable across five modern societies (Argentina, Brazil, Chile, Japan, and the United States) and two traditional groups (the Fore of Papua New Guinea and the Grand Valley Dani of Irian Jaya) (Ekman 1973; see also Boucher 1979, Ekman 1992, Ekman and Friesen 1975, Ekman, Levenson, and Friesen 1983). (Ekman and Friesen [1986] have more recently argued for the generality of another emotion, *contempt.*) Izard (1971) obtained similar results in eight modern societies and among African students studying in Europe. In addition, Scherer and Wallbott (1994), with a cross-cultural questionnaire administered to almost 3000 university students in 37 countries, found that for seven emotions (omitting *surprise* from Ekman's list but adding *shame* and *guilt*), there were stable profiles for each emotion, and all emotions were uniquely different from each other with respect to reports of physiological symptoms, subjective feeling, and expressive behavior. Thus certain basic affective states appear to be general enough that they can be recognized and expressed (and probably experienced) by individuals across a wide variety of cultures.

That regularities of this sort are underlain by fundamental biopsychological factors is given substance by research findings in neuroscience, developmental psychology, and primatology. In several animal species, the amygdala has been linked with the control of emotions and with tying emotions to memory (Barinaga 1992, Davis 1992). Among human beings, converging evidence implies existence of an inborn basis for temperamental traits such as social ease versus shyness (Kagan and Snidman 1991), and especially for negative traits (fearfulness and anxiousness), the heritability of anxiety being calculated at 0.87 in one study (Stavish 1994). In primate research, shyness follows a similar developmental course in rhesus monkeys (Adler 1994, Kerr, Lambert, Stattin, and Klackenberg-Larsson 1994), and such affective disorders as emotional overdependence leading ultimately to lack of coping and early death were observed for chimpanzees in Goodall's (1986) pathbreaking, long-term work.

But the regularities are not the whole story. As White (1994: 223) notes, "The greatest claims for the universality of a small set of core affects have come from studies that have done the greatest amount of decontextualizing, of removing emotion from its social conditions and effects, and of stripping away antecedents and consequents . . ." When anthropologists *have* contextualized emotional expression, they have found unique indigenous configurations, such as Japanese *amae* (something like reciprocal acceptance and dependence) (Doi 1986), or the Ifaluk *song* (something like justified anger) (Lutz 1988). Heider (1993) argues that because for Indonesians it is inappropriate to express strong emotions, especially anger, they may have altered their basic anger face, raising the brows – rather than lowering them, as expected pan-culturally (Ekman and Friesen 1975) – due to the cultural dangerousness of an unambiguous signal of anger. As well, Minangkabau (Indonesian) subjects who made voluntary production of facial expressions for basic emotions registered the predicted autonomic nervous system response patterns, but they also reported the expected subjective feeling of emotion at a much lower rate than did US subjects (Levenson, Ekman, Heider, and Friesen 1992).

Ellsworth's (1994: 23) evaluation is apt: "By now, it should be abundantly clear that some aspects of emotion are very general across cultures, and possibly universal, *and* that people's emotional lives are profoundly influenced by the culture to which they belong" (emphasis added). The study of emotion is facilitated by each of the contributions of comparative research – by its providing an increased range of variation, the investigation of generality, and aid in understanding universals – while being necessarily dependent upon the careful ethnographic delineation of the individual cultural case. Likewise, all the topics discussed herein can be comprehended in their fullness when the comparativist and the particularist are seen as partners in seeking knowledge about human cultural behavior.

Acknowledgments

Thanks are due A. Kimball Romney for comments on an earlier version of this chapter, and an anonymous reviewer for valuable suggestions concerning revisions. Jill Huntley and Pat Streeter ably assisted in the preparation of the manuscript.

NOTES

1 Since a number of sample households in each community contained more than one child, the same score for father presence/absence was necessarily applied to all children from a single home. When a more conservative statistical approach was adopted, by including only one child per household, the Samoan boys displayed the same level of correlation as boys in the other societies (Munroe and

Munroe 1992). For Black Carib boys, however, with a reduced sample the relationship dropped to a nonsignificant level. What this means, though, is that for the two sampling strategies, the association between father absence and attention appeared at least one time within and across all four societies.

2 In a paper delivered in 1940, Benjamin Whorf may have been the first to reach such a conclusion, to wit: "All writing systems . . . symbolize . . . linguistic utterances" (1956: 177).

3 The relationship is not based on factors like diffusion within language families or the simple ratio of vowels to consonants within languages. A replicative study has investigated both these possibilities and found no support for either (Munroe and Silander 1999). We have, however, made the assumption that both speech (usage) and language structure would be shaped by the exigencies of communicative efficiency, and we have been able to measure only language and not usage. Future work on the topic of the CV syllable and its correlates must take up this issue.

REFERENCES

Adler, Tina 1994 Human, Monkey Shyness Varies by Gender. *Science News* 145: 4.

Barinaga, Marcia 1992 How Scary Things Get That Way. *Science* 258: 887–888.

Biller, Henry B. 1976 The Father and Personality Development: Paternal Deprivation and Sex-Role Development. In *The Role of the Father in Child Development*, M. E. Lamb, ed. New York: Wiley. Pp. 89–156.

Boucher, Jerry D. 1979 Culture and Emotion. In *Perspectives on Cross-Cultural Psychology*, A. J. Marsella, R. Tharp, and T. Ciborowski, eds. New York: Academic Press. Pp. 159–178.

Brown, Cecil H., and Stanley R. Witkowski 1980 Appendix B: Language Universals. In *Toward Explaining Human Culture*, D. Levinson and M. J. Malone. New Haven, CT: HRAF Press. Pp. 359–384.

Burton, Michael, and Douglas White 1991 Regional Comparisons, Replications, and Historical Network Analysis. *Behavior Science Research* 25: 55–78.

Burton, Roger, and John W. M. Whiting 1994 The Absent Father and Cross-Sex Identity. In *Culture and Human Development: The Selected Papers of John Whiting*, E. H. Chasdi, ed. Cambridge: Cambridge University Press. Pp. 210–220 (originally published 1961).

Buss, David M. 1994 *The Evolution of Desire*. New York: Basic Books.

Campbell, Donald T. 1965 Variation and Selective Retention in Socio-Cultural Evolution. In *Social Change in Developing Areas*, H. R. Barringer, G. I. Blanksten, and R. W. Mack, eds. Cambridge, MA: Schenkman. Pp. 19–48.

Chagnon, Napoleon A., and William Irons, eds. 1979 *Evolutionary Biology and Human Social Behavior*. North Scituate, MA: Duxbury.

Coe, Michael D. 1992 *Breaking the Maya Code*. New York: Thames and Hudson.

Daly, Martin, and Margo Wilson 1988 *Homicide*. New York: Aldine de Gruyter.

D'Andrade, Roy G. 1971 Procedures for Predicting Kinship Terminologies from Features of Social Organization. In *Explorations in Mathematical Anthropology*, P. Kay, ed. Cambridge, MA: MIT Press. Pp. 60–76.

Davis, Michael 1992 The Role of the Amygdala in Fear and Anxiety. *Review of Neuroscience* 15: 353–375.

Doi, Takeo 1986 *The Anatomy of Self.* Tokyo: Kadansha.

Draper, Patricia, and Henry Harpending 1982 Father Absence and Reproductive Strategy: An Evolutionary Perspective. *Journal of Anthropological Research* 38: 255–273.

Ekman, Paul 1973 Cross-Cultural Studies of Facial Expression. In *Darwin and Facial Expression*, P. Ekman, ed. New York: Academic Press. Pp. 169–222.

1992 Facial Expression of Emotion: New Findings, New Questions. *Psychological Science* 3: 34–38.

Ekman, Paul, and Wallace V. Friesen 1975 *Unmasking the Face.* Englewood Cliffs, NJ: Prentice-Hall.

1986 A New Pan-Cultural Facial Expression of Emotion. *Motivation and Emotion* 10: 159–168.

Ekman, Paul, Robert W. Levenson, and Wallace V. Friesen 1983 Autonomic Nervous System Activity Distinguishes Among Emotions. *Science* 221: 1208–1210.

Ellsworth, Phoebe C. 1994 Sense, Culture, and Sensibility. In *Emotion and Culture*, S. Kitayama and H. R. Markus, eds. Washington, DC: American Psychological Association. Pp. 23–50.

Fox, Robin 1962 Sibling Incest. *British Journal of Sociology* 13: 128–150.

Geertz, Clifford S. 1965 The Impact of the Concept of Culture on the Concept of Man. In *New Views of the Nature of Man*, J. R. Platt, ed. Chicago, IL: University of Chicago Press. Pp. 93–118.

Goodall, Jane 1986 *The Chimpanzees of Gombe.* Cambridge, MA: Harvard University Press.

Greenberg, Joseph H., ed. 1966 *Universals of Language.* 2nd ed. Cambridge, MA: MIT Press.

Heider, Karl G. 1993 An Indonesian Anger Face: Suggestive Evidence for the Interplay of Biology and Culture. Paper presented to the 92nd Annual Meeting of the American Anthropological Association, Washington, DC.

Hewlett, Barry S. 1991 *Intimate Fathers.* Ann Arbor, MI: University of Michigan Press.

Izard, Carroll E. 1971 *The Face of Emotion.* New York: Appleton.

Johnson, Allen 1991 Regional Comparative Field Research. *Behavior Science Research* 25: 3–22.

Kagan, Jerome, and Nancy Snidman 1991 Temperamental Factors in Human Development *American Psychologist* 46: 856–862.

Kerr, Margaret, William W. Lambert, Håkan Stattin, and Ingrid Klackenberg-Larsson 1994 Stability of Inhibition in a Swedish Longitudinal Sample. *Child Development* 65: 138–146.

Knorosov, Yuri V. 1952 Drevniaia Pis'mennost' Tsentral'noi Ameriki. *Sovietskaya Etnografiya* 3: 100–118.

Levenson, Robert W., Paul Ekman, Karl Heider, and Wallace V. Friesen 1992 Emotion and Autonomic Nervous System Activity in the Minangkabau of West Sumatra. *Journal of Personality and Social Psychology* 62: 972–988.

LeVine, Robert A. 1973 *Culture, Behavior, and Personality.* Chicago, IL: Aldine.

Lonner, Walter J. 1980 The Search for Psychological Universals. In *Handbook of Cross-Cultural Psychology*, vol. 1, H. C. Triandis and W. W. Lambert, eds. Boston, MA: Allyn and Bacon. Pp. 143–204.

Lutz, Catherine 1988 *Unnatural Emotions: Everyday Sentiments on a Micronesian Atoll and Their Challenge to Western Theory*. Chicago, IL: University of Chicago Press.

Moore, Carmella C., A. Kimball Romney, Ti-Lien Hsia, and Craig D. Rusch 1999 The Universality of the Semantic Structure of Emotion Terms: Methods for the Study of Inter- and Intra-Cultural Variability. *American Anthropologist* 101: 529–546.

Munroe, Robert L., and Ruth H. Munroe 1992 Fathers in Children's Environments: A Four-Culture Study. In *Father–Child Relations*, B. S. Hewlett, ed. New York: Aldine de Gruyter. Pp. 213–229.

Munroe, Robert L., and Megan Silander 1999 Climate and the Consonant-Vowel (CV) Syllable: A Replication Within Language Families. *Cross-Cultural Research* 33: 43–62.

Munroe, Robert L., Ruth H. Munroe, and John W. M. Whiting 1994 Male Sex-Role Resolutions. In *Culture and Human Development: The Selected Papers of John Whiting*, E. H. Chasdi, ed. Cambridge: Cambridge University Press. Pp. 237–261 (originally published 1981).

Munroe, Robert L., Ruth H. Munroe, and Stephen Winters 1996 Cross-Cultural Correlates of the Consonant-Vowel (CV) Syllable. *Cross-Cultural Research* 30: 60–83.

Nerlove, Sara B., and A. Kimball Romney 1967 Sibling Terminology and Cross-sex Behavior. *American Anthropologist* 69: 179–187.

Oller, D. Kimbrough, and Rebecca E. Eilers 1992 Development of Vocal Signaling in Human Infants: Toward a Methodology for Cross-Species Vocalization Comparisons. In *Nonverbal Vocal Communication*, H. Papousek, U. Jürgens, and M. Papousek, eds. Cambridge: Cambridge University Press. Pp. 174–191.

Romney, A. Kimball, Carmella C. Moore, and Craig D. Rusch 1997 Cultural Universals: Measuring the Semantic Structure of Emotion Terms in English and Japanese. *Proceedings of the National Academy of Sciences* 94: 5489–5494.

Scherer, Klaus R., and Harald G. Wallbott 1994 Evidence for Universality and Cultural Variation of Differential Emotion Response Patterning. *Journal of Personality and Social Psychology* 66: 310–328.

Schlegel, Alice 1994 Cross-Cultural Comparisons in Psychological Anthropology. In *Handbook of Psychological Anthropology*, P. K. Bock, ed. Westport, CT: Greenwood. Pp. 19–39.

Shweder, Richard A. 1979 Rethinking Culture and Personality Theory. Part II: A Critical Examination of Two More Classical Postulates. *Ethos* 7: 279–311.

Slobin, Dan I. 1982 Universal and Particular in the Acquisition of Language. In *Language Acquisition*, E. Wanner and L. R. Gleitman, eds. Cambridge: Cambridge University Press. Pp. 128–170.

Spain, David H. 1994 Entertaining (Im)possibilities. In *The Making of Psychological Anthropology* II, M. M. Suárez-Orozco, G. Spindler, and L. Spindler, eds. Fort Worth, TX: Harcourt Brace. Pp. 103–131.

Sperber, Dan 1994 *On Anthropological Knowledge*. Cambridge: Cambridge University Press (originally published 1985).

Stavish, Sheila 1994 On the Biology of Temperament Development. *APS Observer* 7(3): 7 and 35.

Stevenson, Michael R., and Kathryn N. Black 1988 Paternal Absence and Sex-Role Development: A Meta-Analysis. *Child Development* 59: 793–814.

Studdert-Kennedy, Michael 1976 Speech Perception. In *Contemporary Issues in Experimental Phonetics*, N. J. Lass, ed. New York: Academic Press. Pp. 243–293.

Talmon, Yonina 1964 Mate Selection in Collective Settlements. *American Sociological Review* 29: 491–508.

Talmy, Leonard 1987 Lexicalization Patterns: Typologies and Universals. Cognitive Science Report, No. 47. Berkeley, CA: Cognitive Science Program.

Weisner, Thomas S., Mary Bausano, and Madeleine Kornfein 1983 Putting Family Ideals into Practice: Pronaturalism in Conventional and Nonconventional California Families. *Ethos* 11: 278–304.

White, Geoffrey M. 1994 Affecting Culture: Emotion and Morality in Everyday Life. In *Emotion and Culture*, S. Kitayama and H. R. Markus, eds. Washington, DC: American Psychological Association. Pp. 219–239.

Whiting, John W. M. 1994 The Cross-Cultural Method. In *Culture and Human Development: The Selected Papers of John Whiting*, E. H. Chasdi, ed. Cambridge: Cambridge University Press. Pp. 76–88 (originally published 1954).

Whorf, Benjamin Lee 1956 Decipherment of the Linguistic Portion of the Maya Hieroglyphs. In *Language, Thought, and Reality: Selected Writings of Benjamin Lee Whorf*, J. B. Carroll, ed. New York: Technology Press of Massachusetts Institute of Technology and John Wiley & Sons. Pp. 173–198 (originally published 1942).

Wolf, Arthur P. 1970 Childhood Association and Sexual Attraction: A Further Test of the Westermarck Hypothesis. *American Anthropologist* 72: 503–515.

Name index

Ahnert, L., 95–96
Ainsworth, M., 85–90, 100
Alba, J., 117

Bartlett, F., 109–114, 118, 122–123, 125, 132, 136n.9, 138n.22
Bateson, G., 83
Bausano, M., 223
Benedict, R., 158
Boas, F., 111
Boehm, C., 35
Bourdieu, P., 37
Bowlby, J., 86, 88, 97, 99–101
Brewer, W., 115, 117–118
Brison, K., 152–153
Brown, P., 201
Brown, S., 7, 12–13, 190
Bruce, D., 119–121
Bruner, E., 55, 63n.7
Bruner, J., 108, 116–117, 122, 135n.7

Caudill, W., 83
Chaudhuri, K., 182
Christianson, S., 118
Coe, M., 227
Cole, M., 73–74, 132, 138n.19
Cordua, G., 72
Csordas, T., 49–50, 60–61, 63n.8

Damasio, A., 39–40
D'Andrade, R., 132, 227
Danzinger, E., 11, 14
Davir, R., 96
De Leon, L., 218–219n.4
De Tocqueville, A., 189
De Vos, G., 13
Dewey, J., 70
Douvan, E., 177, 189
Drabman, R., 72
Dube, E., 71

Ekman, P., 232–233
Ellsworth, P., 233

Ember, C., 75
Engels, F., 69–70
Engestrom, Y., 132
Estes, D., 96
Ewing, K., 84

Fairbairn, W., 22
Fajans, J., 157
Feldman, C., 108, 116–117, 121, 135n.7
Fitzgerald, J., 115, 122
Fivush, R., 122, 138–139n.23
Fortune, R., 158
Freud, S., 21–24, 32, 49

Gamson, W., 153–154
Gardner, H., 131, 187
Garro, L., 5–6, 10, 106, 123–124, 129–130
Geertz, C., 225
Goodenough, W., 132
Greenberg, J., 228
Grossmann, K., 89–90, 95–96
Grossmann, K.E., 89–90, 95–96

Haden, C., 122, 138–139n.23
Halbwachs, M., 137n.15
Hallowell, A., 16n.1, 51, 63n.1, 174
Hasher, L., 117
Haviland, J., 201
Heider, K., 232
Hewlett, B., 224
Hollan, D., 6–7, 9, 10, 15, 49, 52, 55–56
Holland, D., 108, 135n.7
Horney, K., 99
Hutchins, E., 132

Ingoldsby, B., 76
Izard, C., 232

Kleinman, A., 59–60
Kleinman, J., 60
Knorosov, Y., 227
Koestner, R., 35
Kohut, H., 22, 49

238

Kornfein, M., 223
Kriyananda, S., 175, 178–179, 182, 186–187
Kroonenberg, P., 96
Kuhn, T., 27
Kulka, R., 177, 189

Lamb, M., 96
Larsen, S., 138n.20
Lave, J., 71–73, 77n.1
Leavitt, S., 4–5, 7, 12–13
Leont'ev, A., 70
LeVine, R., 6–8, 10, 48–49, 51, 83, 95, 97
Levine, N., 76
Levinson, S., 201, 202, 218n.3
Levy, R., 58–59
Lewis, C., 173–174
Lewkowicz, S., 96
Linde, C., 134–135n.5
Linton, R., 83
Lucy, J., 201, 204
Luria, A., 70, 74–75

Mageo, J., 189
Main, M. 96–97
Manier, D., 120
Marx, K., 69–70
Maslow, A., 176
Mathews, H., 35
McClelland, D., 35
McGraw, K., 72
Mead, M., 83
Middleton, D., 120–121
Minoura, Y., 83–84, 98
Mistry, J., 71
Moore, C., 231
Munroe, R. H., vii, 14–15, 224–225, 229, 233–234n.1
Munroe, R. L., 14–15, 224–225, 229, 233–234n.1

Neisser, U., 105, 110, 116–118
Nerlove, S., 227
Nordquist, T., 175, 177
Norman, K., 7–8, 10, 91–94

Paul, R., 49
Peacock, J., 108, 135n.7
Pillemer, D., 116
Potter, J., 121
Price, L., 129n.28

Quinn, N., 4, 42–43, 136n.8, 175

Ratner, C., 7–8, 75
Reese, E., 122, 138–139n.23
Robbins, T., 177
Robinson, J., 115, 118
Romney, A., 227, 231
Rosaldo, R., 135n.5
Rubin, D., 114, 116–117, 124
Rusch, C., 231

Safer, M., 119
Sagi, A., 96
Sapir, E., 11, 16n.1, 50–51, 174
Scherer, K., 232
Schieffelin, E., 157
Schleidt, M., 93
Schmitt, B., 203
Schwartz, T., 158–159, 174–175
Shoham, R., 96
Shore, B., 136n.8, 136–137n.10
Shweder, R., 68–69
Smith, M., 152–153, 159
Sperber, D., 223
Spiro, M., 1, 38, 43
Stearns, P., 76
Strathern, M., 157
Strauss, C., 4, 42–43, 113, 136n.8, 175
Studdert-Kennedy, M., 228
Sullivan, H., 22

Thompson, J., 227
Tolman, E., 38
Tuzin, D., 155, 165

Van IJzendoorn, M., 88, 96
Verhoff, J., 177, 189
Vygotsky, L., 70–71, 74

Walbott, H., 232
Wallace, A., 174, 190
Weinberger, J., 35
Weisner, T., 223–224
Wellenkamp, J., 49, 52, 55–56
Westen, D., 5, 9, 12
White, G., 232
Whiting, J., 14, 83, 224
Whorf, B., 11, 201, 204, 217, 227, 234n.2
Winters, S., 229
Worthman, C., 10

Yogananda, P. 173, 175, 178, 182–183, 186

Zablocki, B., 177, 190

Subject index

activity theory, 8, 69–71
  and cultural psychology, 68–69, 72–73,
    76–77
  and culture change, 8
  and gender roles, 75
  and psychological change, 77
  critique of, 72–76
adaptiveness
  of memory mechanisms, 119
  of sociocultural phenomena, 229–230
affect
  and cultural models, 38–40
  as attitude, 111–113
  implicit, 9
  priming, 34
  regulation, 35–36, 42–43
  states, 232
  unconscious, 9, 34–35
  see also emotion; emotions; memory;
    names of specific affects
Aka Pygmies of the Western Congo, 224,
  231
  father involvement with infants, 224
altruism, 176
  vs. self-interest, 174, 181, 187–189
amae, 233
amamas, 163
Americans, 83, 93, 97, 99
  affluence following World War II, 176
  and sense of self, 12–13, 189–190
  child-rearing, 223
    shift of views of, 98–100, 177
  conflict between emotion and rationality,
    184–186
  in the 1960s, 176–177
  individualism as cultural ideal, 174, 181,
    188–189, 192n.3
    and conflict with community,
      182–184
  see also Ananda Village; baby boomers
Among School Children, 63n.10
Anada Magazine, 174

Anada Village, 13, 173, 190, 192n.7
  and Self-Realization, 178–182
  communal spirit, 188
  description of, 179–181
  economic system, 179–181, 187–188
  meditation, 182–184
  purpose of, 179
  see also Americans; baby boomers;
    religion, revitalization movements;
    social movements
anger, 76, 209, 232
  justified, 233
animals-in-a-row experiment, 203–204, 205,
  211–214
  see also experiments; spatial expression
Anishinaabe (Ojibwa) of Manitoba,
  Canada, 5, 10, 106, 119, 122–131
  and animals, 5, 107, 125, 126–127
  bad medicine, 123, 128, 140n.31
  beliefs about illness, 5, 107, 123
  healers, 106, 107, 123
    comparison with physicians, 124
  high blood pressure, 129–130,
    140n.31
  illness accounts, 106–107, 125–131,
    134n.5, 139n.28
  ondjine, misfortune, 106, 123, 125–127,
    139n.27
anorexia, 41–42
anthropology, 57, 108, 109, 199–200, 201,
  217
  and existential malaise, 200
  and psychiatry, 50
  assumptions, 199
  biological, 10
  cognitive, 71, 113, 114, 132, 201
    linguistic orientation in, 201–202
  culture-centered *vs.* behavior centered,
    51
  educational, 74
  linguistic, 201
  psychoanalytic, 22, 23

psychological, 1, 10, 15, 16n.1, 29, 36, 59,
    60, 83, 84, 170, 223, 229, 231
    and comparative study, 14
    and social movements, 154–155
    methodological techniques, 3, 12
    research agenda for, 3
    vs. cognitive science, 33
anticomparativist view, 14
anxiety, 10, 232
    heritability of, 232
association networks, 3, 4, 26, 28, 33–35
    and affect, 35–36
    and implicit learning, 28, 34–35, 138n.19
    see also, connectionism; memory
Attachment, Separation, and Loss (1969,
    1973, 1980), 100
attachment theory, 11, 85–88
    and irreversibility, 98
    and personality disorders, 97
    Bowlby–Ainsworth model, 86–87, 88, 90,
        96, 99–101
    critique of, 96–98, 100–101
    evolutionary assumptions, 85–86
    range of variation, 97, 100–101
    security of, as a moral ideal, 97, 100
    studies:
        Baltimore, Maryland, 87–88
        Bielefeld, 89–91, 95–97, 100
        East Berlin, 95–96
        Israeli kibbutz, 95–96
        Linden, 91–98
    see also psychoanalytic method and
        theory; Strange Stituation; infancy,
        infant enculturation hypothesis
Autobiography of a Yogi (1985), 174
autonomic nervous system, 233
autonomy, 5, 12, 154–155, 160–161, 169

baby boomers, American, 12, 173, 175, 176,
    177, 184, 190, 192n.3
    and hallucinogenic drugs, 13, 176–178
        meditation as alternative to, 182–184
        relation with Eastern religions, 177,
            192n.4
    see also, Americans; Ananda Village
balam, 227, *228*
Baining of New Britian, 157
Balinese, 83
behavioral environment, 16n.1, 28, 51
Belize, 225, 233n.1
Bielefeld study, *see* attachment theory,
    studies
borderline personality disorder
    and patient histories of sexual abuse,
        32
    cognitive *vs.* psychoanalytic view of, 32

Bumbita Arapash of Papua New Guinea, 5,
    12–13, 14, 155–156
    beliefs in the power of collective action,
        161–164
    Christian revival movement of 1984,
        151–152, 161–164
    clan myths, 159–161
    collapse of revival movement, 166–169
    concepts of spirits, 160–161
    history, 155–156
    initiation grades, 165
    interpersonal conflicts, 167–169
    language affiliation, 155
    men's cult:
        houses, 155, 156, 165–166
        secrets, 151, 159, 162–166, 171n.1
    religious ideology, 164–166, 173n.3
    sense of self, 156–160
    South Sea Evangelical Church (SSEC),
        156
    Tambaran ceremonies, 164–166
    tension in self-schemas, 156–158, 161–164
    see also religion, revitalization
        movements; social movements

cargo, 152, 161, 170, 191
categorization, 26, 30
    of ambiguity, 30
    of color, 75
change
    culture, 8–9, 12, 174–176, 178, 188–191
    psychological, 8–9, 13, 70–71, 77, 98–100,
        174–175
    social, 8, 175
Child Care and the Growth of Love (1953), 99
chronic pain, 59–60
cognitive neuroscience, 28
cognitive science, 4, 9, 25–31, 33, 36, 108,
    131, 132, 199, 200, 217
    modal model of information processing
        in, 25–26
    relationship to activity theory, 71–74
    view of culture, 131–133
    see also psychoanalytic method and
        theory
communitarianism, 190
community formation, 190–191
comparison, 1–3, 11–13, 14–15, 16n.1, 49,
    50, 58, 61,199–200, 223, 218n.1
    advantages of, 14–15, 224, 227
    and generality, 13, 224–226
    and person-centered ethnography, 3,
        14–15, 49–50, 231
    categories of analysis, 3, 15, 49, 199, 204
    comparativists and particularists, 223,
        231, 233

comparison (*cont.*)
  cross-cultural, 217, 223–224
  design of measures for, 11, 213–216
  domain-based studies, 204–205, 219n.5
  history of in anthropology, 14, 224
  implicit *vs.* explicit, 14, 15, 218n.1, 223, 231
  knowledge of universals through, 15, 226
  recent studies, 223–232
  systematic observation, 224, 225
  systems *vs.* units, 199
  types of studies, 231
connectionism (or parallel distributed processing, PDP), 4, 5, 29–31, 43n.1
  constraints, 36
  model of mind, 9
  vs. serial processing, 31
  see also association networks; memory
consciousness, 9–10, 35–36, 69–71
  and information activation, 9–10, 35
  and memory, 115, 139n.24
  and social activities, 69–70
  and the unconscious 29, 34
  psychological awareness of, 176–177
consensus, 152–155, 161–164
consonant-vowel syllables (CV), 228–230, 231
  advantages, 228–229
  association with climate, 229–230, 234n.3
  mean percentage in 53 languages, 229
  qualities of, 228
  range of variation, 229
constructivism, 1, 11, 13, 16n.1
  as particularism, 58
contempt, 232
coping mechanisms, 35–36
  see also defense mechanisms
cultural models, 4, 7, 29, 36–42, 175, 189
  and memory, 136n.10
  conflicts between, 12, 40–42
  differential distribution of, 40, 139n.25
  internalization of, 37–38
  motivational force of, 38–40
  of German child rearing, 89–95, 98, 101
  of interpersonal relations, 84, 91
  see also enculturation; representations; schemas
culture, 68–69, 43n.2
  acquisition of , 83–85, 113
  and activity theory, 69–71
  and cognition, 217
  and experience, 4–5
  and social movements, 153–154
  and the individual, 1–2
  and the study of mind, 108–109, 136n.8
  as activity, 68

as artifacts, 73
as process, 132
as shared meanings, 68
as shared schemas, 4
centripetal and centrifugal tendencies, 175, 189
contradictory elements, 174–175
deaf, 43
distributive model of, 174–175
Goodenough's view of, 132
impersonalized, 50
relationship to psychology, 68–69
salience, 119
transmission, 2
view of in cognitive science, 131–133
  see also enculturation; memory
Culture in Mind (1996), 136n.10

defense mechanisms, 12, 24, 35–36
  compromise formation, 12–13, 23–24, 41–42
    as adaptation, 24
  culturally constituted, 38
  culturally patterned *vs.* idiosyncratic, 41
  see also coping mechanisms; motivation; psychoanalytic method and theory
depression, 59
deprivation
  maternal, 99–100
  paternal, 224
deyatelnost, 69
disgust, 232
dreams, 53, 54, 128–129, 173

Eastern religions, 177–178, 191
einwilligen, 90
emic *vs.* etic, 33
emotion, 10, 15, 58–59, 231–233
  and activity theory, 75–76
  and distress, 59–60
  and facial expression, 85, 111, 232–233
  and rationality, 174, 181, 184–186
  as a basis for memory, 125–129, 136n.9, 137n.17
  conscious *vs.* unconscious, 9–10, 34–35
  profiles of from 37 countries study, 232
  semantic structure of terms, 231–232
  vocabulary, 52
  see also affect; emotions; memory; *names of specific affects*
emotions, 4, 24, 35
  and the amydala, 232
  basic, 232
  disturbance of, 101–102, 232
  in social situations, 75–76
  qualitative character of, 59, 232

pleasurable *vs.* unpleasurable, 12, 35–36
see also affect; emotion; memory; *names of
        specific affects*
enculturation, 98
   and cultural models, 84, 91–94
   and irreversibility, 98
   and precocity, 84, 97–98, 101
   difference from universalist model, 84, 96
   in infancy, 83–85
   pathways of, 86
   see also attachment theory; cultural
        models; infancy; socialization,
        childhood
erziehung, 91, 92
ethnographer(s)
   as participant-observer, 55
   influence of, 134n.5
   of Melanesia, 157, 158
ethnopsychology, 51, 154, 157–158
experience
   acquisition and transmission of, 5–6
   and culture, 1, 16n.1
   and schemas, 4–5
   as a basis for comparison, 15
   behavioral aspects of, 7–8
   childhood, 32, 37–38
   concrete, 116
   embodied aspects of, 2, 6, 9–10, 56–58
   individual, 6, 154, 158, 175, 232
   meditation and mystical, 182–184, 185
   of Tahitians *vs.* Newars, 58–59
   personal, 106, 117, 119, 121, 130, 132
   range of, 154
   reliving, 117
   shared, 120–122
   subjective, 2, 6–7, 9, 57, 233
experience-near approach
   see person-centered ethnography
experiments
   games, 206, 218n.4, 219n.5
   in language and thought studies, 201
      domain-based, 204–205
   judged similarity tasks, 231
   priming, 28, 71, 72
   recall, 27, 72
      cued, 29, 115
      free, 28–29
   recognition, 27
   spatial problem-solving, 202–205
   standardized tasks, 199, 206
   vs. clinical experience, 31
   see also animals-in-a-row; man and tree
        game; memory; route-completion
        task; Strange Situation; Thematic
        Apperception Test
eye gaze, 225

faces
   and "affective attitude," 111
   infant sensitivity to, 85
father absence, 224–226, 231
   and selective attention to males, 224–226
   in relation to females, 226
fear, 5, 10, 34, 37, 232
   as motivation, 23
"fit-for-life," 7, 91–92
14 Steps to Perfect Joy (n.d.), 179

Ganda of Uganda, 86, 87
gehorchen, 90
gender roles
   and activity theory, 75
   and personality, 75
Germans, 86, 99
   patterns of infant socialization, 10, 89–95
   values in child rearing, 91, 93–94, 100
glas meri, 162
grief and bereavement, 49, 58
guilt, 58, 161, 232
Gusii of Kenya, 83, 95, 97

habitus, 35, 37, 62
hallucinogenic drugs, 177–178
happiness, 163, 183, 188, 232
haus tambaran, 155
healing, 60–61
Hindu ideals, 182
*How to Use Money for Your Own Highest
        Good* (1981), 187
human nature, 16n.1, 175, 199, 226
Human Potential Movement, 176

Ilahita Arapesh of Papua New Guinea, 155,
        156
   men's cult houses, 165
   Tambaran ceremonies, 165–166
incest taboo, 227
   avoidance *vs.* taboo, 227
   in matrilineal societies, 227
incommensurability thesis, 1
infancy
   care practices,
      in Germany, 10, 91–95
      in US: between 1920–1950, 98–99;
         following World War II, 99–101,
         177
   developmental theory, 86–87
   infant enculturation hypothesis, 84, 97–98
   psychology, 84–85
   see also attachment theory; enculturation;
        socialization, childhood
intentional communities
   see Ananda Village

intentionality, 68
intentions, 157

Japanese, 83, 97–98, 203, 231, 232, 233
jealousy, 76

Kenya, 226
knowledge
    cultural, 106, 107, 114, 123, 130, 131,
        134n.5, 139n.25
    declarative, 27
    explicit, 27, 37
    failure to integrate, 40
    gendered, 40
    "how to," 28
    implicit, 28, 37
    procedural, 28, 37, 39
    shamanistic, 40
    social origin of, 138n.20
    see also memory
Korsakoff's disorder, 34
Kragur of north coast of Papua New
        Guinea, 152, 159
Kwanga of Papua New Guinea, 152–153
Kwoma of New Guinea, 83

language
    acquisition and development, 85, 98,
        231
    and adaptiveness, 231
    and thought studies, 201
        domain-based, 204, 219n.5
    and writing systems, 227, 234n.2
        Mayan, 227–228
    communicability and constraint, 229
    interviews as natural discourse, 134n.5
    relation to thought, 200, 216–217
    terminology:
        emotion, 231–232
        kinship, 227
        sibling, 227
    universals in, 216, 228, 231
    see also Bumbita Arapash; consonant-
        vowel syllables; linguistic relativity;
        memory; Mopan Maya; spatial
        expression
learning
    explicit, 5, 7, 29, 34–35, 37–38
    implicit, 4, 5, 7, 28, 29, 34–35, 37–38
    theory, 109
    unconscious, 27
lebensfähig, 91, 92
life history studies, 108, 134ns.4, 5, 135n.7
Linden study
    see attachment theory, studies

linguistic relativity, 200, 201–202, 204,
        216–217
    Sapir-Whorf hypothesis, 11, 201, 204
Luo of southwestern Kenya, 75

man and tree game, 207
    discussion of, 206, 216–217
    results:
        in Arandic, 206
        in Dutch, 206
        in Mopan Maya, 206–210
        in Tzeltal, 206
    see also experiments; spatial expression
Manus of New Guinea, 83
Maternal Care and Mental Health (1951),
        99
mathematical thinking, 71
    in shopping activity, 72–73
meaning
    constructivist view of, 1
    cognition as "effort after meaning," 110
    symbolic, 231–232
    understanding vs. emotional significance,
        39
memory
    and amnestic patients, 28–29, 34
    and communication, 120–122
    and culture, 109–114, 119, 123–127,
        129–133
    and emotion, 5, 10, 117, 119–120,
        124–126, 136ns.9, 10, 137n.17, 232
    and language, 138n.23
    and narrative, 107–108, 117, 120–122,
        124–130, 134n.5, 135n.6
    and story recall, 71, 111
    associative, 28, 34
    autobiographical or personal, 105–106,
        114–118
        accuracy of, 117–120, 121
        Bartlett's theory of, 109–114
        methods for studying, 115, 117–118,
            121, 138n.21
    changing views of, 26–27
    collective, 129–131, 137n.15
    construction vs. reproduction, 118–120,
        124–125, 136n.10
    everyday, 105, 132, 133n.1
    explicit vs. implicit, 27–29, 34
    "flashbulb," 137n.17
    hippocampus and temporal lobes, 29
    in children, 116
    individual differences in, 136n.9
    laboratory vs. naturalistic studies of,
        105, 110, 116–119, 124, 133n.1,
        138n.22

long-term *vs.* short-term, 25–26
recall, 107, 110–113, 115, 119–122, 124,
   126, 137n.14
of illness events, 124–127
social contexts of, 120–122, 124,
   126–131
see also affect; association networks;
   connectionism; experiments;
   knowledge
mental processes
conscious, 21–22, 29, 111
preconscious, 21–22
unconscious, 21–22, 34, 111
   cognitive *vs.* dynamic, 29
metapelet, 96
mind
as brain, 27, 30
as computer, 25, 30
model(s) of, 5
   connectionist, 5
   distributed cognition, 109, 139n.25
   experimental *vs.* clinical view, 29
   information processing, 25
   serial processing, 25
   see also psychoanalytic method and
      theory
modal character, 23
Mopan Maya of Belize and Guatemala, 11,
   200, 205, 206
language, 200
performance on spatial experiments,
   206–209, 211–216
spatial expressions in language, 209–210
ritual use of, 209
spontaneous discourse about space,
   209–210
see also spatial expression
motivation, 4, 9, 23–24, 32–33, 35–36, 38–40,
   175
and altruism, 24
bodily origin of, 32
competing, 24, 32
in memory, 111–113
of others, 157–159
unconscious, 34–35, 53
see also defense mechanisms;
   psychoanalytic method and theory
multidisciplinary approach, 2
myths
Bumbita:
   Ambun, 159
   Amoina, 159
   Tembaran, 159–160
of Mexico:
   La Llorona, 37

Nepal, 225
neuroscience, 4, 232
"the neurosis of success," 176
Neurotic Personality of Our Time, The
   (1937), 99
Newars of Bhaktapur, 59
Nyinba of Nepal, 76

object relations theory, 22–23
see also psychoanalytic method and
   theory
Ojibwa
   see Anishinaabe
ondjine
   see Anishinaabe
ordnungsliebe, 91, 92

parallel distributed processing (PDP)
   see connectionism
paranoia, as a world view, 158–159
Path, The (1979), 178
person-centered ethnography, 48–52
and behavioral analyses, 55–56
and embodiment approach, 56–58
and verbal report, 52–54
differences with psychoanalysis, 53–54
historical roots, 50–51
relation to comparative approach, 49–50,
   58
respondents *vs.* informants, 53, 63n.5
phenomenological approach, 9, 61
Philosophy of Meditation (1965), 182
polyandry, 76
postmodernism, 1–2
praxis, 69, 74
primatology, 232
psychiatric theory, 59–60
psychiatry, developmental, 88, 97, 101
psychic unity 58, 136n.8
psychoanalytic method and theory, 4, 22, 29,
   62
contemporary, 21–25
Freudian models of mind, 21–23
neo-Freudian school, 99
relation models in, 22–24
the symptom, 24
transference-countertransference, 51,
   53
vs. cognitive science, 31–33, 36
see also attachment theory; defense
   mechanisms; mental processes;
   motivation; object relations theory
psychology
cultural, 11
   critique of, 70–71, 76–77

psychology (*cont.*)
  cognitive, 201
  developmental, 86, 101, 232
    dominant approach in, 86
  ego, 22, 24
  relational, 22–25
  self, 22, 24, 62
  social, 113

religion
  ideology, 175
  revitalization movements, 4, 12, 174,
    190–191
    appeal of, 170–171
    group's conception of self as source of,
      154–155, 169–171
    in Melanesia, 151–152
    therapeutic function of, 13, 174,
      189–191
    universal aspects of, 169–170
    see also Anada Village; Bumbita
      Arapash; social movements
representations
  and affect, 37
  cultural, 6
  differentiated, 24
  distribution through neurons, 27
  internalization of, 175
  mental, 68, 110
  object, 22
  of heroes, 182
  of semantic structure, 232
  self, 22
  spatial, 38
  see also cultural models; schemas
*Remembering: A Study in Experimental and
  Social Psychology* (1932), 109
Research Society for Creative Altruism,
  176
response latency, 28
route-completion task (Figure 8.1), *203*
  discussion of, 202, 211–214
  solutions:
    absolute, 202, 211, 213–215
    distractor, 202, 213–215
    relative, 202, 211, 213–215
  see also experiments; spatial expression

*Sacred Self: A Cultural Phenomenology of
  Charismatic Healing, The* (1994),
  60
sadness, 232
Samoa, 225, 226
Sapir–Whorf hypothesis
  see linguistic relativity

schemas, 4–5, 26, 38–39, 105, 116–119, 121,
  123, 139n.26
  by verbal report, 52
  definitions, 110–113
  self, 154, 135n.7
    negative, 41
  theory of, 175
  see also cultural models; representations;
    self
selbständigkeit, 91, 92
self, 24–25, 59, 106, 154
  American concepts of, 189
  Bumbita concepts of, 156–159, 169–171
  concept and consumerism, 72
  conflicts with culture, 12–13, 175–176
  construction of, 108, 135n.7, 169–171
  egocentric *vs.* sociocentric concept of, 12,
    154, 157–158, 176–177, 182, 189,
    192n.3
  Melanesian concepts of, 157–158, 169
  presentation of, 134n.5
  psychological view of, 176–177
  public *vs.* private, 134n.5
  reconfiguring, 189
  see also schemas
self-actualization theory, 176–177
self-esteem, 22, 23, 25
self-interest, 187
  reconciled with altruism, 187–188
Self-Realization philosophy, 12, 175,
  181
  Fellowship (SRF), 178, 180, 183
self-reliance, 7, 89, 90, 97–98, 174
senses of the body, 9, 10, 51–52,
  57
shame, 60, 232
shyness, 232
"the sixties," 174
social movements, 13
  and cultural understandings, 154–155,
    169–171
  dynamics of, 153–154
  problems with routinization, 170
  see also Ananda Village; Bumbita
    Arapash; religion, revitalization
    movements
social organization, 68–69, 73
  and kinship terminology 227
socialization
  childhood, 4, 37
  of impluses, 23
  see also enculturation; infancy
song, 233
sorcerers, 162, 164, 166, 171n.1
Socerers of Dobu (1932), 158

sorcery, 160, 161
  as cause of death, 155
  implements of, 151, 152, 156, 162,
    164
spatial expression in language
  absolute *vs.* relative approaches to spatial
    representation, 202–204, 211–213
  and cognition, 200
  in Mopan Mayan, 11, 208–210
  orientation-free encoding of, 11, 210–211,
    216, 219n.7
  orientation-bound encoding of, 11,
    210–211, 214, 216–217, 219n.7
  proximity of parts, 210
  reference systems:
    in Arandic, 202, 210
    in Dutch, 202, 203, 210, 212
    in English, 200, 210
    in Guugu Yimithirr, 201, 202, 210,
      212
    in Japanese, 203, 210
    in Longgu, 203
    in relation to cardinal directions, 201,
      209–210
    in relation to the body, 201
    in Tzeltal, 203
  see also animals-in-a row; man and tree
    game; Mopan Maya; route-
    completion task
stereotypes, racial, 38
Strange Situation (SS) experiment, 86–89,
  91–92, 94–97, 100
  classification from, 87–88
  clinical categories from, 86
  critique of, 97
  procedure, 87
  see also attachment theory
Study of Man, The (1936), 83

surprise, 232
syncretism, 175, 178, 189, 191

Tahitians, 58–59
*Tahitians: Mind and Experience in the
  Society Islands* (1973), 58
tatigkeit, 69
televangelists, 24
Thematic Apperception Test (TAT), 35
Toraja of south Sulawesi, Indonesia, 49, 52,
  57–58
  funeral ceremonies, 55

universals, 11–12, 15, 58, 101–102, 226–231
  and narrative forms, 134n.5
  and psychobiological predisposition, 15,
    232
  as an empirical question, 11–12
  constraints, 11–12, 229
  objections to, 1, 226
  "variform," 226
  vs. particularism, 199
  see also comparison; enculturation;
    language; religion, revitalization
    movements
Uzbekistani color perception, 74–75

Value Orientation Interview, 190, 192n.9
verwöhnt, 92, 93
voice, human, 85

wan bel, 161–162
"War of the Ghosts," Kwakuitl folktale, 111

yoga, 175, 180, 182, 186–187
  and meditation, 182–184
  kriya, 12, 179, 182–184, 186
  raja, 182